DESKTOP MARKETING

LESSONS FROM AMERICA'S BEST

AMERICAN DEMOGRAPHICS BOOKS

AMERICAN
DEMOGRAPHICS BOOKS®
A Division of American Demographics, Inc.
127 West State Street, Ithaca, NY 14850
Telephone: 607-273-6343

First published USA 1991

ISBN 0-936889-09-8
Library of Congress Catalog Number 91-058120

Designed by Rebecca Wilson
Cover design by Michael Rider

Printed in the United States of America

DESKTOP MARKETING

LESSONS FROM AMERICA'S BEST

Richard K. Thomas and Russell J. Kirchner

To the advent of
and advancement of
Relationship Marketing

Acknowledgments

The production of any book requires the input of a large number of people, and this is particularly true with a book of case studies. We have many to thank for their assistance in the completion of this project. The compilation of the case studies required the cooperation of a large number of individuals representing desktop system vendors and the nation's industries. Although all cannot be acknowledged here, we would like to thank Jeff Knebel (Donnelley Marketing Information Services), Jon Voorhees (National Decision Systems), Terri Toomey (National Planning Data Corporation), Rick Byers (Datamap), Nancy Solomon (formerly of National Demographics and Lifestyles), Mary Kay Conlon (The Sachs Group), and Eric Cohen (formerly of CACI), not only for their assistance in the development of the case studies but for their insights into the industry and their guidance in the development of this project.

In preparing this book we interviewed many individuals in the desktop system industry and in consumer industries. For the "insider" perspectives they provided, we would like to thank Dick Raines and Mark Capaldini (Claritas), Andy Paul (National Planning Data Corporation), and Jon Voorhees, Mark Catone and Lou Tazioli (National Decision Systems). We are also grateful for the insights provided by Skip Hunt (Donnelley Marketing Information Services), Tom Colar (Marriott), John Rogozenski (Dunkin' Donuts), Andy Moncla (Lowe's, Inc.) and Kelly Jensen (Illinois Institute of Technology). We would like to especially thank George Hoole (Desktop Marketing Corporation) for his insights.

Of course, many individuals at American Demographics Books played a role in the production of this book. Those who have contributed significantly in one way or another are Peter Francese, Dick Wright, Diane Crispell, Jim Madden, and Kathy Brandenburg. We also appreciate the editorial assistance provided by Tony Phillips.

Finally, we would like to thank our respective employers, Baptist Memorial Hospital and CUNA Mutual Insurance Group, for their support and for creating environments that have provided us the background and the inspiration to pursue undertakings such as this.

Preface

This book is about the ways in which America's most progressive businesses are transforming themselves into customer-driven organizations. The revolution in marketing has resulted in a need for the "quick strike" capabilities that only a desktop marketing system can offer. Indeed, as marketing becomes more database driven, no organization can expect to remain competitive without access to such a system.

Desktop Marketing represents the first attempt to bring together the experiences of various industries with desktop marketing systems. Until now, there has been no ready source of cases in desktop marketing and, to date, America's academicians have largely ignored the importance of this approach to marketing in the nation's business schools. It is hoped that this collection of industry-specific case studies will shed light on the manner in which America's best are using desktop marketing technology to get closer to the consumer and offer the reader insights presently available from no other source.

We believe that "desktop marketing" will become the metaphor of the 1990s, as this decade witnesses the completion of the transition to customer consciousness in American business. We see desktop marketing as the necessary first step in completing the movement away from a traditional product-line orientation that is sales-based to a "customer segment" management approach that is relationship-based. Indeed, the ability of American business to compete in the emerging world market is likely to rest in the hands of those marketers who are creative enough to somehow marry the consumer information resources of desktop systems to the emerging quality revolution. Tomorrow's winners will structure their management around relationships with their customers, and desktop systems will be a primary tool for accomplishing this.

We hope that future editions of this book will bear witness to an incremental improvement in the way American business anticipates and services the needs of its customers. Indeed, we hope to eventually see corporations structured around a constantly improving, long-term relationship with each customer. We hope that you, the reader, will come to embrace this vision that is increasingly being shared by America's "best."

DESKTOP MARKETING
LESSONS FROM AMERICA'S BEST

PART 1

Introduction

The 1980s witnessed a revolution in market analysis capabilities. This revolution was epitomized by the ability to make "desktop decisions" related to a wide variety of corporate activities. Although market research had become very much a science prior to the introduction of desktop marketing systems, consumer marketing was hampered by a number of problems thought to be inherent in the marketing research process. Market researchers were handcuffed by a lack of access to pertinent industry data, a reliance on vendors for current market data, a dependence on mainframe computers, and an inability to integrate, analyze, and report market information in a timely, efficient, and effective manner. The most important drawback, however, was the fact that market researchers and corporate decisionmakers could obtain only numbers, when what they really needed were solutions.

This situation became totally unacceptable in the 1980s, due to overwhelming and irreversible changes in the American marketplace. Defying the futurists of 20 years ago, who said we would all be androgynously alike by 1990, consumers became increasingly fragmented. Diversity was found in all aspects of people's lives—where they come from, where they live, with whom they live, what they do for work and pleasure, how much money they have, and how they spend it. Then, just when marketers got used to the idea of segmenting markets along demographic lines, they realized that two people with the same demographic characteristics could have very different attitudes and lifestyles, and psychographic research came into force. The 1980s witnessed the recognition of the Hispanic market, the geriatric market, and a host of other groups with distinct lifestyles and consumption patterns. To complicate matters even further, many of these niches themselves were segmented—i.e., all Hispanics and elderly are not alike.

During this period, the notion of mass marketing met its demise in virtually every industry, and target marketing became the order of the day as businesses redirected their efforts toward regional marketing, niche marketing, and customer segmentation. It had been one thing to develop marketing plans for a mass market; it was an entirely different matter to identify specific markets and develop customized marketing plans. These new tasks required new tools.

The need to segment the American market led to the emergence of a full-blown consumer information industry. During the 1970s and early 1980s, data companies primarily offered repackaged and value-added census data. With online access to these data, researchers could extract the data they needed for specific population segments and geographic areas.

Despite what appeared at the time to be high-tech solutions to the growing need for timely and detailed market data, these demographic databases did not answer all of the questions. Detailed as they were, census data did not include the consumer- and industry-specific information that market researchers needed. The necessary industry databases often did not exist, and those that did were often difficult to locate and use. Timeliness was another concern; decennial census data quickly became outdated, and there was no way to determine the accuracy of widely varying estimates and projections produced by data companies. Furthermore, online data were often expensive, limiting their use by smaller businesses.

Even organizations with in-house computer capability were often hampered by the bulk and awkwardness of internal databases. Mainframe computers required a great deal of technical expertise to operate, and it was difficult to interface data from outside vendors with existing systems. Research and marketing departments had to have personnel who could interface with systems that could only be defined as user-unfriendly.

Perhaps the greatest barrier facing market researchers and decisionmakers, even those who had overcome all of the above obstacles, was in interpreting the data. Computers can generate a lot of numbers, but numbers are a long way from information. The existing "market analysis systems" offered no way to conveniently manipulate data, merge disparate databases, or cross-reference internal and external sources. In short, no mechanism existed to integrate databases and derive meaningful conclusions.

In March 1985, the first solution to these barriers was offered with the release of the Infomark Laser PC System by National Decision Systems of Encinitas,

California. For the first time, researchers could sit at their desks and conduct a comprehensive market analysis using one system, with all of the required databases and software at the user's fingertips.

These new systems were housed in microcomputers and billed as so user-friendly that staff with no previous computer experience could sit down and operate them with little training. Most important, these systems not only generated numbers; they offered solutions to market research problems.

TECHNOLOGICAL IMPROVEMENTS ADVANCE THE DEVELOPMENT OF DESKTOP MARKETING

For many, desktop market analysis systems transformed marketing research from a slow plodding process of questionable accuracy into a highly accurate and expeditious activity, and it was the desktop computers themselves that were in large part responsible for this capability. Microcomputers had developed to the point that they took on many of the capabilities of mainframes, without the drawbacks and at a much lower cost.

Expanded memory capabilities for microcomputers were especially crucial for the development of desktop systems. Not only could microcomputers handle large datasets, they could manipulate them in a relatively flexible and user-friendly manner. Microcomputers also developed enhanced interface capabilities. These new systems made a major breakthrough in their ability to link databases and programs, model data, connect to mainframes, and merge internal and external data.

But these new hardware and software configurations would have been useless without the concomitant development of large, accessible databases. The demographic data industry expanded its efforts to disseminate a wide range of market-related and industry-specific data. Some data companies devoted themselves to developing forecasting models; others devised mechanisms for data interpretation; industries themselves automated data.This widespread computerization of all aspects of American life, combined with technical advances in information transfer, facilitated the process of getting data from the source to the user.

AN INNOVATIVE APPROACH TO AN OLD PROBLEM

What is it that makes a desktop market analysis system so much of an improvement over previous methods of market research and planning? Desktop systems offer a number of advantages. Because they have been developed by data vendors, they provide a uniquely integrated access to data and software. This integration is perhaps desktop systems' most significant innovation. They can integrate databases from disparate sources; produce standard or custom reports, graphs, and maps; simultaneously use multiple databases; and users can create customized "macros" that manipulate variables for an almost unlimited variety of applications.

The ultimate evaluative criterion, of course, is results, and this is where desktop systems excel. Rather than simply generating numbers, desktop marketing systems are specifically designed to offer solutions. This is not to say that background information, forethought, and interpretive skills are not required. They are. But it does mean that all of the information from which to draw a conclusion is placed at the fingertips. In effect, the systems allow the questions to answer themselves.

For many users, the most appealing aspect of desktop marketing is that all one needs is a personal computer. Desktop systems have freed market researchers from all of the constraints that kept them from operating effectively in a mainframe environment—they can do it themselves.

FEATURES OF DESKTOP MARKETING SYSTEMS

Desktop marketing systems can be grouped into two major categories: so-called market analysis systems and geographic information systems (GIS). Although the two types of systems have similar functions, the latter, as might be inferred from its name, is oriented more toward locational information than behavioral variables. The case studies in this book have been generated using desktop market analysis systems, and these are the focus of this work (with one exception, a GIS study provided by Environmental Systems Research Institute).

Desktop marketing systems come in either a generic or industry-specific form. Most systems on the market are generic; that is, they have a standard set of features and a database that can be used by a variety of industries, such as banks, restaurants, or packaged-goods manufacturers. Industry-specific systems, on the other hand, are designed for a particular industry. The best examples of industry-specific desktop market systems are those designed for the health-care service field, which has many unique characteristics that limit the usefulness of generic systems.

Even in the desktop industry, it seems, the mass market is dead. In a business climate characterized by niche marketing, there is now a rapid movement toward industry specificity even among the leading generic desktop marketing systems. Because the marketing environment and tasks have become so complex, desktop vendors expecting to compete in the 1990s must specialize; they must become industry experts and consultants to their clients.

Although the desktop systems currently on the market offer a wide variety of features, they also share some common ground. Different vendors use different terms to describe their systems, and the following general overview of these common components is offered in the hope of offering insight rather than confusion.

Databases: All desktop marketing analysis systems include databases, and it was in the data business that most desktop vendors got their start. Demographic databases are the bread and butter of these systems and typically drive all other components. Other databases resident on desktop systems depend on the orientation of the vendor, the extent to which the system is industry-specific, and the needs of the specific user.

In general, generic systems usually include databases on income, media and purchase behavior, and business data. Those oriented toward financial services are likely to have detailed business data and credit information. Health-care systems contain data on patient utilization patterns, health-care facilities, and physicians.

These resident databases on desktop systems are usually referred to as external databases. They relate to the external environment and may be national in scope. Internal databases, those generated by system users, include customer, prospect, employee, or patient records, and other internal marketing or business data. The ability to import and incorporate internal data is a standard feature of desktop systems.

Segmentation Systems: Virtually all desktop marketing systems feature a market segmentation system. Some segmentation systems classify the population into a number of distinct groups, categories, or clusters based on demographic or lifestage characteristics. Other segmentation schemes involve psychographic research, which is based on a combination of demographic, lifestyle, and attitude information.

Segmentation systems are most useful when linked to both consumer behavior data and geographic information. For example, national consumer surveys can describe the demographic characteristics of a typical product user. This information can then be applied to the census-based demographic database of a desktop system at a local level. Today, desktop segmentation systems can analyze data at virtually any level of geography, to the census-block-group level in many cases (about 300 households), and even to the individual household level in some cases. Although this level of geography is not appropriate for all marketers, it is necessary for direct marketing.

Modeling: Another feature that all desktop marketing systems share is modeling. Models simulate real-life activities and develop "what if" scenarios. One primary use of modeling on a desktop system is interfacing external and internal databases. For example, a hospital may want to determine what its case mix is likely to be five years from now, given expected changes in population characteristics.

Applications: Vendors also refer to the applications that accompany their systems. Applications may resemble models, but are usually more involved and, in fact, an application may incorporate a number of models. Applications typically represent complete but specialized uses of the desktop system.

A common application for most desktop systems is site selection. The application involves the use of appropriate standard and imported databases, specifically developed models, and outputs designed to offer the desired solution. Applications are often industry-specific, and a vendor of a generic system may enhance its usefulness by creating specific applications.

DESKTOP MARKETING APPLICATIONS

Originally designed as aids to market analysis, desktop systems have rapidly taken on additional functions. Many were never anticipated by their creators, but have been driven by the needs and requests of users. In fact, users have driven much of the growth in desktop applications. Originally conceived as market research tools, desktop systems have expanded their horizons to include marketing planning, strategic planning, and complex monitoring functions. Even as you read these words, new technologies and databases are expanding the capabilities of these systems. The following are just some of the functions that desktop systems can perform and that are generally applicable to all industries.

MARKET RESEARCH: This term covers a wide variety of capabilities, including: ***New market development***—An immediately apparent use for desktop systems is identifying new markets. They can locate markets that are growing, markets that are presently underserved, and pockets of potential customers. ***Existing market evaluation***—Desktop systems can determine the potential market for a specific site or area, forecast market share, and project demand. ***New product development***—Desktop systems can identify unmet needs and new trends in consumer preferences.

SITE ANALYSIS AND SELECTION: Desktop analysis simplifies the otherwise laborious task of identifying potential sites for retail outlets, satellite offices, and sales territories. Integrating databases is key here, because users can simultaneously examine such diverse variables as population trends, market penetration, lifestyle preferences, and traffic patterns.

COMPETITIVE ANALYSIS: Desktop systems can examine a company's performance relative to its competitors, identify respective market strengths and weaknesses, and profile competitor's customers.

DIRECT MAIL: Desktop systems can add precision to direct-mail activities by locating market segments based on virtually any integrated database variable down to the zip+4 level (averaging 10 to 15 households). Many systems can convert identified locales into addresses for direct marketing use.

MEDIA SELECTION: Desktop systems can access media use data and integrate them with product preferences, lifestyle information, and geography to pinpoint the optimal way of reaching target market segments.

FUND-RAISING: With desktop systems, organizations such as hospitals and nonprofit charities can identify potential donors and volunteers and develop fund-raising campaigns.

FINANCIAL ANALYSIS: Desktop systems can integrate financial databases with software packages to develop business plans, pro formas, and so on. Analysts can do realistic modeling with access to the "live" data via integrated databases.

BUSINESS-TO-BUSINESS MARKETING: This is a relatively uncharted area of desktop capabilities that will become increasingly important in the future, as new capabilities emerge to locate and evaluate industrial prospects and customers.

LIMITATIONS OF DESKTOP MARKETING ANALYSIS SYSTEMS

Some words of caution should be inserted at this point. Desktop marketing systems have been designed to enhance expert decisionmaking, not replace it. As powerful as these systems are for performing market analysis, there are some things they cannot do. They can never replace an in-depth, intimate knowledge of the industry in which one is operating. The human ability to read between the lines will always be necessary in any marketing effort. Getting the most out of a desktop system requires experience and intuition that cannot be built into a machine.

Desktop marketing system users should never be lulled into a false sense of security. A desktop site ranking should never have the final say or take the place of an actual physical site evaluation. What appears to be the right solution on paper may not be the right solution in reality. Even the satellite imaging techniques that are being introduced (on National Planning Data Corporation's PrimeLocation system, for example) will not eliminate the need for on-site inspections.

Despite these cautions, it is likely that no major player in the marketing field will be able to successfully compete in the future without desktop capabilities. One can so easily envision a situation in which one research analyst is poring over lists of possible data sources to evaluate a potential site, while a competitor's analyst is already printing maps of the most desirable locations.

We always think back to our experience with a Big Eight accounting firm that does a great deal of consulting for the health-care industry. When one of its executives was asked how he would go about collecting market data for a new client, he responded that he would send an analyst (at $50,000 a year) to visit the local Chamber of Commerce and planning commission to see what demographic data were available. We didn't say so at the time, but we knew that with desktop capabilities, we could have a preliminary site report ready by the time the analyst got off the plane!

2

The Desktop Industry

The emergence of the desktop marketing industry bears witness to the American entrepreneurial spirit. Around the time of the 1970 census, a few pioneers realized that there was a profit to be made in reformatting census data for business use. Today's leading desktop vendors started out as data "boutiques" at that time. On the West Coast, National Decision Systems and Urban Decision Systems started up. On the East Coast, it was CACI, Claritas, and National Planning Data Corporation; and the seeds of an industry were planted.

These early vendors began learning to apply their data to real-world problems. Ironically, they learned this lesson from their first customers, who literally drove the development of the demographic data industry. During this early period, the major customers for market data were real estate developers, restaurateurs, and petroleum retailers; and site selection was the most prevalent application. More and more data were bought and sold as companies opened sites in the blossoming Sunbelt, and soon many progressive companies were spending thousands of dollars a year for demographic and market data.

At the beginning of the 1980s, desktop market analysis was only a twinkle in somebody's eye. By the end of the decade, more than 1,000 systems were in place in various industries around the country. By the time this book is in print, there may be twice that number in operation.

THE EMERGENCE OF DESKTOP MARKETING

By the early 1980s, marketers who spent a lot of money on secondary market data were renting databases on a controlled, fixed cost basis. These marketers were also acquiring personal computers to do database management, research, and a variety of other tasks. At the same time, Jim Shaffer of National Decision Systems stumbled onto laser disc technology at a convention, and as a result, the first desktop marketing system, Infomark, was born in 1985. By the end of the 1980s, virtually all marketing database vendors had desktop marketing products.

This made it possible for marketers to license databases for the entire country and gave them unlimited confidential access to the information. Progressive marketing departments hired computer-literate analysts, while seasoned field-site selectors learned to use the new technology.

The first industries to show an interest in the new systems were national restaurateurs and retailers. Developers were also quick to appreciate the advantages of such systems. As large companies, they were also in a position to afford the relatively expensive early versions of desktop marketing systems.

Other industries came to appreciate desktop marketing, although different factors provided the impetus for different kinds of businesses. Banking and financial-services companies underwent deregulation during this time, and desktop systems provided the basis for the innovative and aggressive promotion of competing services that followed. Indeed, bankers were intrigued by the location modeling applications used by retailers as retail "banking" flourished. The health-care industry became consumer-oriented in the face of increasing competition and declining profits, and social-service agencies faced stiffer competition for fund-raising efforts. In sum, the costs of making any kind of marketing or locational mistake had escalated in virtually every industry, and the need for accurate, timely, and meaningful information had become paramount.

THE DESKTOP MARKETING INDUSTRY MATURES

By the late 1980s, the rush to desktop systems had become a stampede. Over the past six years, more than 1,200 companies have elected to internalize their research by licensing a desktop system. (See Figure 1.) These systems are currently priced from $15,000 to $70,000 for an annual license, depending on the databases included; some may run $100,000 or more. Despite the explosion of sales, industry experts feel that they have only seen the tip of the iceberg so far. While most observers agree that the market for this type of high-end desktop product is limited, the expected introduction of lower-end and less expensive systems will put desktop marketing into the reach of small businesses.

One reason that desktop systems were adopted so readily by many companies was a pent-up demand. As noted earlier, external conditions like deregulation and competition were mandating a much more sophisticated marketing response. Another significant factor in the acceptance of desktop marketing was the fact that many companies were already working with the separate pieces that desktop marketing would bring together. Many had taken steps toward generating and manipulating internal databases; most were used to accessing external databases, either online or in printed reports; and, most important, many had begun to move toward a microcomputer environment. PCs had become standard office equipment, laying the physical groundwork for the introduction of desktop marketing systems.

In the 1990s, however, desktop marketing has to include more than specially designed hardware, software, and databases. As in the general consumer market, desktop system users are asking for more and better customer service. Today's winners in the desktop marketing industry realize that their staff must include

Growth in the Number of Desktop Marketing Systems in Use by American Corporations*

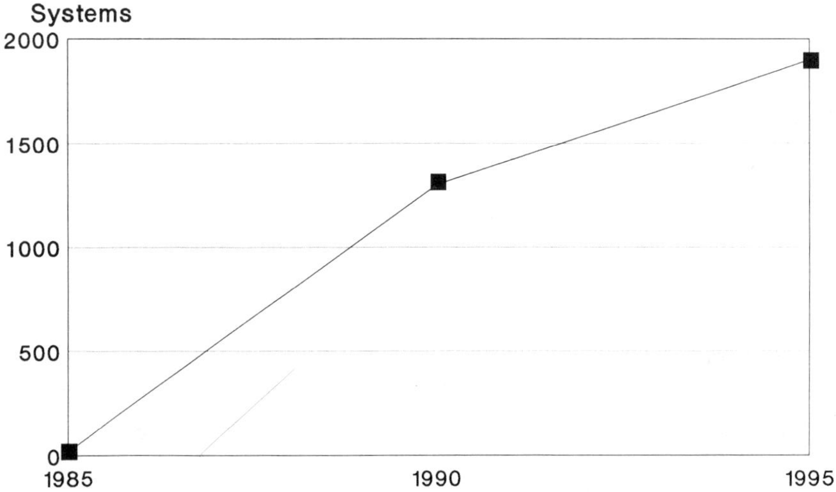

**Infomark, Conquest, PrimeLocation, SCANUSA, Insite, and Compass installations. Estimates derived through a consensus of confidential interviews with leading industry experts.*

FIGURE 1 *Sales of desktop marketing systems grew rapidly in the late 1980s as end users preferred instant access to data over paying online charges.*

vertical industry experts who can act as consultants to help users solve complex marketing problems. Any vendor who relies on a "salesy" approach will be dead in the water.

THE END USERS

The early adopters of desktop marketing systems within companies were typically marketing and real-estate departments, because the systems were initially designed to provide research support for market segmentation and locational analysis. It was soon obvious, however, that there were many more applications possible, such as projecting product demand and use, calculating market share, and targeting areas for direct-mail and other promotions. This expansion of applications quickly drew the attention of other departments—planning, personnel, product development, public relations, and, in selected industries, fund-raising.

Who uses desktop marketing? The distribution of systems in place among selected industries is estimated as follows: financial services (30 percent), retailing (25 percent), health care (20 percent), and restaurant (10 percent), with assorted industries making up the balance. (See Figure 2.) A sleeping giant is the media industry, which could grow from its current 4 percent share of systems to 15 percent

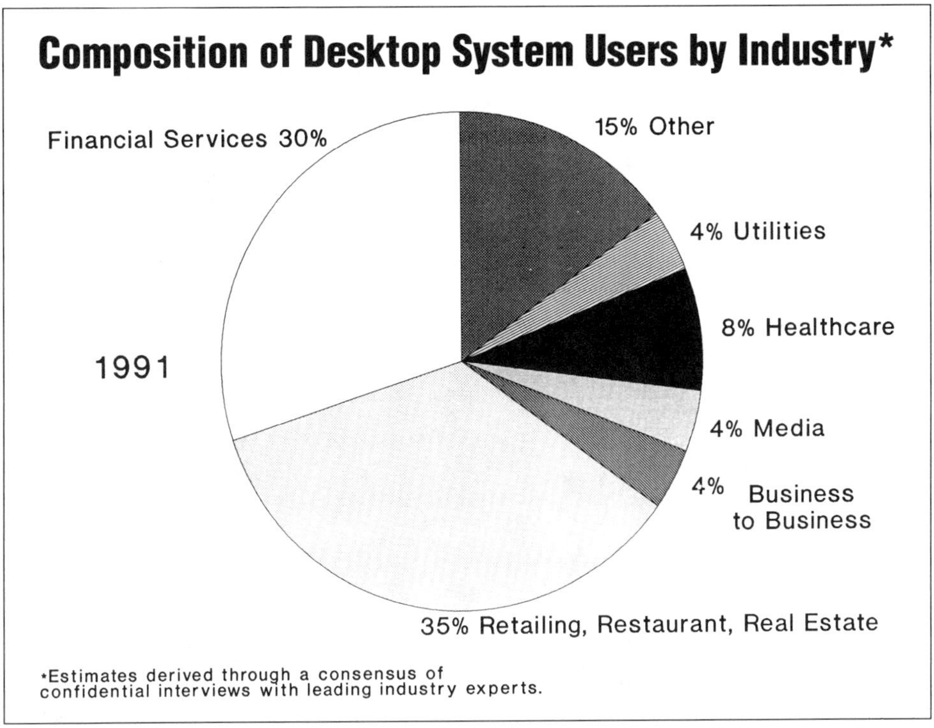

FIGURE 2 *While desktop systems originally appealed primarily to site-oriented marketers, advances in databases and applications have given rise to growth in new industries such as media, utilities, and business-to-business.*

by 1993. The use of systems in utilities and telecommunications companies is also expected to grow, as vendors develop more applications for these industries.

Other industries may be approaching the saturation point. Health-care industry use will probably grow slowly and may actually shrink as a share of desktop users, reflecting the fact that there are a finite number of hospitals nationwide that are candidates for the systems, many of which already have them in place. According to Michael Sachs of The Sachs Group, a health-care-specific vendor, "Our future business will involve delivering new solutions to established relationships."

At the other extreme is desktop marketing use in the business-to-business sector, which is in its embryonic stages. Some speculate that the demand for desktop systems among business-to-business users will reach 1,000 by 1995, although the authors foresee a more modest expansion in this area, because of the need to educate the market.

THE FUTURE OF DESKTOP MARKETING

The desktop marketing industry is currently undergoing a transition that should culminate in an explosion of interest in the 1990s. Steady industry growth is expected to result from improvements in databases, delivery platforms, and applications, and,

Source: Spot Image Corporation and National Planning Data Corporation

FIGURE 3 *Rapid advances in PC hardware and software may soon make satellite images a realistic tool for location analysis.*

perhaps most important, a new generation of affordable "user easy" desktop products. Furthermore, the marketing information industry is increasingly focusing on delivering solutions and investing more human capital in its relationships with clients. As Tom Gay of National Decision Systems puts it, "We will do more to step into the customer's shoes."

The potential for desktop marketing is growing all the time. Vendors like Donnelley Marketing Information Services (DMIS), National Decision Systems, and Spectra (a Claritas affiliate in Chicago) are developing new and innovative applications for utilities that are expected to make headway into the packaged-goods industry. DMIS and VNU are creating media targeting solutions that could very well affect how advertising is bought and sold in the U.S.

In the future, we might use satellites to zoom into a neighborhood, assess its potential market value, and print out the names, addresses, and telephone numbers of the people who live there. Figure 3 demonstrates the promise of this technology; it shows a satellite map from National Planning Data Corporation's PrimeLocationX product.

Database Developments: According to Dick Raines of Claritas, the data on tomorrow's desktop systems will be behaviorally based, localized, and industry-specific. Indeed, demographic (census-based) variables will yield to a new wave of media, purchase, and other consumer databases. Watch for "live" consumer data from TRW, Equifax, and other credit agencies. Also watch for "cleaned up" business-to-business lists and summary data. Some companies already maintain millions of customer records on PCs.

Delivery Platforms: Until recently, the desktop marketing software that linked data and users was deemed cumbersome by many novice users. According to one West Coast user, "Our system is about as user-friendly as a cello." In contrast, "Tomorrow's systems will work in concert with how the human mind works," contends George Hoole of Desktop Marketing Corporation (DMC). The increasing use of the Windows™ environment on PCs will shorten the learning curve for desktop systems and facilitate the integration of iterative geographic information systems and Marketing Customer Information Files with traditional demographic and market data.

Data Democratization: The Windows™ environment for PC desktop marketing systems will also lower the cost of desktop marketing. "Users in the past have been conditioned to think that desktop marketing has to cost $30,000 plus," says DMC's Hoole. This means that small businesses—which constitute 90 percent of all U.S. firms—will be able to acquire desktop systems as a matter of routine.

DMC plans to roll out a system, code-named MERLIN, which will link a company's internal customer files and the world of external data—including mailing lists, demographics, and other marketing information provided by participating vendors. The system will be oriented toward sales and marketing managers, salespeople, and company executives. A point-and-click approach will guide users not only in retrieving data but in incorporating the knowledge thus gained into a comprehensive process that encourages creative thinking. The best part is that these systems will cost between $800 and $7,000.

Customer Service: Tomorrow's desktop marketers will demand, and receive, more advice about desktop applications. This is partly because many marketing departments are experiencing a cyclical downscaling that may not reverse itself for several years, and until such time, will require extra help from outside experts. In addition, the number of databases and applications for desktop marketing systems are growing, increasing the range of choices that users have to make.

Desktop marketing vendors recognize that they have to move further from their original technical and product-based approach toward a consultation-based value-added approach. Tom Ratkovich of National Demographics and Lifestyles states, "We evaluate our corporate moves based on their effect on our customers." Tom Holland of National Decision Systems points out, "We evaluate how we can help our customers get the most from their system. By doing this, we are able to make the most of the relationship we have with the user." Hopefully, the thinking of Ratkovich and Holland will epitomize that of the entire desktop marketing industry in the 1990s.

PART 2

Industry Case Studies

This chapter includes more than 40 case studies representing a variety of consumer industries. Case studies were originally solicited from all known vendors of desktop market analysis systems. Ultimately, many more cases were compiled than could be published in the book, and the authors used several criteria in the selection process for inclusion. Every effort was made to ensure that all vendors were represented. Similarly, every effort was made to ensure that there were representative cases from all relevant industries. Beyond these criteria, cases were selected on the basis of variety of applications, quality of presentation, and variety and quality of graphics. In the final analysis, the selections were made with the perceived needs of the reader in mind.

The main objectives of the authors were to ensure that certain key points were included and that there was some uniformity of presentation. Criteria were established for length and number of exhibits, and these were generally adhered to. In some cases, fictitious names were used to maintain business confidentiality and are identified as such by disclaimers.

The cases are organized for the most part to introduce the reader to the company on which the case study focuses and the problem that the company faced. Subsequent sections of each case describe the desktop system used to solve the problem, the methodology followed, and the solution ultimately developed.

Periodic revisions of this book are anticipated. Hopefully, readers will provide useful feedback about the types of cases they would like to see in subsequent editions.

3

Media and Advertising

There was a time when marketers associated the task of promotion with the mass media. This sort of thinking, of course, is in the past. For the sake of cost efficiency, targets are now more refined, and the desktop industry has helped marketers manage this media mix.

Many contend that the heyday of the large superfluous national media budget is past. According to studies by Robert Coen of the McCann-Erickson advertising agency in New York, national media still comprise roughly 50 percent of total media expenditures. However, this is down 25 percentage points from the 1960 share of 75 percent. It is argued that national media's percent of total media expenditures will drop even further in the 1990s, as marketers embrace micromarketing technology.

This move toward media targeting has largely been forced upon advertising agencies and the media by users of desktop segmentation systems. A southern retailer says, "We are picking new sites using the VISION geodemographic system to locate our best customers. It only makes sense to target these same people with our media budget."

Economic conditions today, coupled with target marketing techniques, are turning the advertising and media industry on its head. The result is increasing chaos in the ad industry and rapidly declining aggregate expenditures for mass media. This chaos signals opportunity for progressive agencies and media.

When we speak of promotional media, we mean any type of communication that provides a link to the customer and/or most promising prospect. Figure 1 matches types of media with their ability to reach various levels of consumer targets. The discussion that follows explores the strengths and weaknesses of these media and their potential for tomorrow's marketer.

With the invaluable input of Mark Capaldini of Claritas Corporation, a paradigm has been developed to evaluate media options in terms of their "levels of

Potential Strength of Media at the Four Efficiency Levels, 1991

Target Levels	National Network TV	Local Spot/Cable	Radio	Newspapers/ Magazines	Direct Response	Outdoor
Individual Level	Incapable	Incapable	Incapable	Incapable	Very Strong	Incapable
Household Level	Incapable	Presently Incapable	Incapable	Strongly Developing	Very Strong	Incapable
Geographic Level	Incapable	Strongly Developing	Incapable	Strong	Very Strong	Sufficient
Mass Media Level	Very Strong	Cost Inefficient	Sufficient	Strong	Inefficient	Inefficient

FIGURE 1 *(above) At one extreme, network TV is ideal for reaching a mass market; at the other extreme, direct-response marketing is the only way to reach individual households and persons.* **FIGURE 2** *(facing page) Growth in individual, household, and neighborhood-level targeting opportunities has come at the expense of the mass media, expected to continue its decline into the next century.*

targeting efficiency." Capaldini sees the future of media in terms of its ability to achieve varying efficiencies at mass- to micro-levels of audience contact.

Mass Media

Traditionally, mass media were perceived as efficient, because they had the "lowest cost per thousand impressions made." Today, marketers realize that true efficiency lies in getting the "lowest cost per thousand *viable* prospects," and mass media are well on their way to becoming a minority share of media expenditures. Even so, "mass media will always be with us," says Capaldini. "Many products have mass appeal, and many corporations will still want to reinforce target media with limited network approaches." Indeed, tomorrow's national marketers will use a mix of these levels.

Geographic Targeting

The advent of demographic desktop systems in 1985 spurred the spread of geographic target marketing, as marketers gained access to small-area demographics and linked them to media use. Today, everything from site selection to media selection is done at this level of proficiency. Many media can now be targeted at very small levels of geography, and this capacity will grow as marketers pressure ad agencies and media to deliver such information.

Percent Composition of Media Targeting Efficiency Yesterday, Today, and Tomorrow

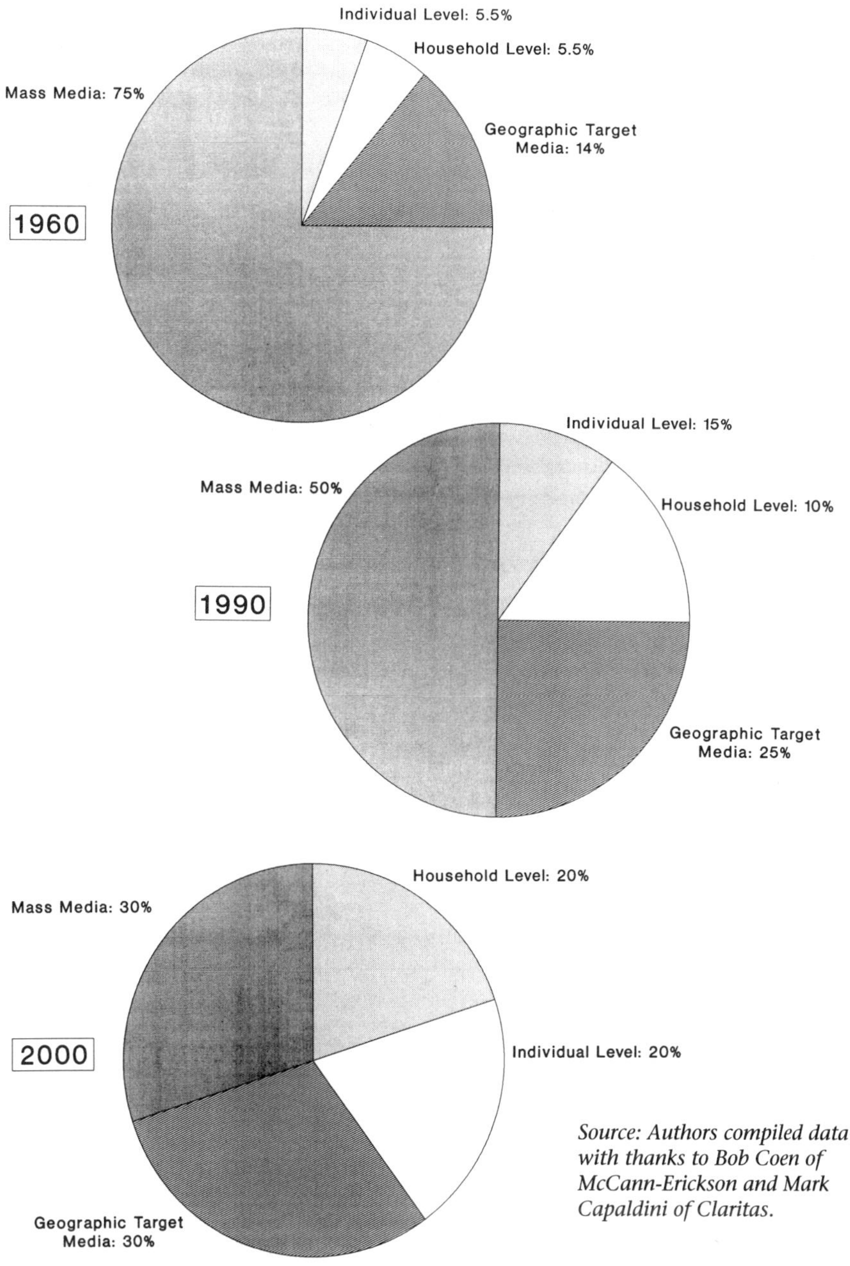

Source: Authors compiled data with thanks to Bob Coen of McCann-Erickson and Mark Capaldini of Claritas.

Household Level

Marketers can now use geodemographic segmentation systems such as ACORN, PRIZM, ClusterPLUS, and MicroVISION to classify customers at the household level. Back in the 1970s, marketers learned to classify consumers by demographics such as age, sex, and income, but lacked the means to target these optimal customers beyond the zip-code and census-tract levels. Today, individual households can be targeted using direct response and free-standing inserts (FSIs) offered by progressive newspaper and magazine companies. The share of media targeting that is done at the household level is expected to grow 5 percentage points from now until the year 2000. But even this level of targeting may gradually be superceded by improvements in the ability to target at the individual level.

Individual Level

For many products, the most appropriate target is the individual consumer. In 1960, individual targeting comprised 5.5 percent of total media expenditures; this share has tripled to 15 percent of today's media budget. But in direct-mail marketing, segmentation at the individual level is already a reality, an example being EQUIS (individual targeting by Equifax). With this system, more than one EQUIS segment can exist within a given household. By the year 2000, corporations may spend as much as 20 percent of their media budgets targeting individuals.

THE FUTURE OF MEDIA USAGE

The growth and very survival of various media will be contingent upon their ability to deliver targeted communications to the various levels of markets—individuals, households, geographic areas, and mass. The paragraphs that follow explore the current state of media and offer some predictions for their future.

Network Television

National network television used to be the only game in town. In 1970, it comprised more than 60 percent of television advertising expenditures and just under 10 percent of total expenditures for all types of media, including direct response. Network television's share of total media expenditures peaked in 1980, and has fallen to roughly 7 percent of total media expenditures today. National media will continue to be a way to reinforce local (spot) media for the largest national retailers, but we project that national network television media consumption will account for less than 5 percent of total media expenditures by 1995.

Spot and Cable TV

With the advent of micromarketing in the 1980s and cutbacks in media budgets, the future for spot promotions and cable television looks bright. Any growth in total television expenditures will be driven by spot and cable at the expense of national television and print media.

Radio

For the most part, radio is a spot-media solution for marketers who wish to reach their targets. As a result, radio has increased its share of total national media expenditures between 1970 and 1990. Radio is an efficient buy because formats are becoming increasingly distinct, referred to as *format fragmentation* by Capaldini. Today, a local radio station might be considered a market leader with only a 9 percent "listenshare." Back in 1970, a larger percent denoted a leadership position because there were fewer stations offering broader formats. Radio will see a bright future and account for a growing proportion of total media expenditures by 1995.

Newspapers and Magazines

Back in 1970, newspapers and magazines accounted for 29 percent of national media expenditures. This media share declined to 27 percent in 1980 and 25 percent in 1990. In 1970, most newspapers delivered 1.6 tabloids per household; today, this figure is down to 0.7 deliveries per household. People simply don't seem to be reading as much. The demise of print media can be attributed to three major forces:

Changing Demographics—Syndicated research points out that younger people are less likely than older people to read print media. Some believe that the young will take on their parents' reading habits as they age. We believe that this may not be true because of what demographers call the "cohort effect." The cohort effect, simplified, says that today's youngsters may not behave as their elders do when they themselves get older, because their unique life experiences will mold their media consumption habits. Because of this cohort effect, it is difficult to subscribe to the theory that an aging population means a bright future for print media.

Electronic Competition—We live in an age of instant gratification, and media consumption is certainly no exception to this. The introduction of electronic media has changed the nature of the industry. At the time of this writing, we are witnessing a war in the Persian gulf reported to us live. Electronic services often offer the most up-to-date news and financial information. New electronic competitors will continue to eat away at print media's dwindling market share during the 1990s.

Target Marketing—Many advertisers in the 1980s wanted to target print advertising to specific households. Many in the print media industry resisted because they feared that targeted advertising would result in "cherry picking" and diminished print media expenditures. They were right, and today, newspapers have been forced to incorporate free-standing inserts (FSIs) to keep their advertising customers. Meanwhile, direct-response media continue to make print obsolete as an efficient media option.

Advertising expenditures on newspapers and magazines will continue to erode. The best in the business will survive by adopting customer information systems and continuing the development of FSIs and binding technologies.

Direct Mail and Telemarketing

Direct response is today's fastest-growing medium. In 1960, less than 6 percent of media budgets were allocated to this technique. This share grew to 15 percent by 1990, and may comprise as much as 20 percent of total media expenditures by 2000. The advantage of direct-response marketing is that its rate of success can be directly measured. In addition, many companies are developing internal customer databases to help them use mail and telecommunications to talk directly with their customers.

One cloud in the blue sky of direct response is the privacy issue, something that marketers will have to resolve in the coming years. Other challenges include escalating postal rates, new telemarketing laws, and the possibility that more states will introduce sales and use taxes. The case studies that follow illustrate how all kinds of media currently use desktop marketing systems to target their advertisers' consumers.

CASE STUDY

KCPQ - TV 13

COMPANY BACKGROUND

KCPQ-13 is a television station in Washington that serves the Seattle-Tacoma Designated Market Area (DMA) as defined by the Nielsen rating service. KCPQ has recently institutionalized and implemented a custom value-added program called "On Target Marketing." The idea behind the program was to go beyond simply selling commercial airtime to providing a service to existing and prospective advertising clients. According to Chris Kelly, research director for KCPQ, "We're becoming consultants to our clients and, as advisers, we offer more than a commodity for sale. We want to do more in the way of understanding our customers."

THE PROBLEM

The challenge facing KCPQ and other television stations is to locate and quantify potential product and service markets and link these markets to their media consumption patterns. More important, with shrinking media budgets, the station needed to demonstrate that it was providing more benefits for the media dollar. For example, says Kelly, "If you're a bank trying to sell IRA accounts, you don't necessarily want to be on 'Funniest Home Videos' even though it delivers huge household ratings." Indeed, today's advertiser wants to know more about the audience and is demanding this type of decision support information. As part of this program, KCPQ-TV recently performed an analysis for their theatrical movie clients that wanted to profile their customer base and select the optimal advertising media. It needed to determine how to best reach potential movie-goers.

THE SYSTEM

Competing stations in the Seattle area were already using various market analysis systems. As a foundation for its "On Target Marketing" program, KCPQ acquired the TV CONQUEST™ system. TV CONQUEST is an adaption of the CONQUEST system developed by Donnelley Marketing Information Services (DMIS) that has Nielsen audience ratings resident in the system. CONQUEST is a PC-based geodemographic marketing information system that includes a number of demographic, consumer, business-related, and media databases. (For more information about the system and vendor, consult the descriptions in Appendix 1.)

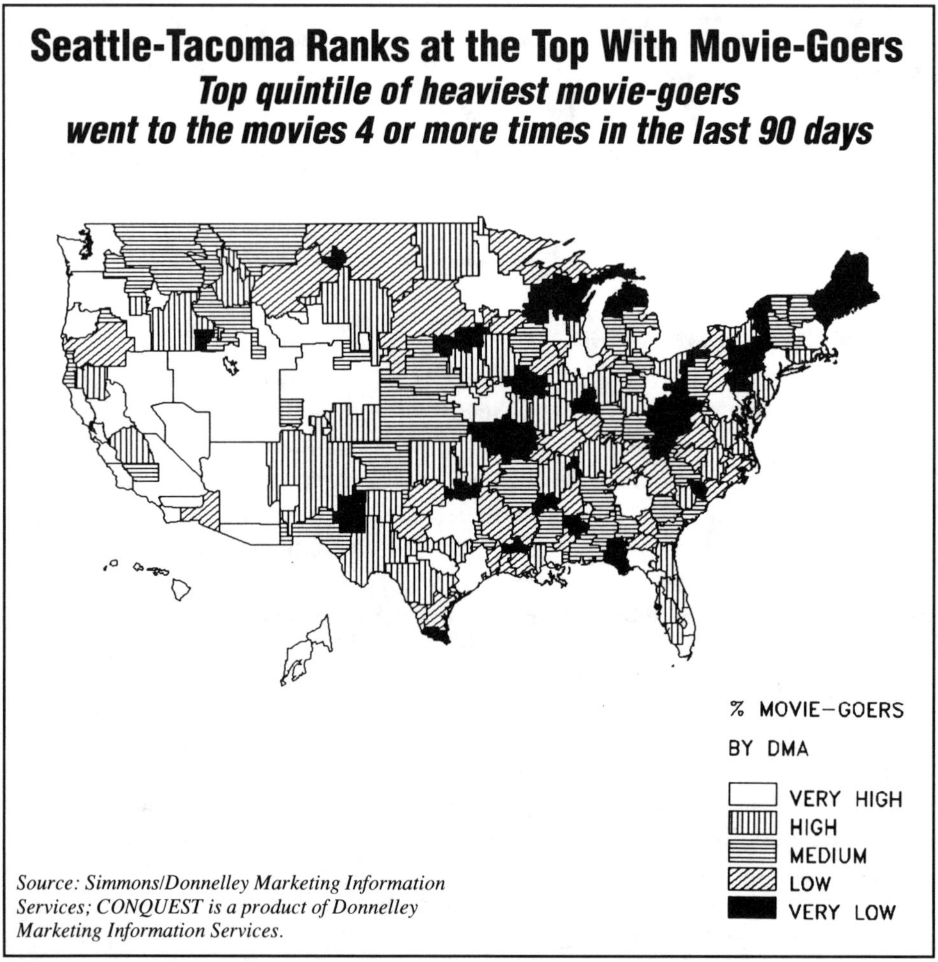

FIGURE 1 *By comparing the demographic profiles of heavy movie-goers with tthose of Designated Market Areas, KCPQ was able to demonstrate that its market ranked in the top 20 percent of the nation.*

METHODOLOGY

The first step was to determine the extent to which residents of the Seattle-Tacoma DMA went to the movies relative to the rest of the nation. This was done linking movie-going data from Simmons Market Research Bureau with demographic characteristics of market areas. The results revealed that residents of the target DMA are among the heaviest movie-goers in the nation. Figure 1 illustrates the levels of movie attendance nationwide.

KCPQ-TV worked with the theater client to interpret the data for marketing purposes. "What we like to do is look at the top quintile, the top 20 percent of the various lifestyle categories." By examining the top customer segments for movie attendance, KCPQ-TV can also access valued information on the target customers'

ClusterPLUS Product Quintile Report

Product : S1561: WENT TO MOVIES 4+ TIMES IN LAST 90 DAYS
Market : D819: SEATTLE-TACOMA
Base : Adult Population
Ranking : Usage Index

Rank	Code	Description	Base	% Base	Users	% Users	% Pen	Index
		Totals	2616064	100.00	360753	100.00	13.79	105
1	S 17	Well educated, young, mobile, singles, apartment dwellers	81715	3.12	18919	5.24	23.15	175
2	S 03	Younger mobile professionals, homeowners, children	89038	3.40	19728	5.47	22.16	168
3	S 44	Urban blacks, singles, large metro areas	13331	0.51	2766	0.77	20.75	157
4	S 07	Apartments & condos, high rent, professionals, singles	87471	3.34	17833	4.94	20.39	155
5	S 01	Top income, highly educated, professionals, prestige homes	20631	0.79	4119	1.14	19.97	151
6	S 24	Young mobile singles, urban, ethnic, low income, apartments	120332	4.60	23121	6.41	19.21	146
7	S 02	Well educated, mobile professionals, new homes & condos	13133	0.50	2457	0.68	18.71	142
8	S 14	Retirees, apartments & condos, high home values & rents	12011	0.46	2176	0.60	18.12	137
9	S 38	Old, low income, retirees, urban apartment areas	39509	1.51	6826	1.89	17.28	131
10	S 10	Well educated, young singles, apartments, professionals	105501	4.03	17852	4.95	16.92	128
		Quintile 1	582672	22.27	115797	32.10	19.87	151
11	S 05	Non-mobile professionals, established communities	74601	2.85	12052	3.34	16.16	122
12	S 04	Mature professionals, larger families, teenagers	57519	2.20	9242	2.56	16.07	122
13	S 29	Older, non-mobile, avg income, northeast urban ethnic areas	7462	0.29	1177	0.33	15.77	120
14	S 35	Young, mobile, avg educated, old homes & apartments	26542	1.01	4173	1.16	15.72	119
15	S 16	Non-mobile working couples, older homes, urban areas	54916	2.10	8310	2.30	15.13	115
16	S 12	Young mobile working couples, young children, new homes	187346	7.16	27601	7.65	14.73	112
17	S 15	Older, non-mobile, urban, white collar, old housing	68548	2.62	10074	2.79	14.70	111
		Quintile 2	476934	18.23	72629	20.13	15.23	115
18	S 18	Working couples, children, larger families, homeowners	16586	0.63	2374	0.66	14.31	108
19	S 27	Lower valued single family, homes built in 50s & 60s	100089	3.83	13549	3.76	13.54	103
20	S 40	Older, singles, retirees, old homes & apartments	15053	0.58	2028	0.56	13.47	102
21	S 11	Average educated homeowners, teenagers, homes built in 60s	44683	1.71	5854	1.62	13.10	99
22	S 06	Younger mobile large families, children, new homes	168143	6.43	21961	6.09	13.06	99
23	S 08	Older, fewer children, white collar workers	123594	4.72	15792	4.38	12.78	97
24	S 26	Below avg income, retirees, mobile homes, fewer children	82761	3.16	10079	2.79	12.18	92
		Quintile 3	550909	21.06	71637	19.86	13.00	99
25	S 45	Unskilled urban blacks, old housing	7391	0.28	871	0.24	11.78	89
26	S 13	Older non-mobile homeowners, fewer children, older homes	26863	1.03	3084	0.85	11.48	87
27	S 25	Young, below average income, apartment dwellers	202056	7.72	23170	6.42	11.47	87
28	S 47	Unemployed, urban areas, black females with children	2098	0.08	239	0.07	11.39	86
29	S 09	Average education, two incomes, homes built in 60s & 70s	206165	7.88	22769	6.31	11.04	84
30	S 32	Old, low income, singles, retirees, few children	40158	1.54	4263	1.18	10.62	80
		Quintile 4	484731	18.53	54396	15.08	11.22	85
31	S 22	Older, fewer children, single family homes	44350	1.70	4408	1.22	9.94	75
32	S 37	Average income, blue collar, primarily north central region	11276	0.43	1092	0.30	9.68	73
33	S 28	Younger mobile families, children, mobile homes	109876	4.20	10488	2.91	9.55	72
34	S 39	Older, non-mobile, blue collar, very old housing	8095	0.31	768	0.21	9.49	72
35	S 19	Younger, married homeowners, larger families, children	142735	5.46	12807	3.55	8.97	68
36	S 34	Older, avg educated, rural, non-mobile blue collar workers	16603	0.63	1450	0.40	8.73	66
37	S 21	Blue collar workers, children, homeowners, rural areas	59270	2.27	4773	1.32	8.05	61
38	S 41	Blue collar workers, rural, manufacturing areas	29324	1.12	2272	0.63	7.75	59
39	S 43	Unskilled southern blacks, families with children	1218	0.05	90	0.02	7.39	56
40	S 33	Non-mobile blue collar workers, low home values, older homes	13441	0.51	986	0.27	7.34	56
41	S 31	Older, non-mobile, low income, retirees, old housing	13715	0.52	997	0.28	7.27	55
42	S 42	Poorly educated, non-mobile, blue collar, rural south	64	0.00	4	0.00	6.25	47
43	S 30	Poorly educated, low income, farm families, rural areas	50376	1.93	2898	0.80	5.75	44
44	S 36	Avg income, Hispanic families with children	0	0.00	0	0.00	0.00	0
45	S 46	Unskilled, Hispanic families with children, apartments	0	0.00	0	0.00	0.00	0
46	S 20*	Group quarters: college dorms, hospitals, institutions	17554	0.67	2928	0.81	16.68	126
47	S 23*	Non-mobile married couples, old homes, farm areas	2921	0.11	333	0.09	11.40	86
		Quintile 5	520818	19.91	46294	12.83	8.89	67

* Results should be viewed with caution--insufficient sample size.

FIGURE 2 *The ClusterPLUS profile used to generate the shading on the map in Figure 1.*

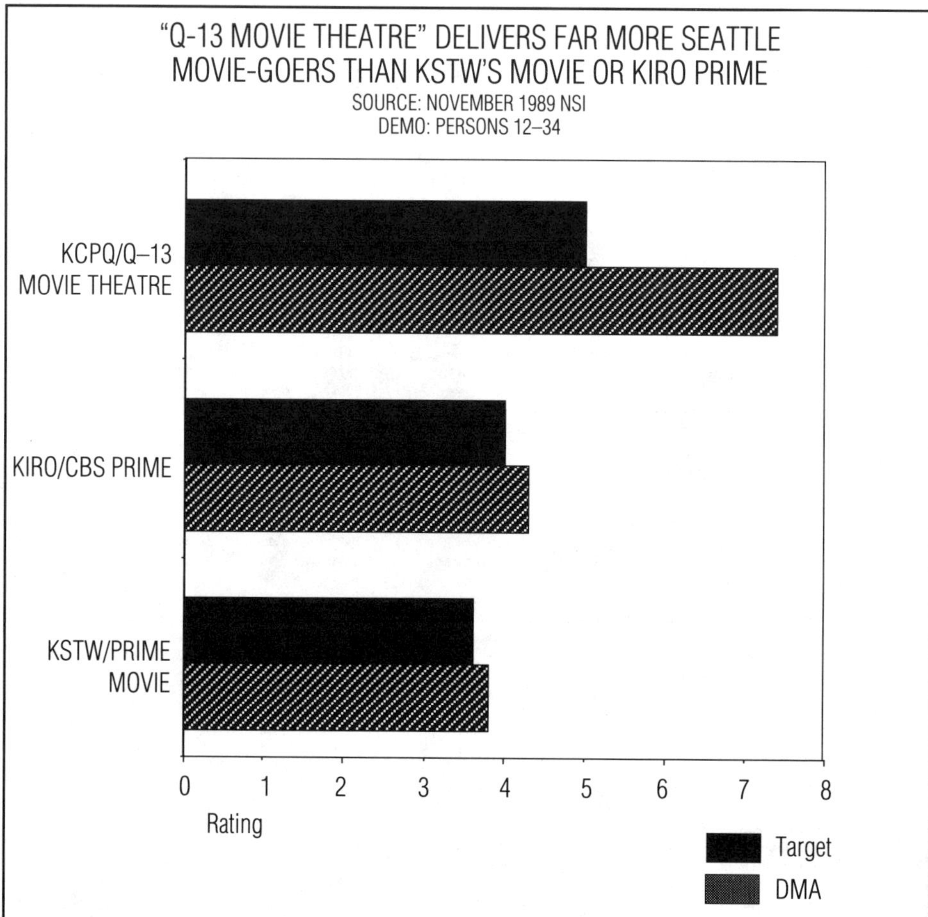

Source: 1989 TV/CONQUEST, Nielsen Media Research & Donnelley Marketing Information Services

leisure pursuits and other product preferences, which identifies areas for cross-promotion. "If you know they like to eat at Mexican restaurants, you can do some type of cross-promotion with a Mexican restaurant and the cinema client.... It has been very effective," says Gary Pazoff, KCPQ's marketing analyst.

The researchers at KCPQ used Nielsen NSI ratings and Simmons media data from CONQUEST to link ClusterPLUS segments (including product consumption) with their television watching preferences. "What makes TV CONQUEST different from regular CONQUEST is the fact that we have the Nielsen Module and we can actually go in and look at ratings. But what makes it even better is we can look at ClusterPLUS group ratings," says Pazoff. "It can really help make a better decision on what shows are best. You can't just think—OK, 'Entertainment Tonight,' that's a great show..."

MARRIED WITH CHILDREN ON KCPQ IS THE #1 PRIME TIME PROGRAM WITH SEATTLE MOVIE-GOERS!

Market: Seattle-Tacoma
Simmons Product Category: Went to Movies 4+ times in last 90 days
NSI ratings: 11/89
Demo: Persons 18-34

RANK	PROGRAM	STATION	NET	DAY	TIME	RTG MOVIE GOER P 18-34	DMA RTG P 18-34	INDEX
1.	**MARRIED WITH CHILDREN**	**KCPQ**	**FOX**	**SU**	**9:00PM**	**24.4**	**15.4**	**160**
2.	Cosby	KING	NBC	TH	8:00PM	24.1	20.7	115
3.	Different World	KING	NBC	TH	8:30PM	23.9	18.5	128
4.	ThirtySomething	KOMO	ABC	TU	10:00PM	23.7	18.3	128
5.	Roseanne	KOMO	ABC	TU	9:00PM	23.2	26.2	88
6.	Cheers	KING	NBC	TH	9:00PM	23.1	22.3	103
7.	LA Law	KING	NBC	TH	10:00PM	22.1	16.5	134
8.	Wonder Years	KOMO	ABC	TU	8:30PM	21.3	26.0	82
9.	Dear John	KING	NBC	TH	9:30PM	19.0	18.1	105
10.	**AMERICA'S MOST WANTED**	**KCPQ**	**FOX**	**SU**	**8:00PM**	**18.9**	**11.5**	**163**

Source: 1990 TV Conquest

FIGURE 3 *(facing page) Syndicated survey data reveal which local TV station scores best with movie fans.*
FIGURE 4 *(above) Although other programs had higher overall ratings in the Seattle-Tacoma DMA, 'Married With Children' scored highest against the target of heavy movie-goers.*

The next step was to access a Simmons profile of consumers who have attended four or more movies in the last three months. Heavy movie-goers were profiled and their characteristics used to develop media campaigns. Figure 2 categorizes heavy movie-goers by geodemographic cluster.

Once heavy movie-goers were identified, they could be matched with their media use. As it turned out, KCPQ viewers were among the heaviest movie-goers, and heavy movie-goers were more likely to watch KCPQ's television movies than the movies on other networks. (See Figure 3.)

In addition, the research indicated which programs heavy movie-goers watched other than movies. Again, a KCPQ program was most popular among heavy movie-goers. As can be seen in Figure 4, "Married With Children" was the most popular series with heavy movie-goers in the18-to-34 age group.

SOLUTION

KCPQ-TV uses TV CONQUEST as a sales device to enhance prospective and current customers. "We can now identify the heaviest users of packaged goods, automobiles, and even financial products," says Pazoff. In addition, it uses TV CONQUEST-based data to sell the entire Seattle-Tacoma DMA to national advertisers for spot television. The station circulates a pamphlet, "Six Reasons to Advertise in the Seattle-Tacoma Market," which features TV CONQUEST data. According to Pazoff, "Seattle-Tacoma is in many ways unique. Everybody knows that television advertising is flat, but that's not true in Seattle. Seattle has a very vibrant economy. Our mission is to relay this to national advertisers who may not be aware of that fact."

This case study was based on a presentation by:

Gary Pazoff, Marketing Analyst
Chris Kelly, Research Director
KCPQ-TV
100 S. King Street, Suite 405
Seattle, WA 98104

CASE STUDY

Gannett Outdoor Network

COMPANY BACKGROUND

Gannett Outdoor Network is the leading "out-of-home" media company in North America, with a network of more than 40 leading independent companies. Gannett Outdoor provides coverage in more than 85 of the top 100 Areas of Dominant Influence (ADIs). Gannett Outdoor falls under the Gannett Corporation banner, which includes *USA Today, USA Weekend,* a number of television and radio stations, the Louis Harris organization, and many newspapers. These holdings make Gannett the largest newspaper chain and third-largest media company in the U.S.

THE PROBLEM

Both national and local advertisers have found that outdoor advertising allows them to specifically target ethnic markets without the waste associated with other advertising media. Billboards can be placed in the neighborhoods where blacks, Hispanics, and Asians work, shop, and play. With different subcultures and even different languages, the challenge is to tailor out-of-home messages to a diverse group of customer segments. The following project illustrates Gannett's efforts at targeting the black population in Cook, Dupage, and Lake Counties in Illinois.

THE SYSTEM

Because the out-of-home industry has a targeted story to tell, the CONQUEST desktop marketing system has numerous applications. CONQUEST is a PC-based marketing system developed by Donnelley Marketing Information Services. CONQUEST provides access to Donnelley's demographic, economic, and geographic databases. (For more information about the system and vendor, consult the descriptions in Appendix 1.)

METHODOLOGY

Using CONQUEST, a map was created showing the concentration of the black population by zip code within the three-county target area of the Chicago metropoli-

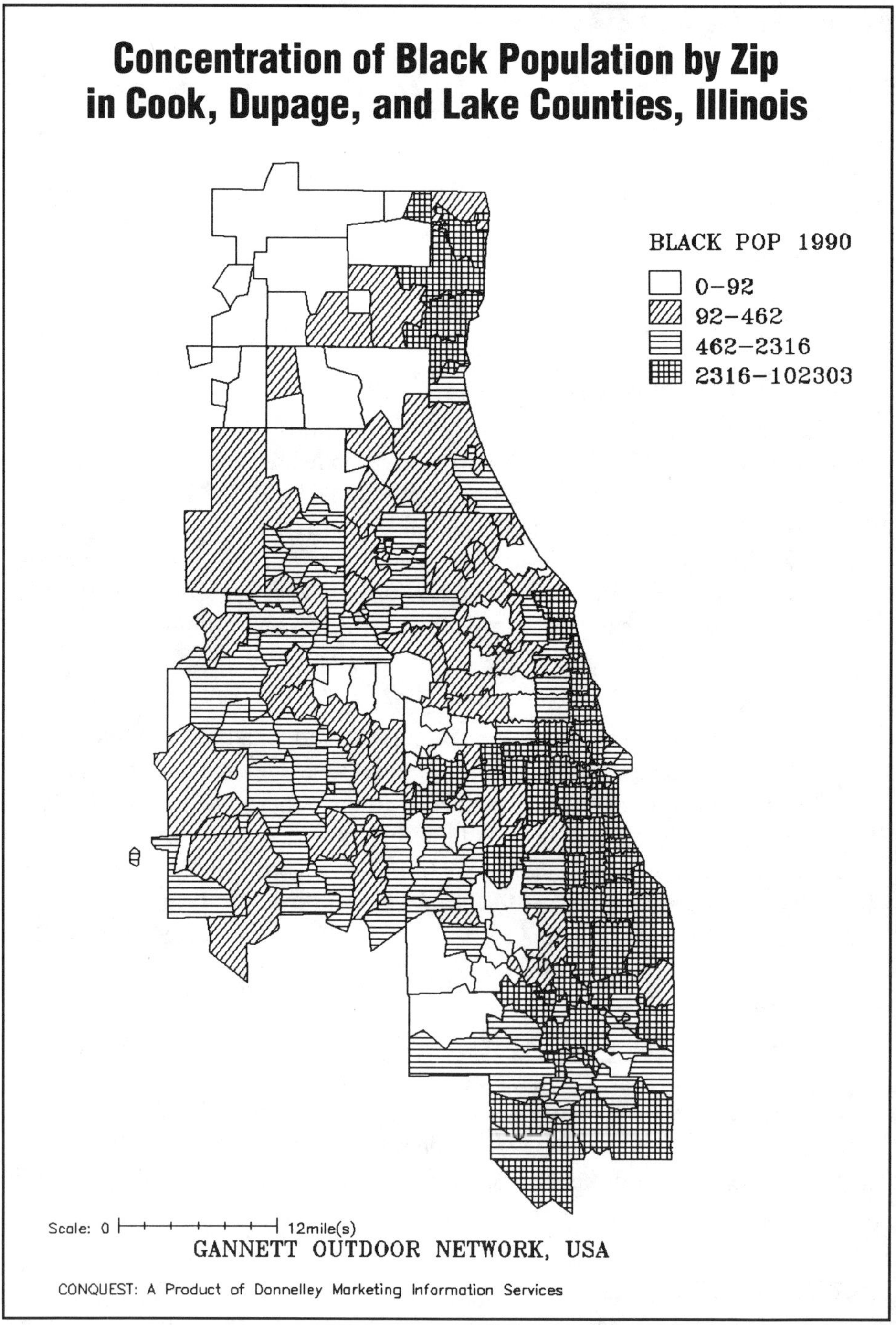

FIGURE 1 *Outdoor advertising, by definition a geographically oriented medium, is well suited to desktop thematic mapping applications.*

Percent Concentration of Black Population by Zip in Cook, Dupage, and Lake Counties, Illinois

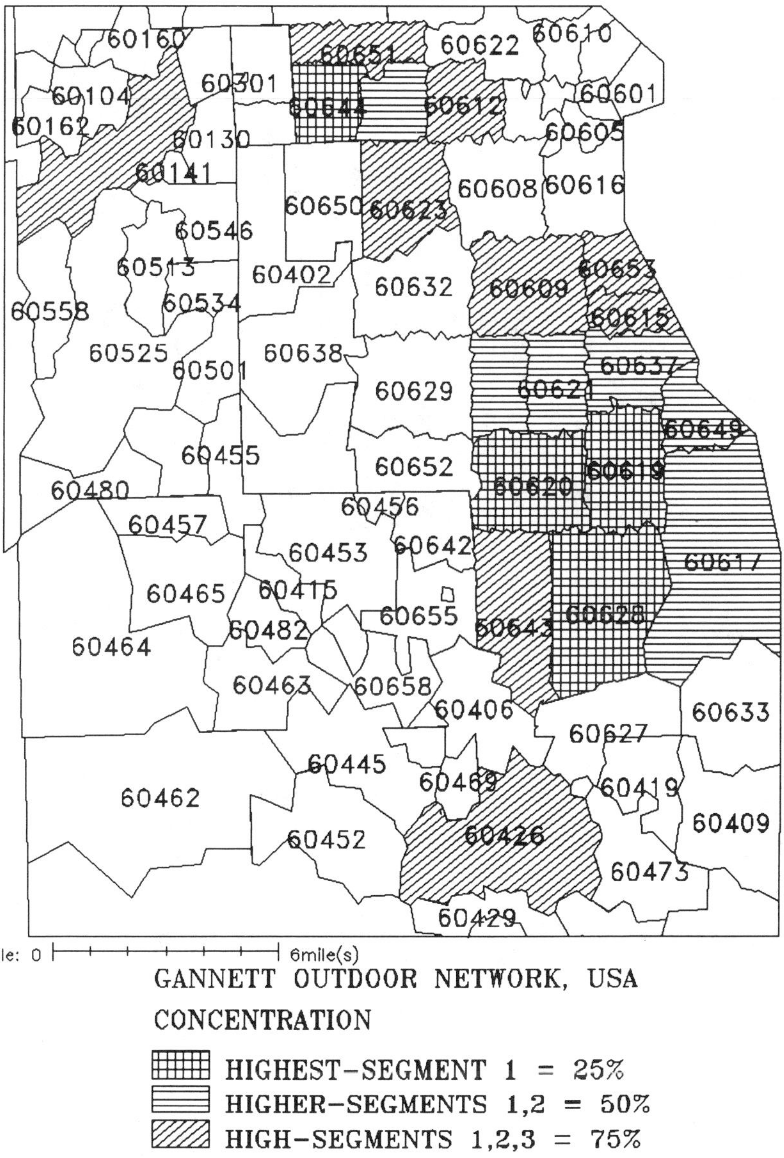

CONQUEST: A Product of Donnelley Marketing Information Services

FIGURE 2 *The Chicago area's black population tends to cluster in adjacent zip codes.*

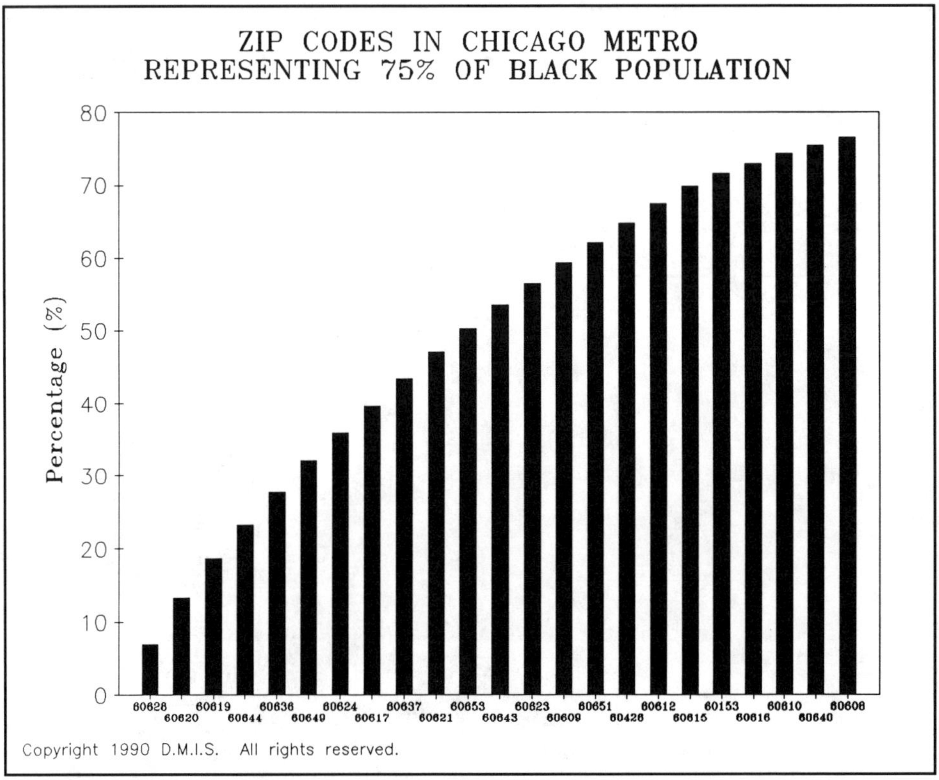

FIGURE 3 *A bar chart ranking the top 23 zip codes in the Chicago metro by share of black population.*

tan area. (See Figure 1.) This offered a broad-brush view of racial distribution in the metropolitan area.

The map not only pinpoints zip codes with the highest concentrations of blacks, it also displays the overall distribution of the total black population. It was then possible with CONQUEST's mapping capabilities to "zoom" into the areas with the greatest concentrations of the black population and create a more targeted map. (See Figure 2.)

For comparison purposes, a bar graph was created to show the distribution of black population within the most concentrated areas. The chart demonstrates that for the portion of the metropolitan area with the highest concentration of blacks, the degree of concentration for zip codes in the area ranges from less than 10 percent to nearly 80 percent. (See Figure 3.)

THE SOLUTION

The CONQUEST system facilitated a detailed analysis of the racial distribution within the Chicago ADI. This analysis identified the codes making up 25 percent, 50 percent, and 75 percent of the total black population of the three-county area. It was determined that 75 percent of the black population in the Chicago metropolitan area lived within a ten-mile radius. This provided the supporting information to convince an advertiser to use outdoor advertising rather than another medium to reach black consumers in this three-county area. The system was further used to pinpoint specific sites providing the most exposure.

This case study was submitted by:
Vonda K. Heimbouch and Megan O'Meara
Gannett Outdoor Network
444 N. Michigan Avenue
Chicago, IL 60611

CASE STUDY

Satellite Music Network

COMPANY BACKGROUND

Satellite Music Network (SMN) is a national radio network that distributes ten live 24-hour-a-day radio program formats to more than 1,000 affiliates throughout the U.S. The radio listening formats span a range that includes hard rock, adult contemporary, traditional country, and big-band music.

THE PROBLEM

Since the target audience for radio music programs varies widely from market to market, listener formats must be selected accordingly. As one example, SMN was looking for the best target markets for big-band music in the New Orleans metropolitan area. The first task was to get both primary and syndicated information about the population of the area to find the target market. The second problem was to convert this information into promotion targeting, direct-mail distribution, and billboard placement.

THE SYSTEM

SMN uses Claritas Corporation's Compass desktop marketing system to identify appropriate formats for current and potential affiliate stations. The data that SMN analyzes in Compass include data from Mediamark Research, as well as listener data collected from its affiliates. (For more information about the system and vendor, consult the descriptions in Appendix 1.)

METHODOLOGY

Listeners throughout the country can call an 800 number to request songs from SMN. Using the Claritas Compass system, SMN logs the caller's residential zip code into a database to create a profile of listener preferences and lifestyles by radio format. Affiliates also collect zip-code-level data gleaned from promotions and diaries kept by listeners. SMN then uses Compass to link format profiles of listener preference with demographic data to produce reports and maps that show the potential appeal for various radio formats in any market. A typical profile includes at least 10,000 listener request records for each format. Affiliates use the format potential maps to target billboard locations and direct-mail campaigns.

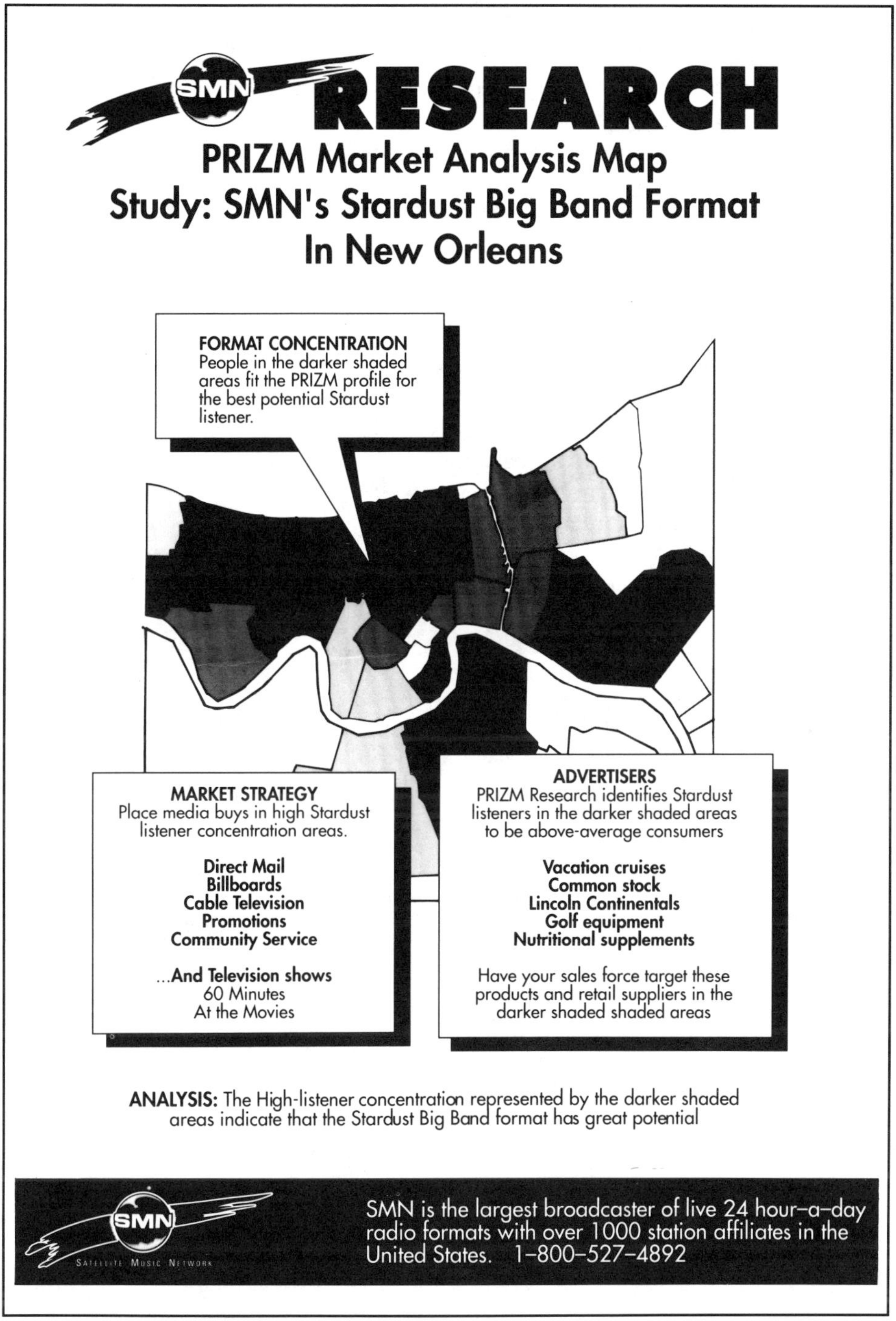

FIGURE 1 *By combining PRIZM audience profiles with syndicated research and COMPASS thematic mapping software, SMN is able to identify the best neighborhoods for its programming and the best ways to reach listeners.*

SMN also uses Compass to link format preference with other types of data to boost listening and ratings performance. For example, Arbitron's radio listenership data can be incorporated to help improve radio ratings for SMN's affiliates by comparing actual return zip codes to potential zips. The analysis also helps optimize advertising revenue, since listenership as measured by ratings determines advertising costs.

THE SOLUTION

SMN uses Compass in advertising sales for its affiliates by analyzing and mapping retail sales potential, auto dealer, syndicated product preference, PRIZM cluster, and other types of data. In the case of big-band listening preferences in New Orleans, Compass allowed SMN to identify the "best" neighborhoods for this type of programming (see Figure 1), as well as reveal the product preferences of these consumers and the best ways to reach them.

This case study was submitted by:

June Barnes
Satellite Music Network
12655 N. Central Expressway
Dallas, TX 75243

CASE STUDY

ATC Cablevision

COMPANY BACKGROUND

Cablevision of Fayetteville is a cable television system operated by ATC in Fayetteville, North Carolina. The system has 38 channels, including 4 pay services and Viewer's Choice 1, a pay-per-view service. With the U.S. Army's Fort Bragg close by, Fayetteville has a young, transient population characteristic of military towns—families with children and mid- to lower-income households. Out of all homes passed by cable service, the system has a penetration of 70 percent for basic service and 56 percent for pay service.

THE PROBLEM

Precise targeting is particularly important for Cablevision's pay-per-view marketing because the system has no "barker channel." A barker channel is dedicated to continuous advertising for pay-per-view events and movies, and is highly effective in boosting viewers.

THE SYSTEM

Cablevision uses Claritas Corporation's Compass system to analyze its subscribers' purchase of cable service, producing maps of pay-per-view buy rates by census tract. Compass is a PC-based desktop marketing system that integrates a variety of databases. The station also analyzes subscribers with the PRIZM lifestyle segmentation system. (For more information about the system and vendor, consult the descriptions in Appendix 1.)

METHODOLOGY

Cablevision analyzed its subscriber database at the block-group level to develop PRIZM lifestyle profiles for several categories of cable-TV customers. These categories included: active users, basic subscribers, pay subscribers, and pay-per-view buyers. It found that, overall, subscribers consist of four main clusters: "New Homesteaders" (young, middle-class families with white-and blue-collar employment); "Norma Rae-Ville" (lower-middle-class blue-collar families); "Downtown Dixie-Style" (inner-city, downscale, blue-collar singles and elderly); and "Single City Blues" (blue-and white-collar singles living in modest apartments).

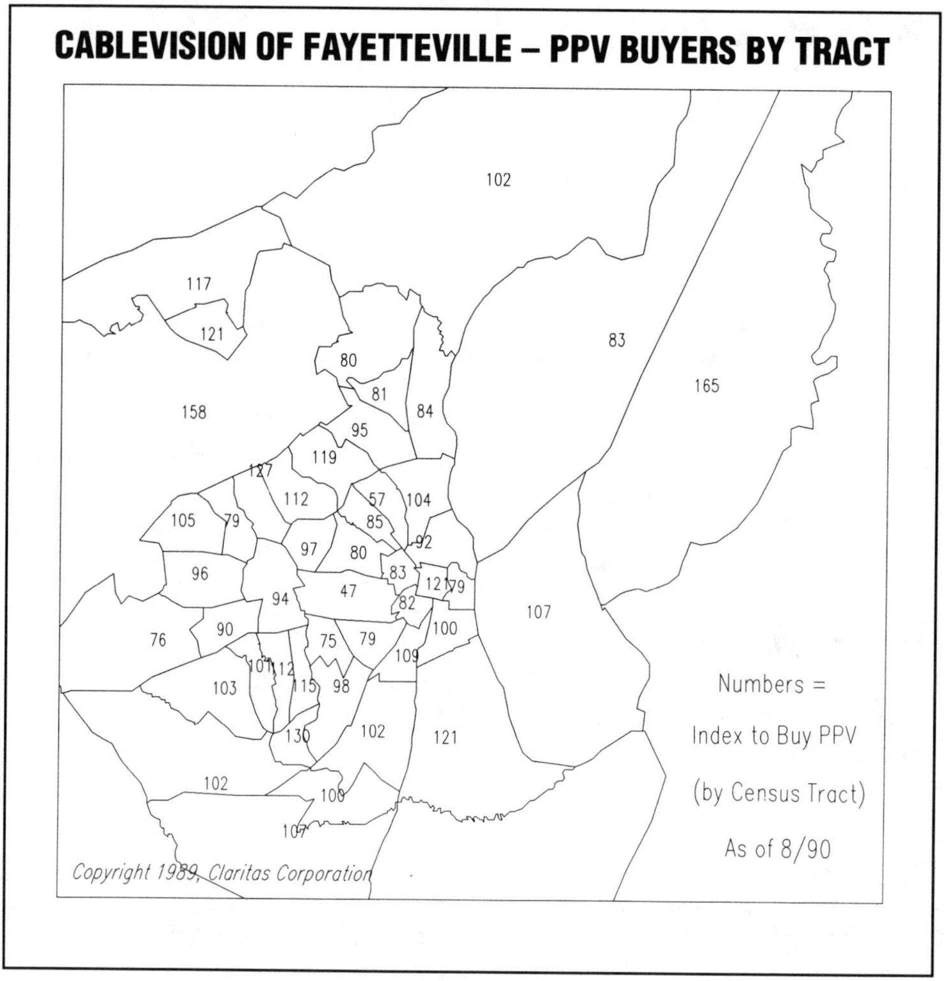

FIGURE 1 *Using PRIZM profiles of its subscriber base, ATC is able to target promotions for pay-per-view events at households most likely to order the programming.*

The highest users of pay-per-view services, however, were Single City Blues households. Fort Bragg, as it turns out, accounts for most of the Single City Blues households in Fayetteville. (A dramatic decline in Single City Blues buyers for an October 1990 pay-per-view boxing event was attributed to the deployment of troops to Saudi Arabia.) Further cluster analysis of specific pay-per-view programs found that wrestling appeals to Norma Rae-Ville, Single City Blues, and Downtown Dixie-Style clusters in Fayetteville, while auto racing events appeal to the small Mines and Mills cluster. New Homesteaders were not heavy pay-per-view users, but when they did buy pay-per-view, they purchased movies more frequently than special events. Compass allowed ATC to map the distribution of potential pay-per-view customers (see Figure 1).

THE SOLUTION

Based on PRIZM analysis and census tract maps, Cablevision is able to promote pay-per-view events using direct mail and telemarketing to targeted cluster neighborhoods. The system supplements this marketing with cross-channel promotion on eight cable networks, as well as radio and newspaper advertising. Direct mail typically consists of a postcard mailed to all subscribers in a particular target cluster. For instance, to promote an auto racing event on pay-per-view, Cablevision mails to Mines and Mills households, because they purchase auto events at three times the rate of all of Cablevision's pay-per-view households.

This case study submitted by:

Nadine Cualoping
Director of Marketing
ATC - Fayetteville Division
6205 Raeford Road
Fayetteville, NC 28309-3608

CASE STUDY

Canadian Products, Inc.

COMPANY BACKGROUND

Canadian Products, Inc. is a national advertiser in Canada. It promotes a variety of products and uses a wide variety of media. As in the U.S., media costs are high, and the marketplace is increasingly fragmented.

THE PROBLEM

The director of communications for Canadian Products, Inc. perceived a need to increase the effectiveness of his advertising campaigns. Previous media strategies had taken a wide scattergun approach using all types of advertising. The director's major concerns were that the advertising message was not reaching the target market and that the company was not using its advertising budget as effectively as possible. Although the company's products had been highly successful on the market, the director felt it was time to adopt a more streamlined and targeted approach. The consulting firm of Peat, Marwick, Stevenson and Kellogg provided assistance in the endeavor.

THE SYSTEM

The consultants used Compusearch's CONQUEST/Canada desktop marketing system in their analysis of media markets. The system's Lifestyles market segmentation system, developed by Compusearch Market and Social Research of Canada, was crucial to the analysis. Used in conjunction with CONQUEST/Canada, the system can perform market analysis for any market in Canada. (For more information about the system and vendor, consult the descriptions in Appendix 1.)

METHODOLOGY

The Lifestyles system allows an advertiser to identify its customers by unique segments, each with its own demographic and consumer characteristics. A strategic subset of lifestyle clusters was selected as the target market, followed by an analysis of each group's media habits (e.g., newspaper, television, outdoor, radio, and magazine) using Print Measurement Bureau (PMB) data. (The PMB survey measures magazine readership, product usage, and other media habits in Canada.)

The media habits of the target lifestyles were different for urban and rural target markets:

Urban Target Market

- Newspaper—Entertainment section
- Radio—Different time slots and radio formats were found to be more effective across lifestyle segments
- Television—Late-night news programming

Rural Target Market

- Newspaper—Dailies
- Direct Mail—Magazine subscriber lists
- Television—Game shows

SOLUTION

Once this information was presented, the advertiser was able to develop a new media strategy. The media plan introduced a newspaper campaign as the base for both urban and rural markets, thereby saving on production costs. Direct-mail campaigns were used to "heavy up the reach" in rural areas, using key magazine lists, and copy was written specifically for the target Lifestyles groups. For the urban areas, radio messages were designed to appeal to the different preferences of each Lifestyles segment.

This case study was based on material prepared by:

Kelly Woodcock
Compusearch Market and Social Research, LTD
330 Front Street West, Suite 1100
Toronto, Ontario, CANADA M5V 3B7

This study is based on an actual case, but due to the proprietary nature of the topic, fictitious names are used to maintain confidentiality with the company and its personnel.

CASE STUDY

A Major Market Newspaper

COMPANY BACKGROUND

The market area for a newspaper in southern California covers 2,800 square miles, with its population essentially concentrated in a string of communities in valleys connected by freeways. In the late 1980s, the paper's management set out to expand its local markets by fulfilling readers' needs for local and national news and advertisers' need to reach the area's residents.

THE PROBLEM

Newspapers have been using geographic and demographic information for many years to define their markets. In this instance, however, the traditional forms of information were inadequate for identifying local markets. In response, the newspaper surveyed the opinions, attitudes, and interests of market-area residents. The challenge was to translate this information into a form that could address circulation and advertising issues.

The paper also faced a more specific problem. One of its top advertisers is a home-improvement retail chain with many stores in southern California. The advertiser recognized that changes in the marketplace and shifts in national demographics offered opportunities to develop a market niche. The retailer wanted to develop a product mix that would match the needs of shoppers and residents within a five-mile radius of each store.

THE SYSTEM

The newspaper's marketers used the OASYS desktop system to conduct a demographic and lifestyle analysis of the market-area residents. Developed by National Demographics & Lifestyles (NDL), OASYS is a PC-based delivery system that provides national consumer and market data. (For more information about the system and vendor, consult the descriptions in Appendix 1.)

The OASYS system also allows users to incorporate their own data and conduct demographic and lifestyle analyses for particular service areas. Users can construct custom market areas and key the relevant database to those specific areas.

METHODOLOGY 1

Expenditure information collected through the resident survey was incorporated into OASYS to develop purchase potential for specific product categories and available advertising revenue. All data were geocoded and mapped to reveal key market segments. Maps indicated areas of homogeneity in which residents shared similar interests and attitudes. These were seen as areas in which the paper could establish common editorial and advertising zones. Figure 1 illustrates the distribution of family income within the target area.

SOLUTION 1

Based on the solution offered by the OASYS system, the newspaper established

FIGURE 1 *OASYS enables the newspaper to provide its client with maps like these that show the demographic and behavioral characteristics of the neighborhoods around each of its stores.*

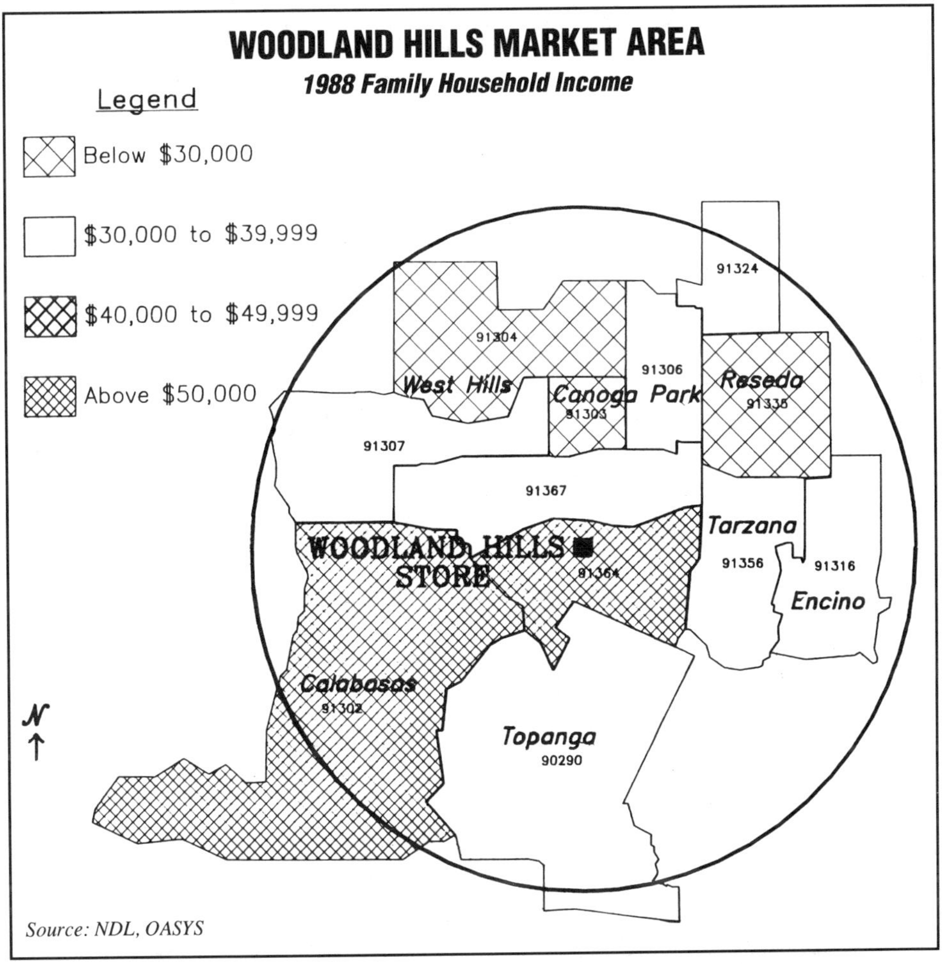

initial editorial and advertising zones. In each zone, the editorial content focused on subjects of interest and concern in keeping with the lifestyle characteristics of the residents, increasing the paper's value and readership. Within the first year, circulation and advertising increased almost 100 percent in the targeted zones. In view of this initial success, the paper added additional zones of targeted readership using the same methodology. Figure 2 illustrates the distribution of residents interested in gardening activities.

METHODOLOGY 2

A home-improvement chain asked each newspaper in which it advertised for demographic and shopping behavior information for each of its individual markets.

FIGURE 2 *By mapping lifestyle characteristics, the newspaper could geographically target its editorial content to its readers' interests.*

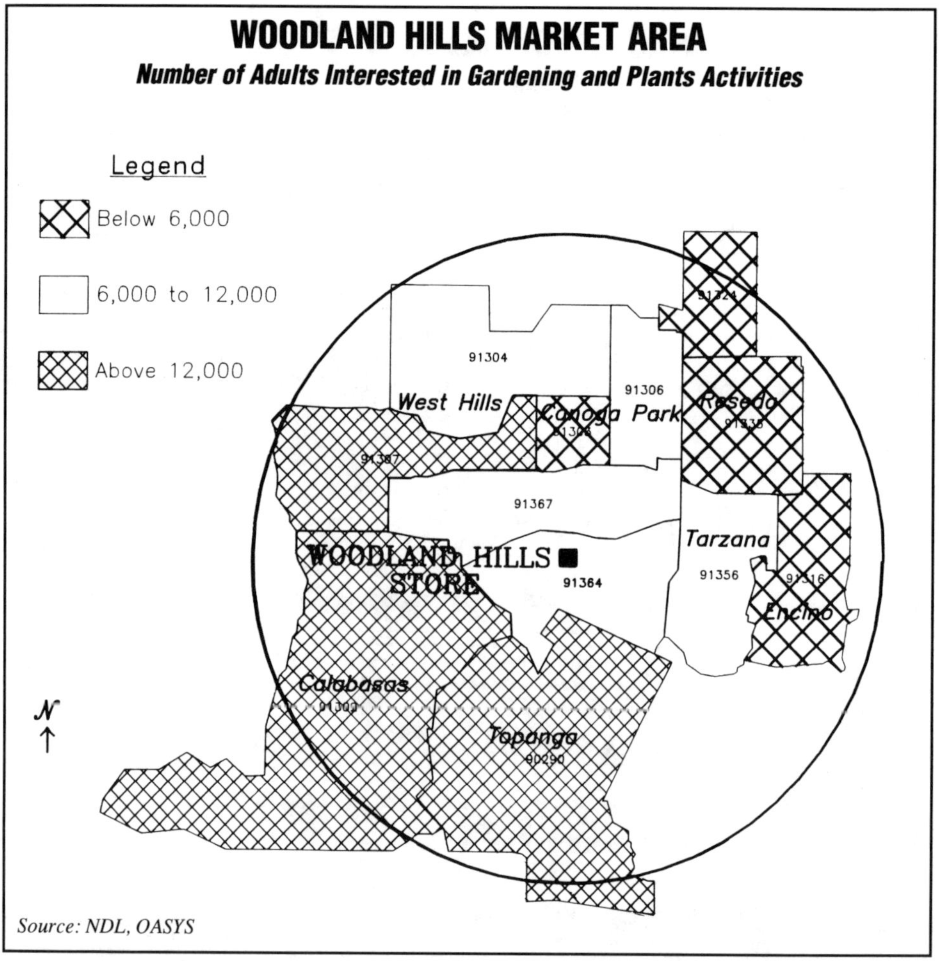

By using OASYS, NDL's client was able to provide the retailer with information about the market as a whole, as well as information about specific locations indexed back to the market as a measure of potential. The demographic and expenditure data were also mapped to provide visual depictions of the markets' characteristics.

SOLUTION 2

Because of its access to the OASYS system, NDL's client was the only newspaper that could provide this level and type of analysis to the advertiser. It was also the only newspaper to suggest creative ways of combining "run-of-print" advertising with a targeted pre-print campaign. The ensuing advertising campaign resulted in considerable media savings for the retailer, while the paper was able to capture more of this client's advertising.

This case study was submitted by:

Nancy Solomon
Marketing Communications
National Demographics & Lifestyles, Inc.
1621 Eighteenth Street
Denver, CO 80202-1211

CASE STUDY

INTELIMAIL

COMPANY BACKGROUND

The INTELIMAIL™ Division of Data Documents, Inc., is a full-service direct-mail marketing firm. One of its clients is a major petroleum company with 9,800 retail locations nationwide.

THE PROBLEM

The client had conducted direct-mail campaigns previously, targeting potential consumers in zip codes surrounding its retail locations. Considering the size of most zip codes, the client had been squandering direct-mail dollars on prospects who lived outside the retail trade zones of its stores. As a result, the client's cost per response had grown beyond an acceptable level. The client needed to identify a much more refined methodology for targeting prospects, and reduce its cost per response.

THE SYSTEM

INTELIMAIL used the CONQUEST system to target direct-mail prospects for its retail customers. CONQUEST is a PC-based geodemographic marketing information system developed by Donnelley Marketing Information Services (DMIS). CONQUEST provides access to DMIS's demographic, economic, and geographic databases. (For more information about the system and vendor, consult the descriptions in Appendix 1.)

METHODOLOGY

The client was initially skeptical of INTELIMAIL's ability to improve its "hit rate." To test this new marketing tool, it identified several store locations and developed maps that highlighted the census tracts within a one-, three-, and five-mile radius of each store. Using D.O.N.E. (Donnelley On-Line Express), which provides mainframe access to Donnelley Marketing's residential file of more than 85 million households and 120 million individuals, the client retrieved list counts of consumer households for all surrounding census tracts. Figure 1 shows household concentrations by census tract. In addition, the income levels of relevant census tracts could be graphed on the system.

The mailing size was set at 2,000 pieces per store, and mailed to census tracts

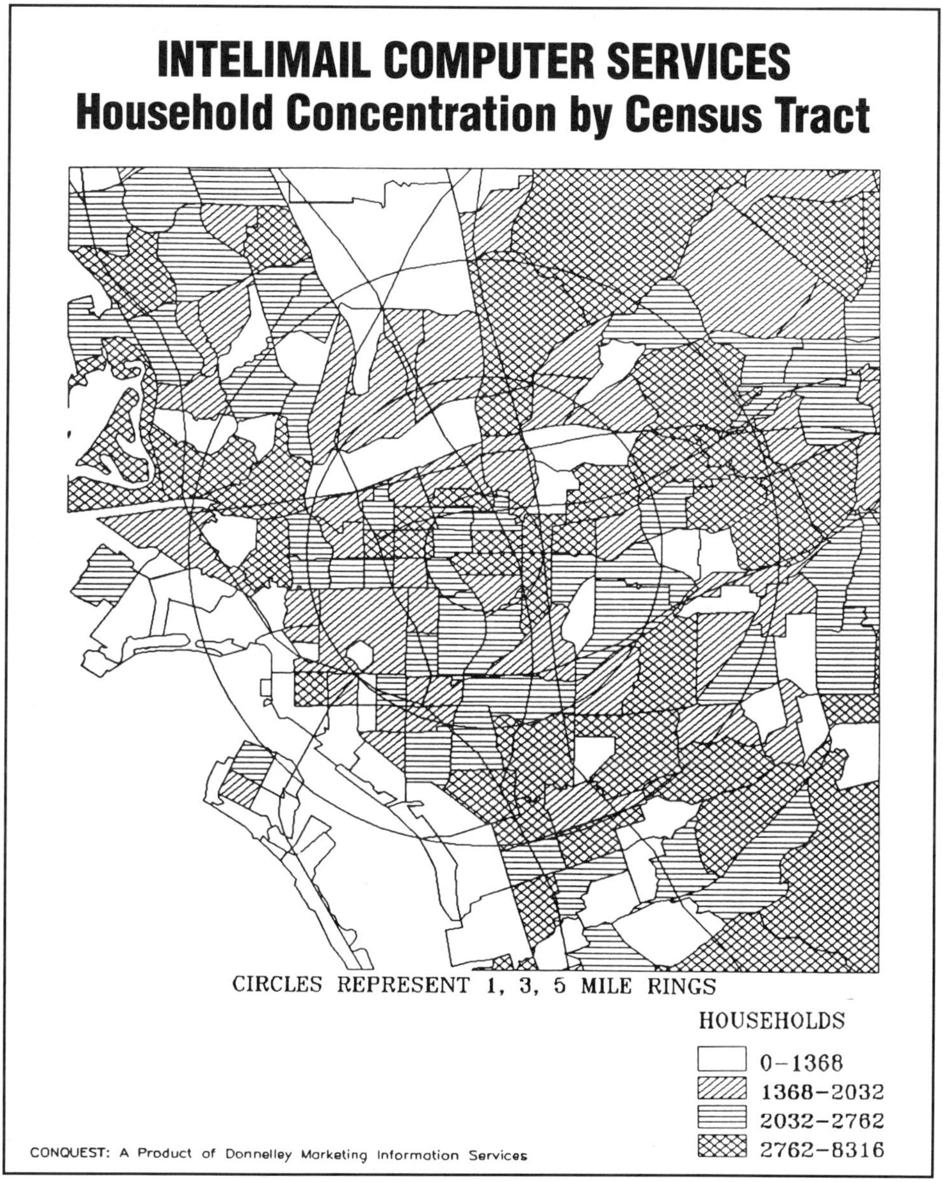

FIGURE 1 *Geocoding to the census-tract level of geography improved INTELIMAIL's response rate over previous mailings.*

surrounding the stores, more effectively covering each store's retail trade zone. By specifically targeting consumers in close proximity to the store, response improved and cost per response dropped, because the client was no longer wasting efforts targeting prospects who lived too far away from the stores. An additional feature of the system, CONQUEST/BYWAYS, allowed the client to identify physical barriers, such as rivers, lakes, bays, and highways that could limit or impede access to a store. This feature further lowered promotion cost by eliminating consumers who couldn't easily get to the stores.

THE SOLUTION

Based on the success of the initial test, the client has rolled out this program to all of its outlets. The client's store managers access INTELIMAIL's system by faxing an order form with the store address to be mapped. After CONQUEST identifies the census tracts, the D.O.N.E. system generates list counts by tract to reach the 2,000 mail quantity per store. The mailing lists are then ordered directly through the D.O.N.E. system. INTELIMAIL achieved its client's objective of reducing the cost per response while increasing total response.

This case study submitted by:

Michael O'Brien, Marketing Manager
INTELIMAIL Division
Data Documents, Inc.
14601 West 99th Street
Lenexa, KS 66215

CASE STUDY

DME/Manne Furniture

COMPANY BACKGROUND

Direct Mail Express Inc. (DME) produces customized direct-mail marketing campaigns for a variety of industries in the United States and Europe. DME's in-house capabilities include: promotion conception, copy writing, graphic arts production, printing, laser personalization, complete lettershop, list brokerage, and database development management services. Originally a division of US Trade Distributors (an international incentive marketing company founded in 1980), Direct Mail Express opened its Daytona Beach, Florida, operation in October 1987. The 1990 production volume was approximately 50 million pieces of mail.

THE PROBLEM

Success with any direct-mail promotion requires a mailing list that is accurate, current, highly deliverable, and most important, targeted to the right consumers. DME needed to provide its client, Manne Furniture, with a comprehensive customer profile that identified the demographic and lifestyle characteristics that best differentiate Manne's customers from noncustomers. It also needed to identify the neighborhood cluster list selection criteria that yield a mailing universe large enough for future mailing programs, yet effectively segmented to meet desirable response performance levels.

THE SYSTEM

DME used the CONQUEST system to target direct-mail prospects for its retail customers. CONQUEST is a PC-based geodemographic marketing information system developed by Donnelley Marketing Information Services (DMIS). CONQUEST provides access to DMIS's demographic, economic, and geographic databases. (For more information about the system and vendor, consult the descriptions in Appendix 1.)

METHODOLOGY

Donnelley Marketing's 85-million name DQI2 consumer database is the core of DME's customer list analysis. "We begin our analysis by sending our client's customer file to DMIS to have ClusterPLUS codes appended," explains Robbie

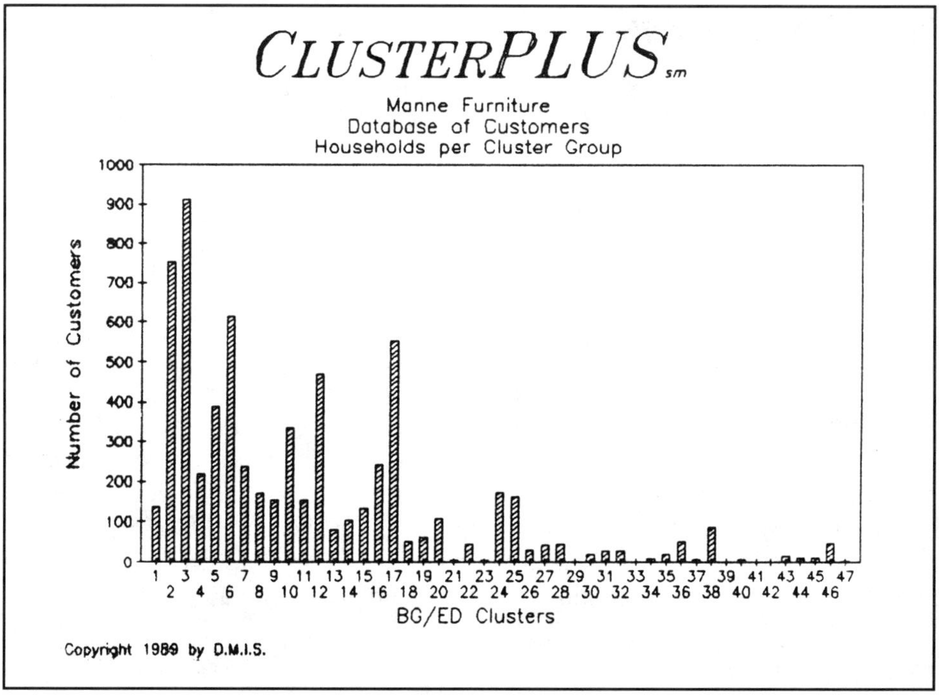
CLUSTERPLUS sm
Manne Furniture
Database of Customers
Households per Cluster Group
Number of Customers
BG/ED Clusters
Copyright 1989 by D.M.I.S.

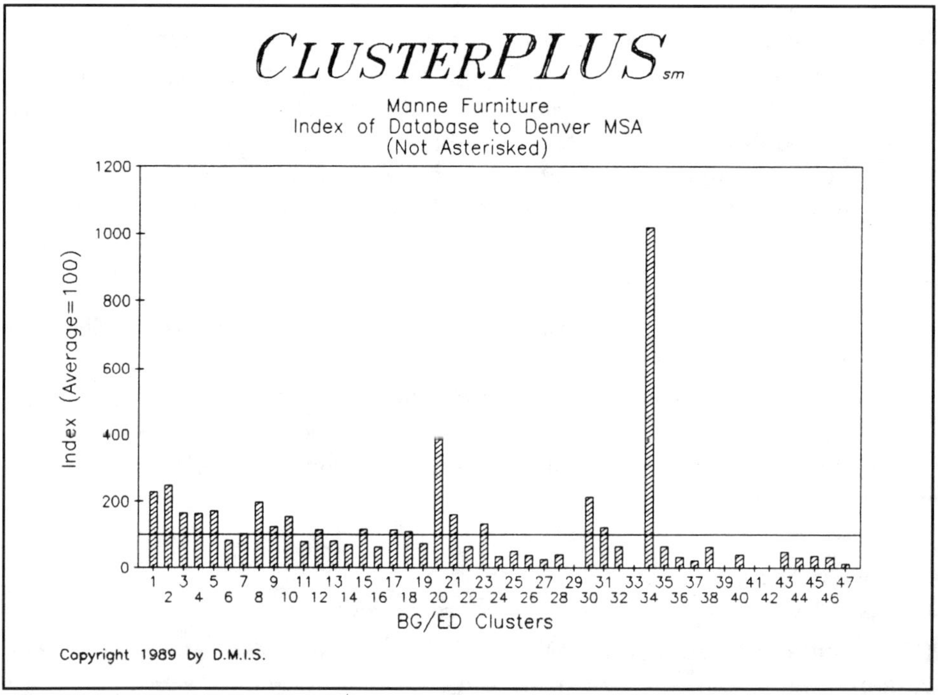
CLUSTERPLUS sm
Manne Furniture
Index of Database to Denver MSA
(Not Asterisked)
Index (Average=100)
BG/ED Clusters
Copyright 1989 by D.M.I.S.

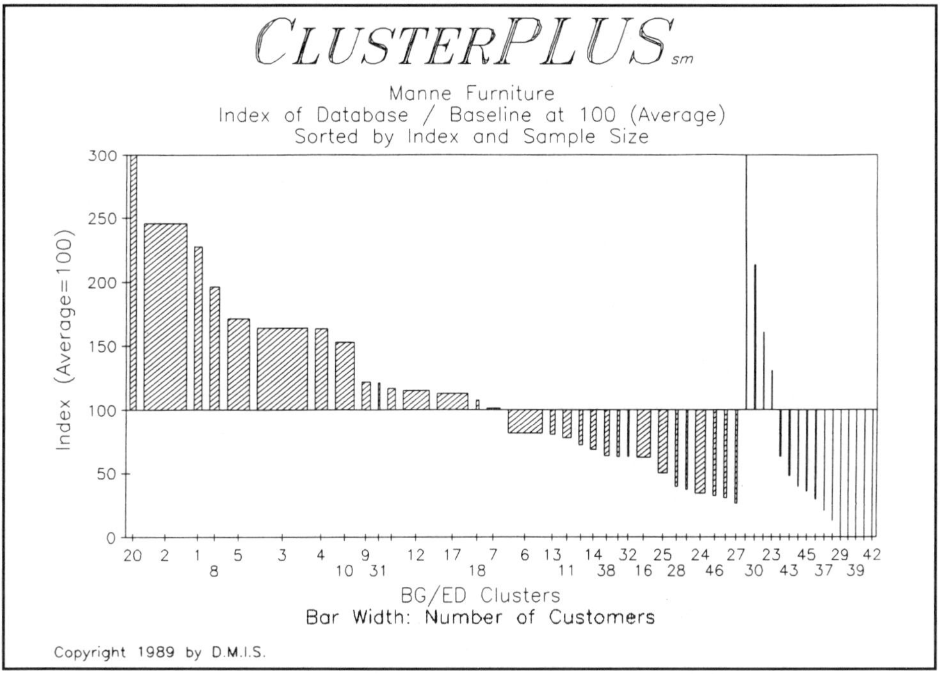

FIGURES 1 AND 2 *(facing page) and* **FIGURE 3** *(above) ClusterPLUS profiles indicate market segments that have the greatest propensity to be customers. Figure 1 shows the overall customer profile, while Figure 2 indexes this profile to the Denver MSA. In Figure 3, greater analytical significance is derived by combining two variables—penetration index and segment size.*

Tuttle, director of marketing. "We receive back specific information as to which of the 47 lifestyle segments each record represents. The match rate to Donnelley's file is usually between 80 and 90 percent."

In this case, using DMIS's CONQUEST system, DME compared Manne's customer profile against that of the general Denver metropolitan area market. Using DMIS's CONQUEST system, Figure 1 shows the distribution of Manne customers by cluster, while Figure 2 shows the penetration index of Manne customers by cluster—that is, their distribution compared with that of the overall market. Clusters with indexes above the 100 average indicate high-potential lifestyle segments.

The next step was to find large numbers of high-potential cluster groups. Figure 3 graphically illustrates a rank-ordering of clusters by both penetration index and size of population in the market area.

The final step was to locate the high-potential clusters by mapping their concentration in the market area. (See Figure 4.)

THE SOLUTION

Based on the recommendations of DME representatives, Manne Furniture targeted subsequent direct-mail campaigns to a combination of previous customers and new

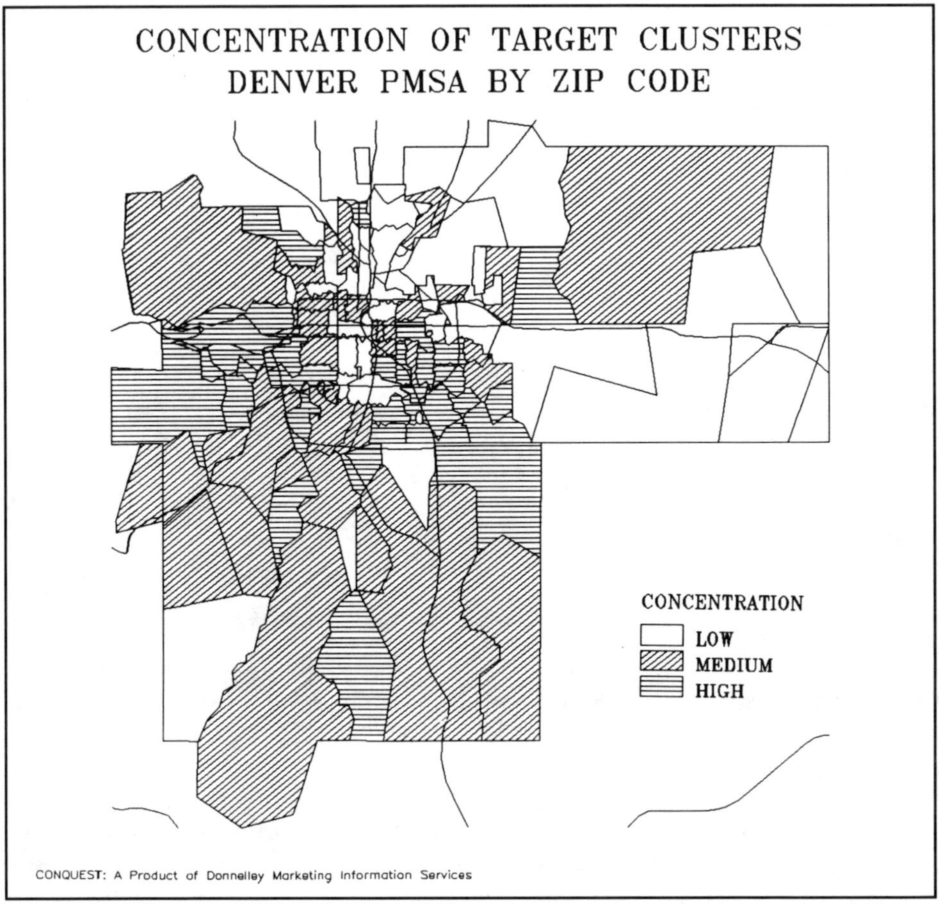

FIGURE 4 *High-potential segments are pinpointed by mapping their concentration by zip code in the Denver PMSA.*

prospects pinpointed by both cluster group and geographic proximity to the Denver retail store. The targeted promotion drew 1,278 people to a private invitational sale event, a response rate of 2.2 percent. In the past, nontargeted mailings had received 1 percent response rates. Average sales also increased with the targeted mailing, to $300, from $270. In all, sales from the promotion totaled $380,000, up $218,000 from a similar effort the previous year.

This case was submitted by:

Robbie Tuttle
Director of Marketing
Direct Mail Express
2441 Bellevue Avenue
Daytona Beach, FL 32114

4

Restaurant Industry

The restaurant industry faced a number of challenges in the late 1980s, and the 1990s promise to be no different. According to Susan Mills of the National Restaurant Association, the restaurant industry as a whole is sustaining a meager growth rate of less than 1 percent per year, slower than that of the U.S. population. According to Dun & Bradstreet, this represents a significant decline from the mid-1980s, when over 38,000 new restaurants were opened in a three-year period. The small growth that has been sustained reflects the demand for restaurant convenience generated by members of dual-earner households who are short on time.

"Many feel that the restaurant industry is overbuilt," says Jane Crossman of National Decision Systems. "The restaurant industry saw its brick-and-mortar expansion heyday in the 1980s," adds Tom Colaw, an independent consultant in Bethesda, Maryland. "Many expanding chains used locational criteria derived from the gasoline company strategies of the 1960s." Despite the overbuilding, restaurant developers contend that there are still many more sites available to them than to retailers in general. This is true even in Canada, according to Kelly Woodcock of Compusearch: "Chains in other retail sectors have expanded through acquisitions. This has not happened to the same extent in the restaurant industry."

Historically, many chains looked for sites based on the belief that retail activity functioned as a drawing mechanism for restaurant consumption. Many firms employed site-location analysts who had experience locating service stations in the 1960s and 1970s. The approach was to "window scan" sites by driving major roads to identify shopping centers assumed to generate restaurant business. Field analysts made a quick-and-dirty assessment of competitors already in the marketplace by taking a "head count" of customers at peak hours. Some firms even absconded with the menus of potential competitors to assess their products and price positioning. Hence, restaurant location analysts spent the lion's share of their time tracking competitors instead of customers. Today, the increasingly competitive nature of the industry will force restaurateurs to constantly reevaluate their marketing mix and to anticipate changes in consumer demand. "The slowed growth and a more competitive environment have resulted in a demand for up-to-date, actionable marketing intelligence," says Cochran.

According to Colaw, "Only 20 percent of restaurant consumers eat where they shop. Most restaurant consumers make their decisions on restaurant choice independent of their retail shopping choices." Furthermore, restaurant chains, whether fast food or upscale, do not necessarily locate their outlets in demographically similar neighborhoods. A particular chain may operate very profitable units in both densely populated urban areas and in more sparsely settled (and more affluent) suburbs. These realizations necessitate getting closer to the customer and spurred the placement of desktop marketing systems in most larger restaurant headquarters. Indeed, restaurant chains were among the first wave of desktop marketing users, and today there are over 150 restaurant organizations using these marketing and demographic information systems.

The challenges facing the restaurant industry are exacerbated by some of the unique characteristics of the hospitality industry. Restaurants do not necessarily draw their customers based on local demographics. In addition, a great deal of the hospitality industry's business is handled through third parties such as travel agents and tour operators. The restaurant business also has a high degree of turnover, and successes are often based on current fads.

The desktop marketing information industry will continue to respond to the needs of the restaurant industry with more consumer and competitive information. Of particular importance will be the further refinement of geographic information using census TIGER files and zip+4 analysis to get ever closer to the elusive customer.

CASE STUDY

Southwest Burger

COMPANY BACKGROUND

Southwest Burger is a regional chain of company-owned fast-food restaurants operating throughout major metropolitan markets in the southwestern U.S. Like most restaurant operators, Southwest Burger pays close to the minimum wage to most employees in order to minimize costs.

The problem of staffing restaurant operations effectively is compounded by the fact that the nation's population base is growing older. As a result, there are fewer entry-level employees available and willing to work for minimum wage, particularly in more affluent suburban areas, because attractive higher-paying jobs are available. It is becoming increasingly important for site analysts to identify convenient and viable employee sources for given locations.

THE PROBLEM

Southwest Burger's management team constantly evaluates the performance of all units. Senior management concluded that unit manager turnover, employee turnover, and the inability to hire stable, competent, and motivated employees were the major contributors to poor sales performance in many units. Management concluded, quite simply, that if a restaurant is not properly staffed, it will not generate a high sales volume. While this problem is extremely prevalent throughout the food-service—and especially fast-food-industry, Southwest Burger wanted to attack the employee issue by identifying high-potential employee recruitment residential areas.

Southwest Burger expressed several objectives in conducting this employee research:

- Determine who its employees are in terms of demographic and lifestyle characteristics,
- Locate large concentrations of these potential employees in existing and prospective metropolitan markets,
- Provide information to unit managers for recruiting employees from these high-potential areas,
- Develop data for the Southwest Burger site-acquisition function to influence the location of future company restaurants.

THE SYSTEM

Southwest Burger chose the VISION® lifestyle segmentation system to help identify the characteristics of residents in areas targeted for restaurant development. Developed by National Decision Systems, VISION divides the population into 48 lifestyle and behavioral segments. This segmentation system allows for analysis to the census-block-group level. (For more information about the system and vendor, consult the descriptions in Appendix 1.)

METHODOLOGY

Personnel records were accessed to obtain residential addresses for all unit employees employed during the past three years. Only present and past workers who had at least six months tenure with a Southwest Burger restaurant were included in this profile. The VISION system categorized each employee into one of the 48 distinct lifestyle groups based on census-block-group characteristics in which each worker resides. Once this profile was developed for all present and recent employees, a VISION Game Plan was prepared to organize the profile for action. This Employee Game Plan is graphically depicted in Figure 1.

The 48 VISION segments are shown relative to their percentage of total employees (scaled on the horizontal axis), and relative to their propensity to be

FIGURE 1 *The VISION Profile Game Plan enables Southwest Burger to analyze its employee profile on two dimensions—overall segment size (pct comp) and relative propensity (index).*

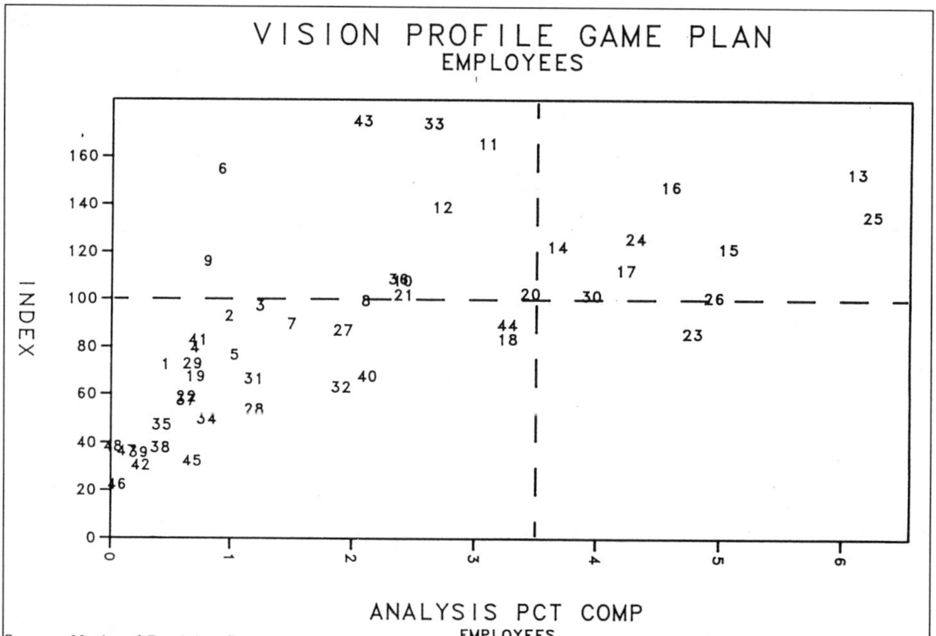

Source: National Decision Systems

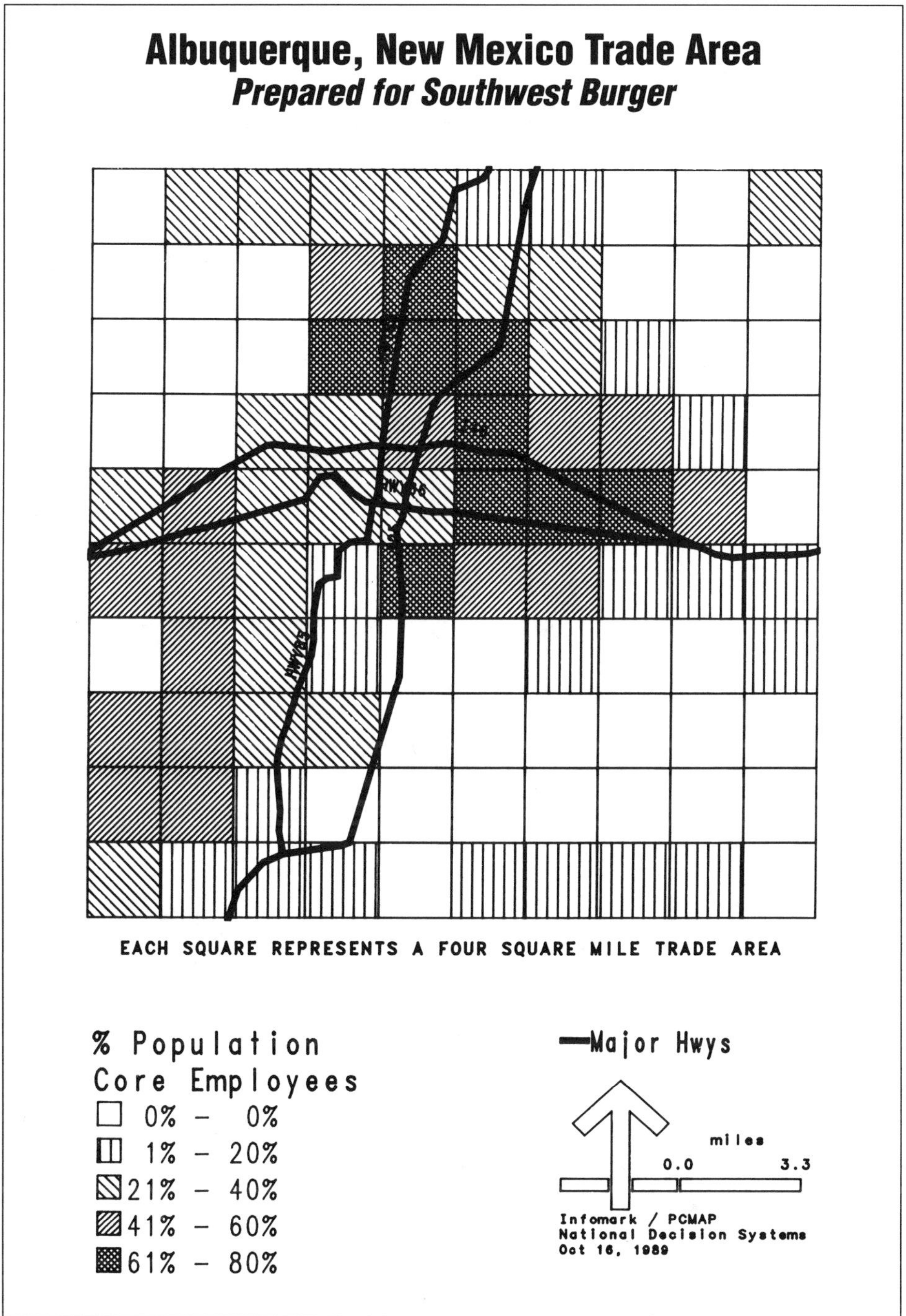

FIGURE 2 *Grid mapping normalizes geography, making it possible to make direct comparisons among geographies while compensating for the "density effect" of odd-shaped standard areas like zip codes and census tracts.*

ALBUQUERQUE, NEW MEXICO TRADE AREA
WITH 4 SQUARE MILE GRID CELLS

GRID CELL NUMBER	% POP LITTLE LEAGUE & BBQ	% POP BABY BOOM AGAIN	% POP INDUSTRIAL UPPER DECK	% POP PORCH SWINGS & APPLE PIE	% POP CARPORTS & KIDS	% POP TOWN & COUNTRY
1	0.00	0.00	0.00	0.00	0.00	0.00
2	0.00	36.12	0.00	0.00	0.00	0.00
3	0.00	35.10	0.00	0.00	0.00	0.00
4	0.00	36.12	0.00	0.00	0.00	0.00
5	26.97	0.31	0.00	0.00	0.00	0.00
6	13.11	1.60	0.00	0.00	0.00	0.00
7	0.28	15.40	0.00	0.00	0.00	0.00
8	0.00	0.00	0.00	0.00	0.00	0.00
9	0.00	0.00	0.00	0.00	0.00	0.00
10	20.36	0.00	0.00	0.00	0.00	0.00
11	0.00	0.00	0.00	0.00	0.00	0.00
12	0.00	0.00	0.00	0.00	0.00	0.00
13	0.00	0.00	0.00	0.00	0.00	0.00
14	0.00	0.56	25.40	0.00	20.81	0.00
15	0.00	0.00	30.03	0.00	34.79	0.00
16	0.00	21.19	0.00	0.00	0.00	0.00
17	6.47	15.01	0.00	0.00	0.00	0.00
18	0.00	0.00	0.00	0.00	0.00	0.00
19	0.00	0.00	0.00	0.00	0.00	0.00
20	0.00	0.00	0.00	0.00	0.00	0.00
21	0.00	0.00	0.00	0.00	0.00	0.00
22	0.00	0.00	0.00	0.00	0.00	0.00
23	0.00	0.00	0.00	0.00	0.90	0.00
24	0.00	0.00	49.98	0.00	14.36	0.00
25	0.00	0.00	31.88	0.00	34.70	0.00
26	0.00	2.17	7.26	7.72	6.29	0.00
27	5.26	3.14	0.00	3.95	0.00	0.00
28	10.85	0.00	0.00	0.00	0.00	0.00
29	0.00	0.00	0.00	0.00	0.00	0.00
30	0.00	0.00	0.00	0.00	0.00	0.00
31	0.00	0.00	0.00	0.00	0.00	0.00
32	0.00	0.00	0.00	0.00	0.00	0.00
33	0.00	10.05	3.70	0.00	7.36	0.00
34	0.00	0.00	27.47	0.00	8.31	0.00
35	0.00	0.00	3.57	31.61	0.00	0.00
36	0.00	0.00	36.83	13.17	11.24	0.00
37	2.20	0.00	21.60	6.99	9.70	0.00
38	12.67	1.75	20.57	0.00	13.46	0.00
39	9.62	2.46	0.00	0.00	4.69	0.00
40	0.00	0.00	0.00	0.00	0.00	0.00
41	0.00	25.77	0.00	0.00	0.00	0.00
42	0.00	53.06	0.00	0.00	0.00	0.00
43	0.00	17.52	9.53	0.00	0.00	0.00
44	0.00	0.00	0.07	6.52	0.00	0.00
45	0.00	0.00	0.00	13.00	3.06	0.00
46	0.00	0.00	2.00	23.33	4.63	0.00
47	0.00	0.00	12.78	4.70	29.93	0.00
48	14.09	9.55	15.66	0.00	29.02	0.00
49	0.00	44.43	0.00	0.00	3.07	0.00
50	0.00	0.00	0.00	0.00	0.00	0.00
51	0.00	57.41	0.00	0.00	0.00	0.00
52	0.00	58.27	0.00	0.00	0.00	0.00

Southwest Burger employees (scaled on the vertical axis). An index of 100 indicates an average propensity to work at Southwest Burger.

The upper right-hand quadrant of the chart represents core employee segments for Southwest Burger. These are VISION segments with an above-average propensity to be employees and that represent a substantial share of the total employee base. These nine core employee segments are:

Segment No.	Name
13	Little League & Barbecues
14	Baby Boom Again
15	Industrial Upper Deck

% POP HAMLETS & HARDHATS	% POP TOM SAWYER-VILLE	% POP YOUNG BEGINNERS	TOTAL % POP OF CORE SEGMENTS
0.00	0.00	0.00	0.00
0.00	0.00	0.00	36.12
0.00	0.00	0.00	35.10
0.00	0.00	0.00	36.12
0.00	0.00	0.00	27.29
0.00	0.00	0.00	14.71
0.00	0.00	0.00	15.68
0.00	0.00	0.00	0.00
0.00	0.00	0.00	0.00
0.00	0.00	0.00	20.36
0.00	0.00	0.00	0.00
0.00	0.00	0.00	0.00
0.00	0.00	0.00	0.00
0.00	0.00	0.00	46.77
0.00	0.00	0.00	64.82
0.00	0.00	0.00	21.19
0.00	0.00	0.00	21.47
0.00	0.00	0.00	0.00
0.00	0.00	0.00	0.00
0.00	0.00	0.00	0.00
0.00	0.00	0.00	0.00
0.00	0.00	0.00	0.00
0.00	0.00	0.00	0.90
0.00	0.00	0.00	64.34
0.00	0.00	2.44	69.02
0.00	0.00	47.88	71.32
0.00	0.00	18.68	31.04
0.00	0.00	0.00	10.85
0.00	0.00	0.00	0.00
0.00	0.00	0.00	0.00
0.00	0.00	0.00	0.00
0.00	0.00	0.00	0.00
0.00	0.00	0.00	21.11
2.10	0.00	1.92	39.80
4.45	0.00	19.35	58.99
0.00	0.00	15.26	76.50
0.00	0.00	9.19	49.68
0.00	0.00	6.23	54.69
0.00	0.00	0.00	16.78
0.00	0.00	0.00	0.00
0.00	0.00	0.00	25.77
0.00	0.00	0.00	53.06
0.00	0.00	0.00	27.05
0.00	0.00	20.81	27.41
0.00	0.00	10.71	26.77
0.00	0.00	40.67	70.63
0.00	0.00	28.75	76.16
0.00	0.00	0.00	68.32
0.00	0.00	0.00	47.50
0.00	0.00	0.00	0.00
0.00	0.00	0.00	57.41
0.00	0.00	0.00	58.27

FIGURE 3 *Individual grid cells can be treated like any geographic unit and access demographic and other data for further analysis.*

16	Porch Swings & Apple Pie
17	Carports & Kids
24	Town & Country
25	Hamlets & Hardhats
26	Tom Sawyerville
30	Young Beginners

To find these "core" segments within a given market, Southwest Burger mapped the data. As an example, the metropolitan area of Albuquerque, New Mexico, one of Southwest Burger's existing markets, is shown in simplified form in Figure 2, gridded into 2 mile by 2 mile squares or cells. This process highlights specific residential cells in Albuquerque with a high density of core VISION segments. When Southwest Burger locations are overlaid on this map, individual restaurant managers can pinpoint the closest high-priority employee neighborhoods.

Figure 3 shows the specific "core" segment composition for individual grid cells in Albuquerque. Certain segments, such as Town & Country and Hamlets & Hardhats, are virtually nonexistent in the Albuquerque market, although they are more prevalent in other markets where Southwest Burger operates.

THE SOLUTION

With VISION, the Southwest Burger management team was able to develop valuable information about its base of restaurant employees. It identified the core Lifestyle segments likely to be the right type of employee. By mapping the location of these core segments, management created a powerful decision-making tool for each existing (and prospective) market. Southwest Burger has been successful in reducing restaurant employee turnover by focusing recruiting efforts on high-density segments. These efforts include local newspaper and mail inserts to high-priority neighborhoods, referrals from current employees residing in high-priority neighborhoods, and high school and college recruiting efforts in high-priority employee areas. Management is also using its knowledge of employee profiles to influence the location of new stores. By incorporating the profile information into standard site-selection methodology, the company is confident of not only a successful location in terms of sales potential, but also one with a convenient base of the right type of employee.

This case study was submitted by:

Terry Munoz
Vice President, Traditional Markets
National Decision Systems
539 Encinitas Boulevard
Encinitas, CA 92024-9007

This study is based on an actual case, but due to the proprietary nature of the topic, fictitious names are used to maintain confidentiality with the company and its personnel.

CASE STUDY

Dunkin' Donuts

COMPANY BACKGROUND

Dunkin' Donuts is the world's largest retail coffee and donut shop chain, with over 1,500 outlets worldwide. The Development/Operations Division is responsible for new shop expansion throughout the U.S. and Canada. The Market Planning Department within the division provides data and services to its executives, as well as to other departments throughout the company.

THE PROBLEM

The Market Planning Department provides demographic information that assists Development executives in the selection process for potential new shop sites. In this case, the department was asked to evaluate the Dallas metropolitan market to determine the overall growth potential of the area. A later phase would evaluate specific sites for future development.

THE SYSTEM

Dunkin' Donuts chose National Decision Systems' Infomark system for its desktop marketing needs. This menu-driven system includes a demographic file with census data and selected third-party databases. The Infomark components of most use to Dunkin' Donuts are the Pop-Facts demographic database containing updated estimates and projections of key population indicators like age and income, the Business Facts business establishment and employment database, and the Shopping Center database. (For more information about the system and vendor, consult the description in Appendix 1.)

METHODOLOGY

The first step in evaluating the Dallas area was to generate demographic and shopping-center data. Infomark allows users to view selected demographic data by major sub-geographies (counties and zip codes), as well as specific locations (major road intersections). This provides information about the potential residential customer base in a market. The employment data from Business Facts offer insight into the daytime market of a local area, i.e., the people who work there.

The shopping-center and business databases also provide information about

FIGURE 1 *Dunkin' Donuts uses Infomark maps like this to determine high-potential neighborhoods for additional sites.*

competing and complementary retail sites. In the latter case, Dunkin' Donuts researchers systematically use business data to look for potential and mutually beneficial tie-ins with other local retailers, such as gas stations.

Once the initial customer profile was completed, researchers conducted an analysis that got closer to the ground. Infomark's PCMAP module merges roads and highways with other levels of geography to produce a microgeographic look at a site, trade area, or entire market. Figure 1 illustrates the customer potential in the Dallas metro area by zip code. The high-potential areas would be analyzed further to determine the availability of sites and whether such sites met the company's selection criteria for new donut-shop locations.

THE SOLUTION

By combining customer-potential data, demographic data, and employment data at the zip-code level on one integrated system, the direction for future development in the Dallas area became clear. Shopping-center information was helpful in pinpointing site-specific locations, and mapping functions depicted data in a visual format. The end result of the desktop analysis was a complete market plan for the metropolitan Dallas area. This plan became a working tool to help field executives effectively develop the market.

Dunkin' Donuts researchers process 60 to 70 requests like the above example from both its field organization and in-house demands each month. With this volume of demographic analysis, the company has realized a substantial cost savings with the desktop marketing system.

This case study was submitted by:

John E. Rogozenski, Jr.
Director of Market Planning and Administration
Dunkin' Donuts, Inc.
14 Pacella Park Drive
Randolph, MA 02370

CASE STUDY

Sonic Industries

COMPANY BACKGROUND

Sonic Industries is a 32-year-old Oklahoma City-based chain of approximately 1,100 1950s-style drive-in restaurants that specialize in hamburgers, hot dogs, and onion rings. The units feature a nostalgic in-car dining atmosphere with carhop service to customers in covered parking stalls. With the majority of the chain's units in the South Central United States, current expansion efforts are focused in the Southeast and Southwest.

THE PROBLEM

Historically, Sonic has expanded by selling additional franchises. It has been its policy not to grant exclusive territorial rights to franchise holders. However, the recent growth in per-unit sales has boosted franchisers' interest in developing new units, and Sonic has begun to grant exclusive territorial agreements to eliminate conflicts in areas with more than one franchise group.

In the case of one major metropolitan area, there were five long-time Sonic franchisees in the process of developing new units. One of these groups had previously been granted an exclusive territory for a portion of the city. The other four groups continued to develop on a unit-by-unit basis, and conflicts over certain locations were becoming more and more common.

THE SYSTEM

CONQUEST is a personal computer-based geodemographic marketing information system developed by Donnelley Marketing Information Services (DMIS). It provides access to Donnelley's demographic, economic, and geographic databases. (For more information about the system and vendor, consult the description in Appendix 1.)

Sonic Industries has also worked with Blake, Silverman & Partners, a micromarket planning company, to develop a proprietary system that integrates the functions of the Corporate Planning, Franchise Development, Operations, and Marketing Divisions into a single customized information planning environment. Sonic uses a customized version of the Donnelley desktop decision-making system as the "engine" driving its proprietary system.

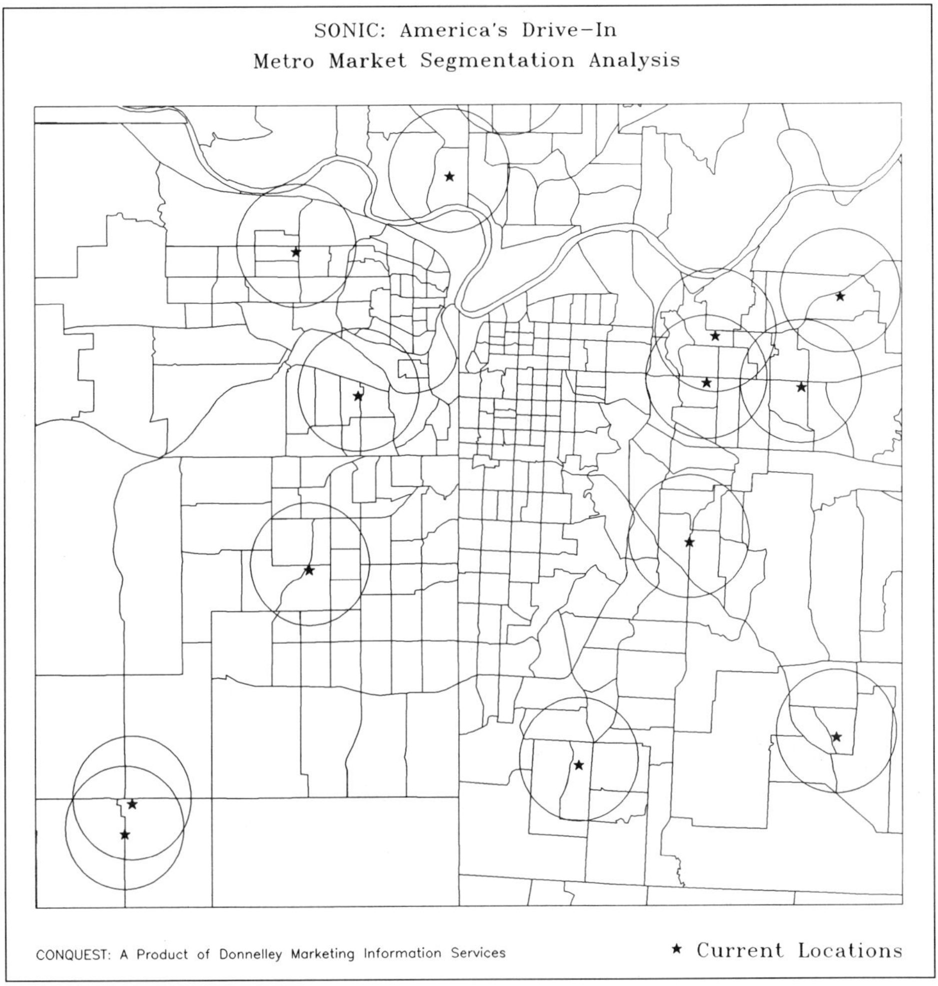

FIGURE 1 *Sonic Industries uses CONQUEST to map the locations and trade area radii for each of its existing franchise units in a major metropolitan area.*

METHODOLOGY

Using CONQUEST and the profiles developed jointly with Blake, Silverman & Partners, Sonic segmented the "unclaimed" portion of the metro market into four exclusive territories. This was achieved by creating proprietary customer and trading-area profiles. These profiles were then linked directly to a customized market-potential model.

The first step was to segment the metropolitan area into four separate areas to be assigned to particular franchise groups. This involved determining market characteristics by mapping each of the existing 13 units and its contractually protected trade-area radius. This baseline information is depicted in Figure 1.

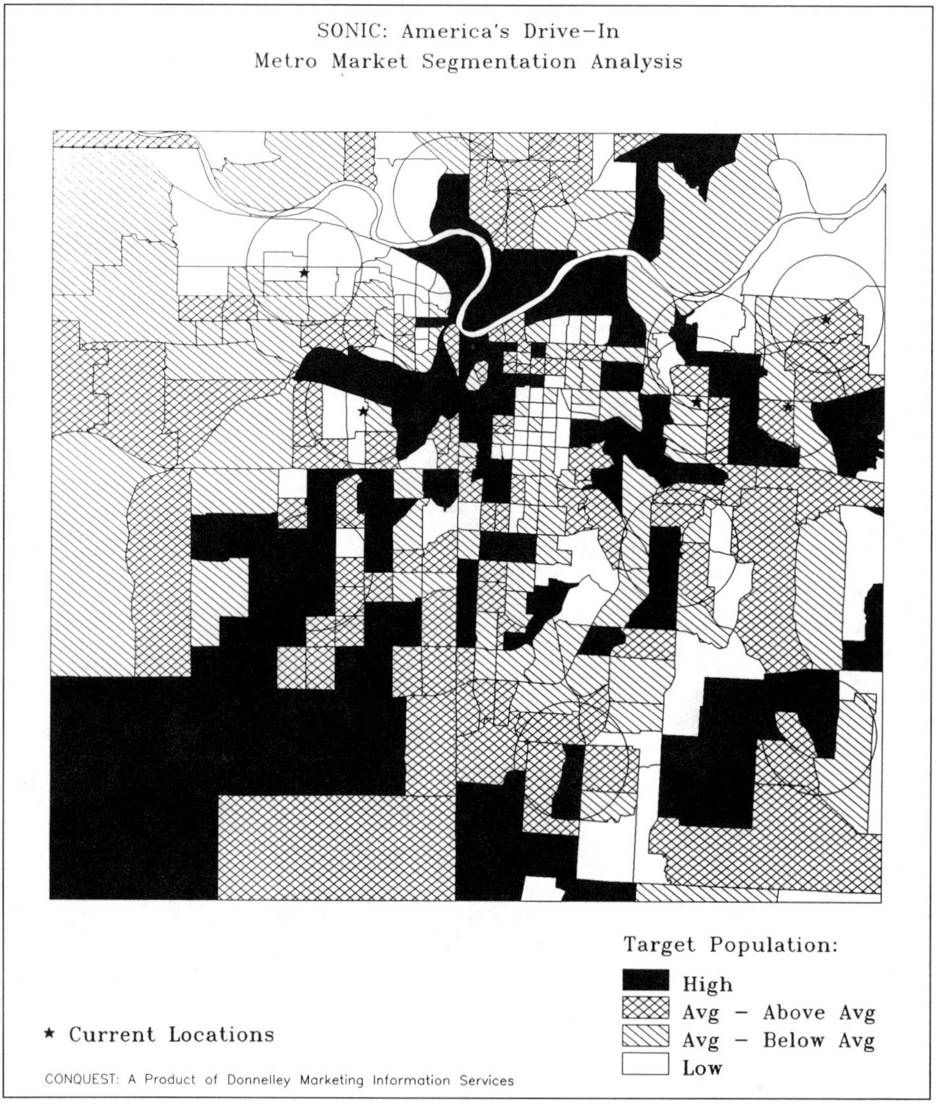

FIGURE 2 *(Facing page) The trade areas are then compared using segmentation clusters to measure market potential.*

The next step was to generate demographic data on the remaining portions of the market area. These were merged with data on the volume of retail trade and number of employees working in the area, and mapped to determine the nature and location of unserved markets. Figure 2 depicts the characteristics of the area's population in terms of segmentation clusters. Figure 3 presents the same information in a different manner, illustrating the location of concentrations of target populations along with shopping centers, schools, and existing competitors.

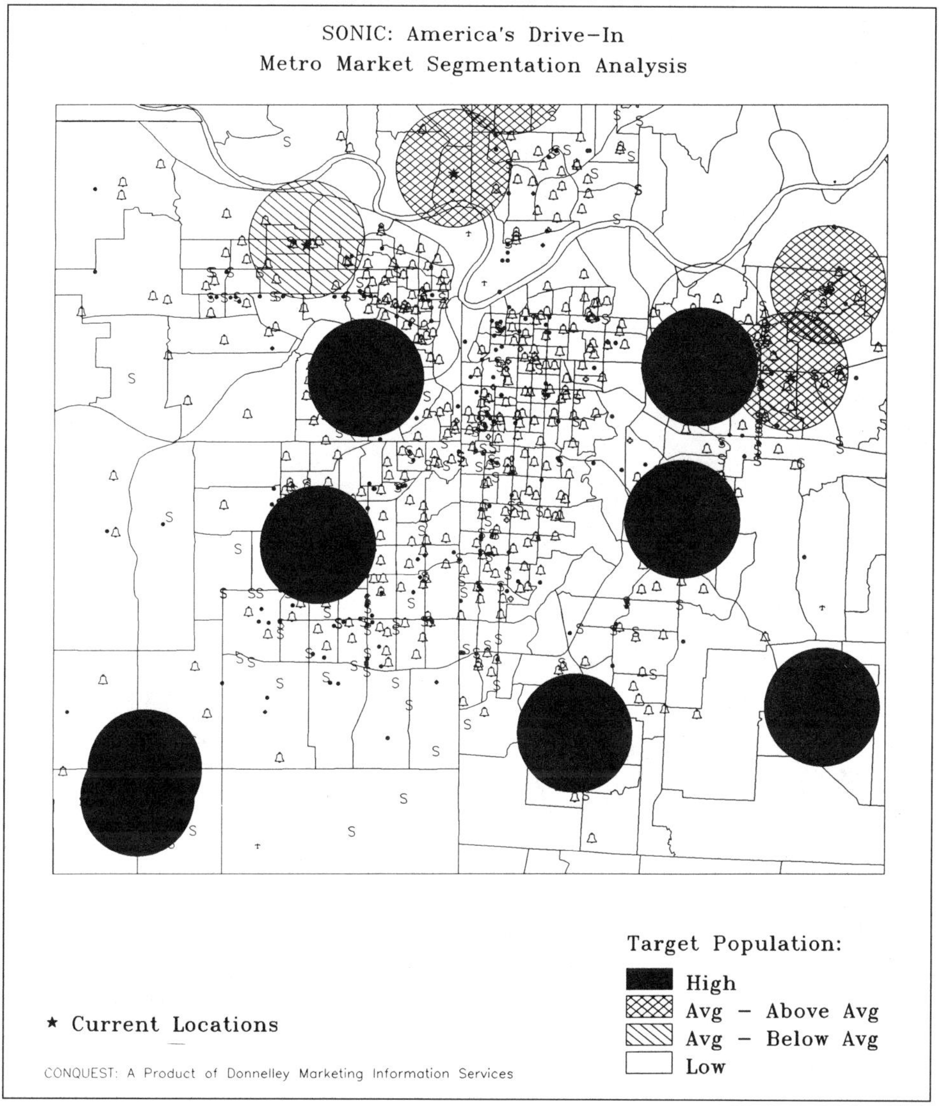

FIGURE 3 *(Above) Finally, this information is mapped using standard geography and merged with data on shopping centers, schools, and competitor locations to provide a complete picture of the market.*

The last step involved dividing the city into four areas, matching opportunities to specific franchisees according to operational and financial abilities, and grouping new target market opportunities with existing locations.

THE SOLUTION

With this approach, Sonic was able to successfully segment the market and assign development territories to the appropriate franchise developers. The company and the franchisees could then plan and begin to implement five-year growth plans for the city. Each franchise group was provided with an area suited to its own growth needs and abilities and to those of the franchise.

This case study was submitted by:

J. A. Archer
Director of Real Estate
Sonic Industries
120 Robert S. Kerr Avenue
Oklahoma City, OK 73102

Gary Blake
Director
Blake, Silverman & Partners
3690 SW Brooklane Drive
Corvallis, OR 97333

CASE STUDY

Friary Meux Pubs

COMPANY BACKGROUND

Friary Meux is a subsidiary of Allied Breweries, the United Kingdom's largest pub retailer. With 600 pubs across Great Britain, the company is heavily involved in site analysis. Two important activities of Friary Meux are identifying pubs for acquisition and upgrading existing ones to their fullest potential. Although a long-time user of geodemographic data, Friary Meux found the accuracy of market data was a problem due to the variety in size and shape of pub trade areas.

THE PROBLEM

Pub retailers (and similar small organizations such as betting shops, news agents, convenience stores, etc.) typically have smaller trade areas than do larger operations. For this reason, it is essential to have demographic data at the most detailed level possible. In the U.K., this means data at the census enumeration district levels, i.e., census geographies that describe areas as small as 150 households. Using the wrong level of geographic building block may result in an inaccurate demographic profile around a site, but this problem is not immediately apparent to the user.

THE SYSTEM

Developed by CACI, the InSite desktop system is a PC-based geographic information system for site location and market analysis. CACI's ACORN segmentation system was the first geodemographic clustering system developed for the British market. (For more information about the system and vendor, consult the description in Appendix 1.)

METHODOLOGY

The kind of information needed (the average age, social class, and ACORN housing profile of people living near a pub) is not provided by postal-code sector data. This is because the areas that postal code sectors cover are much larger than the average trade area of a pub. U.S. marketers face the same problem when dealing with large geographies, such as zip codes and counties.

Friary Meux has attained a fine level of detail by having both postal sector data and enumeration district data on its system. Friary Meux's sales data are incorporated in the InSite system, providing a profile of all outlets within the investigated trade area. (This particular database was also extended to give each pub a grid reference based on the Ordnance Survey Map.)

All requests for expenditures on new site or pub refurbishments require authorization, usually by the company's Board of Directors. An InSite demographic report is regularly included as an integral part of the document justifying the expenditure. The demographic profiles developed in the report are used to prove there is a sufficient market to provide adequate return on the investment, and subsequently, to justify the style of pub being proposed.

THE SOLUTION

Friary Meux can now build detailed models of trade areas that allow it to compare existing sites with new ones, and to repeat successful pubs. Since obtaining InSite, the marketing regions of Allied Breweries have undergone reorganization, and Friary Meux has also used the InSite system to evaluate a large number of pubs for which it has taken responsibility for development.

This case study was submitted by:

CACI Marketing Systems
9302 Lee Highway
Fairfax, VA 22031

5

Retail Industry

The retail sector comprises the largest current user group for desktop systems. Indeed, over 30 percent of the systems in place today are on the desktops of American retailers. The retailing sector underwent a rash of brick-and-mortar expansion in the 1970s and 1980s. Desktop systems were introduced at that time to evaluate sites; they largely used basic demographics without benefit of psychographic or consumer data.

The effect of this fast-paced expansion is coming home to roost in the 1990s in the form of a shakeout in the retail industry. According to Scott Purlee of National Decision Systems, "Retailers will have to treat each individual store as if it were their only store." This new focus on exacting the optimal product mixes for each outlet will be the challenge of the 1990s.

Linda Hyde of Management Horizons sees the current state of the retail industry as problematic. According to Hyde, there are already too many stores in the marketplace due to overexpansion in the 1980s. Furthermore, many chains have become so homogeneous that their merchandise layout and service have opened the window of opportunity for specialty retailers. Eric Cohen (formerly of CACI) agrees. "The increase in competition has been tremendous, and this, coupled with a downturn in the economy, has put retailers in a bind." This situation is not limited to the United States. Kelly Woodcock of Compusearch in Toronto notes, "In Canada today, not only is there a smaller pie to fight over, but there is an increasing shortage of viable retail locations."

The 1990s are being viewed as a struggle for retail survival, and it appears that desktop systems may be the deciding factor in many cases. Both national chains and localized niche retailers must be able to carefully target their markets and make the right siting decision the first time because the cost of selecting the wrong site is increasing dramatically.

Efficient marketing has been hampered somewhat by the way the industry operates. While marketers have always believed that location decisions are marketing decisions, this has not always been the case among those handling the location decision. In the past, the real estate and marketing groups often did not speak to each other, let alone work together. The new retail environment requires a philosophical shift in thinking as marketing departments gain a stronger voice. Real estate decisions are beginning to be directed by marketing people as a part of the total development package.

The 1990s will be a time of contraction for many retailers. According to Jim Harper of National Decision Systems, "Our clientele are using information to determine which 'dog' sites to eliminate, as retailers brace themselves for the forthcoming shakeout in the 1990s." Some of the trends likely to characterize the retail industry of the 1990s are discussed below.

The Un-malling of America

We have seen the end of development of regional malls with their tremendous amounts of gross leasable area (GLA). According to Hyde, "New centers will be multi-use complexes that offer combined living, workplace, entertainment, and shopping facilities." Poorly performing malls will either be razed or converted for different (more profitable) business use.

Relationship Merchandising

Many retailers are learning from bankers and smart insurance companies the concept of relationship marketing. Bankers have known for years that it costs five times more to acquire a new customer than it does to keep an established one. Now retailers have embraced this tried-and-true paradigm and are compiling marketing customer information files (MCIFs) to manage their customer relationships. The new focus will move from mass merchandising, with its emphasis on products and suppliers, to relationship merchandising that takes customer needs into account. Survivors of the 1990s will use cross-selling strategies. Ultimately, this trend could evolve into a "one-stop shop" where the optimal product mix is available to each customer who has been constantly kept in communication via direct-response tools. According to Purlee, this approach is picking up momentum. "We are doing a lot of work in the area of MCIFs. Retailers are getting our assistance in constructing customer databases to survive the 1990s."

Stronger Retail/Supplier Alliances

Manufacturers and wholesale distributors want to deal with retailers who will dominate and flourish in the 1990s. As a result, we will see stronger value-added partnerships between manufacturers and retailers with a vested interest in each others' success. For example, Supervalue, a wholesale grocery distributor based in Minneapolis, works to achieve this type of value-added partnership with grocery retailers such as Cub Foods.

Other developments likely to characterize the retail industry of the 1990s include increases in advertising to reach a more diverse audience, more locational concerns related to drive times of customers, and increasing overlap of store trade areas. These trends all herald a more significant role for desktop systems. According to Robert Galvin of Donnelley Marketing Information Services, "The use of desktop systems will proliferate in the 1990s, particularly among high-end users." Vendors will custom-integrate marketing information with users' executive information systems and other management decision systems. On the high end, users will integrate desktop marketing systems with their own MCIFs. At the lower end, inexpensive localized databases will make it possible for "Mom and Pop" operations to compete more successfully against the major players. The major players, on the other hand, are likely to use desktop tools to become better "niche" players. More finely tuned geographic data will enhance efforts at both ends. As Eric Cohen notes, TIGER and street-level data will make these systems more useful and economic.

Databases that use retail credit activity as a variable for segmentation schemes will become increasingly available. "If we have complete empirical knowledge of people's retail activity, we can better predict consumer behavior," says Mike Pugliese of National Decision Systems. With all of these system enhancements becoming available, he adds, "The 1990s will be a trying, yet exciting time for retailers."

CASE STUDY

Rent-to-Own, Inc.

COMPANY BACKGROUND

Rent-to Own, Inc. is a large regional corporation that provides furniture, appliances, and household electronics on a rent-to-own basis to residential consumers. While it has historically oriented its products, services, pricing, and merchandising techniques toward the lower demographic population groups, this retailer had never specifically identified a profile of its most important customers. As a result, its efforts at locating successful sites, as well as promoting to the proper customer base, were severely handicapped.

THE PROBLEM

Rent-to-Own identified a number of marketing research and location research concerns associated with the nationwide development of its stores and sales of products and services to the general public. A number of specific tasks were determined: profiling existing customers, locating potential customers, media targeting, analyzing product and marketing mixes and locations, evaluating competing sites, providing decision support for existing stores about remodeling and re-leasing, and identifying underserved markets. In short, Rent-to-Own faced all of the marketing challenges of a national retailer. This example follows the initial process of developing a way to locate areas of high-potential customers.

THE SYSTEM

The retailer chose the VISION® lifestyle segmentation system as the basis for profile development. Developed by National Decision Systems, VISION is a segmentation system that divides the population into 48 distinct lifestyle and behavioral segments. This segmentation system allows analysis at the census-block-group level. (For more information about the system and vendor, consult the descriptions in Appendix 1.)

METHODOLOGY

The first step was to compile customer records and match them demographically and geographically with the VISION lifestyle segments. Figure 1 shows the resulting distribution of nearly 17,000 customers in a given trade among the 48 VISION segments. The table also has an index that compares the share of customers in each

Figure 1. VISION PROFILE REPORT BY SEGMENT

BASE AREA: TOTAL CUSTOMERS
BASE VAR: HOUSEHOLDS IN TRADE AREA - COUNTY

GROUP	DESCRIPTION	ANALYSIS TOTAL	ANALYSIS PCT.	BASE TOTAL	BASE PCT.	PERCENT PENETRATION	VISION INDEX	
SU 1	Suburban Gentry	5	0.0	194701	0.7	0.003	100	*
SU 2	Nouveau Riche	58	0.3	436887	1.5	0.013	24	
SU 3	Tuition & Braces	56	0.3	639373	2.2	0.009	16	
UU 4	Urban Gentry	8	0.0	147921	0.5	0.005	100	*
UU 5	Young Urban Professionals	24	0.1	235149	0.8	0.010	18	
UU 6	Condos & Palms	10	0.1	35907	0.1	0.028	100	*
SH 7	Suburban Up & Comers	41	0.2	574454	1.9	0.007	13	
SH 8	High Tech Frontiers	147	0.9	703792	2.4	0.021	37	
SH 9	The Good Life	3	0.0	64821	0.2	0.005	100	*
SH 10	Comfortable Suburbanites	136	0.8	887628	3.0	0.015	27	
SH 11	Leave It To Beaver	40	0.2	465956	1.6	0.009	15	
SH 12	A Good Start	365	2.2	681021	2.3	0.054	96	
SM 13	Little League & Barbecues	677	4.1	1776061	6.0	0.038	68	
SM 14	Baby Boom Again	663	4.0	1065311	3.6	0.062	111	
SM 15	Industrial Upper Deck	502	3.0	2085703	7.0	0.024	43	
SM 16	Porch Swings & Apple Pie	256	1.5	1340325	4.5	0.019	34	
SM 17	Carports & Kids	1604	9.6	1389389	4.7	0.115	206	
SM 18	Declining Suburbia	1219	7.3	1882435	6.3	0.065	115	
SM 19	Ethnic Industrial	1	0.0	547766	1.8	0.000	100	*
UM 20	Brownstones & Whitesteps	205	1.2	1746294	5.9	0.012	21	
UM 21	Black Middle Class	1185	7.1	993499	3.3	0.119	213	
UM 22	High Rise Blues	3	0.0	216818	0.7	0.001	100	*
TM 23	Mainstreet, USA	607	3.6	1720530	5.8	0.035	63	
TM 24	Town & Country	108	0.6	452463	1.5	0.024	43	
TM 25	Hamlets & Hardhats	136	0.8	953104	3.2	0.014	25	
TM 26	Tom Sawyerville	594	3.6	538365	1.8	0.110	197	
RM 27	Mobile Homeville	290	1.7	472636	1.6	0.061	109	
RM 28	Ranches & Farmlands	31	0.2	167118	0.6	0.019	33	
RM 29	Country Pleasure	4	0.0	142481	0.5	0.003	100	*
SL 30	Young Beginners	962	5.8	1400692	4.7	0.069	122	
SL 31	Young Hispanics	0	0.0	276051	0.9	0.000	100	*
SL 32	Just Making It	2315	13.9	1654140	5.6	0.140	249	
UL 33	Single Starters	328	2.0	670048	2.3	0.049	87	
UL 34	Metro Hispanic Mix	0	0.0	171909	0.6	0.000	100	*
UL 35	Urban Melting Pot	0	0.0	52152	0.2	0.000	100	*
UL 36	Black Urban Fringe	2031	12.2	1152021	3.9	0.176	314	
UL 37	Fixed Income Blues	266	1.6	521780	1.8	0.051	91	
UL 38	Teeming Tenements	1012	6.1	381826	1.3	0.265	472	
TL 39	Sun City	0	0.0	24315	0.1	0.000	100	*
TL 40	Appalachian Trail	260	1.6	106093	0.4	0.245	437	
TL 41	Collegetown, USA	110	0.7	233373	0.8	0.047	84	
RL 42	Tractors & Pickups	4	0.0	19506	0.1	0.021	100	*
RL 43	Golden Years	3	0.0	52788	0.2	0.006	100	*
RL 44	Prairie People	122	0.7	175520	0.6	0.070	124	
RL 45	Tough Times	200	1.2	87701	0.3	0.228	406	
XX 46	Books & Beer	43	0.3	72857	0.2	0.059	105	
XX 47	GI Joe	21	0.1	69834	0.2	0.030	54	
XX 48	Institutions&Unclassified	9	0.1	12360	0.0	0.073	100	*
	TOTALS	16662	100.0	29692874	100.0	0.056	100	

* UNSTABLE INDEX--SET TO 100

FIGURE 1 *Rent-to-Own VISION-coded its customer file so it could be profiled across the 48 VISION segments, ranked here in socioeconomic order.*

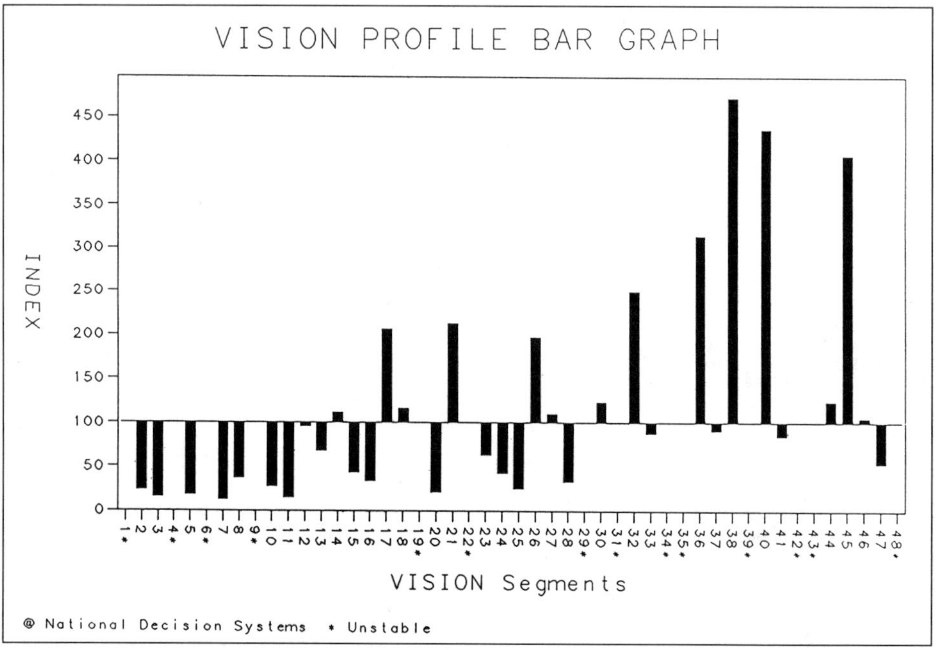

FIGURE 2 *This bar chart displays the relative propensity (index) of each lifestyle segment to be a Rent-to-Own customer.*

segment with the share of all householders in that segment. For example, the 206 index for the Carports and Kids segment indicates that this group is a little more than twice as likely as the average household in the area to be a Rent-to-Own customer. Figure 2 charts these indexes for all 48 segments.

The analysis was carried further by creating a VISION Game Plan. Figure 3 shows the segments plotted in relation to their index and the share of customers they represent, providing a way to analyze both customer quality and customer quantity.

The upper-right quadrant of the graph represents the "core" customer segments for this retailer. These segments represent above-average propensity to be customers and are overrepresented in the area. These are the retailers' best customer groups, whose buying habits, media preferences, and economic tendencies have been well documented within the VISION system.

THE SOLUTION

Having identified the VISION segments that represent their best customers, Rent-to-Own used National Decision Systems' Infomark system to solve a variety of marketing problems. For existing stores, it used Infomark to locate and quantify pockets of key customers within each trade area in order to better target direct-mail and media promotions. In addition, it used the VISION profiles to improve cross-selling efforts among existing customer bases. Rent-to-Own also used the system to find areas with high concentrations of key VISION customer segments. This enabled

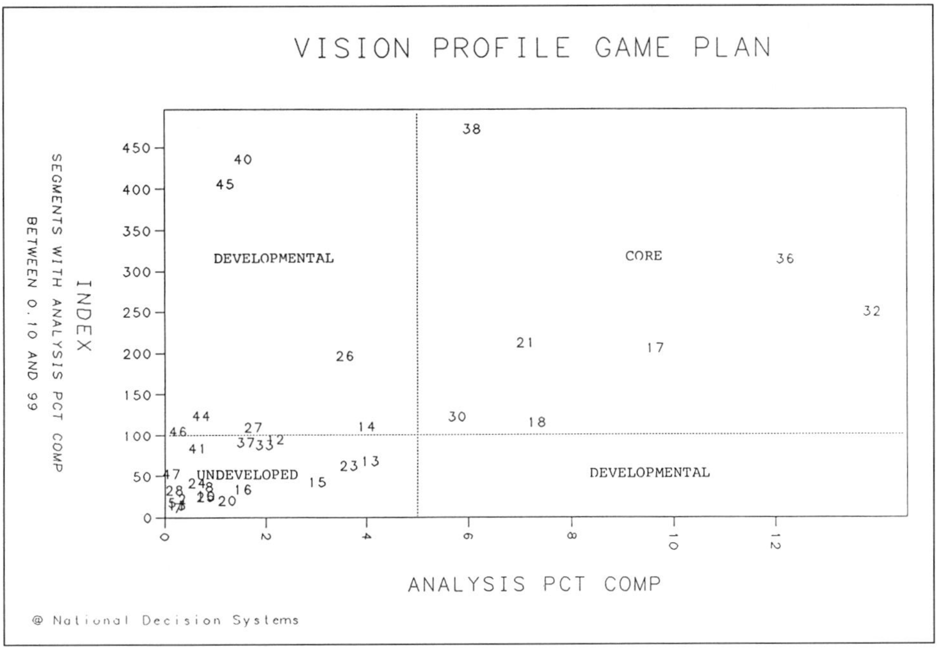

FIGURE 3 *The VISION Game Plan graphically indicates the marketing strategies that can be used to effectively reach each group of market segments.*

Rent-to-Own to better identify the specific available sites that would provide high sales potential.

This case study was submitted by:

Terry Munoz
Vice President, Traditional Markets
National Decision Systems
539 Encinitas Blvd.
Encinitas, CA 92024

This study is based on an actual case, but due to the proprietary nature of the topic, fictitious names are used to maintain confidentiality with the company and its personnel.

CASE STUDY

Lowe's Companies

COMPANY BACKGROUND

Lowe's Companies, Inc., based in North Wilkesboro, North Carolina, is in three distinct businesses. Its outlets sell to "do-it-yourself" (D-I-Y) consumers, durable-goods customers, and home-building contractors. Lowe's 300 stores provide merchandise and service in 20 states, primarily in the South Atlantic and South Central regions of the United States. Lowe's stores range in size from approximately 5,000 to 100,000 square feet. This wide range of store sizes reflects Lowe's transformation from its origins as a contractor supply company in 1958 to the retail-driven home center of today. The shift towards D-I-Y retailing has created the need for a more analytical approach to store location selection.

THE PROBLEM

One market that exemplifies this shift is Greenville, South Carolina. In Greenville, Lowe's was the leading D-I-Y retailer until Hechinger and Home Depot entered the market. Lowe's previous strategy of having several smaller stores dispersed throughout the market was no match for these new larger competitors with more extensive product offerings. The task for Lowe's Corporate Research Department was to determine an optimum area and site for Greenville, utilizing a new large format prototype, so Lowe's could effectively compete with Home Depot and Hechinger.

THE SYSTEM

To answer this question, the Research Department chose the CONQUEST system. CONQUEST is a desktop geodemographic marketing information system developed by Donnelley Marketing Information Services (DMIS). The GEOCOMP Huff Gravity Model, when used in conjunction with CONQUEST, determines probabilistic patronage patterns based on store size, store image, location of the competition, and sites under consideration. (For more information about the system and vendor, consult the descriptions in Appendix 1.)

METHODOLOGY

Based on the demographic and socioeconomic data retrieved from CONQUEST and local planning sources, two distinct areas emerged as viable possibilities for Lowe's.

Probabilities of Attracting Customers to Proposed Site in the Greenville, South Carolina Market

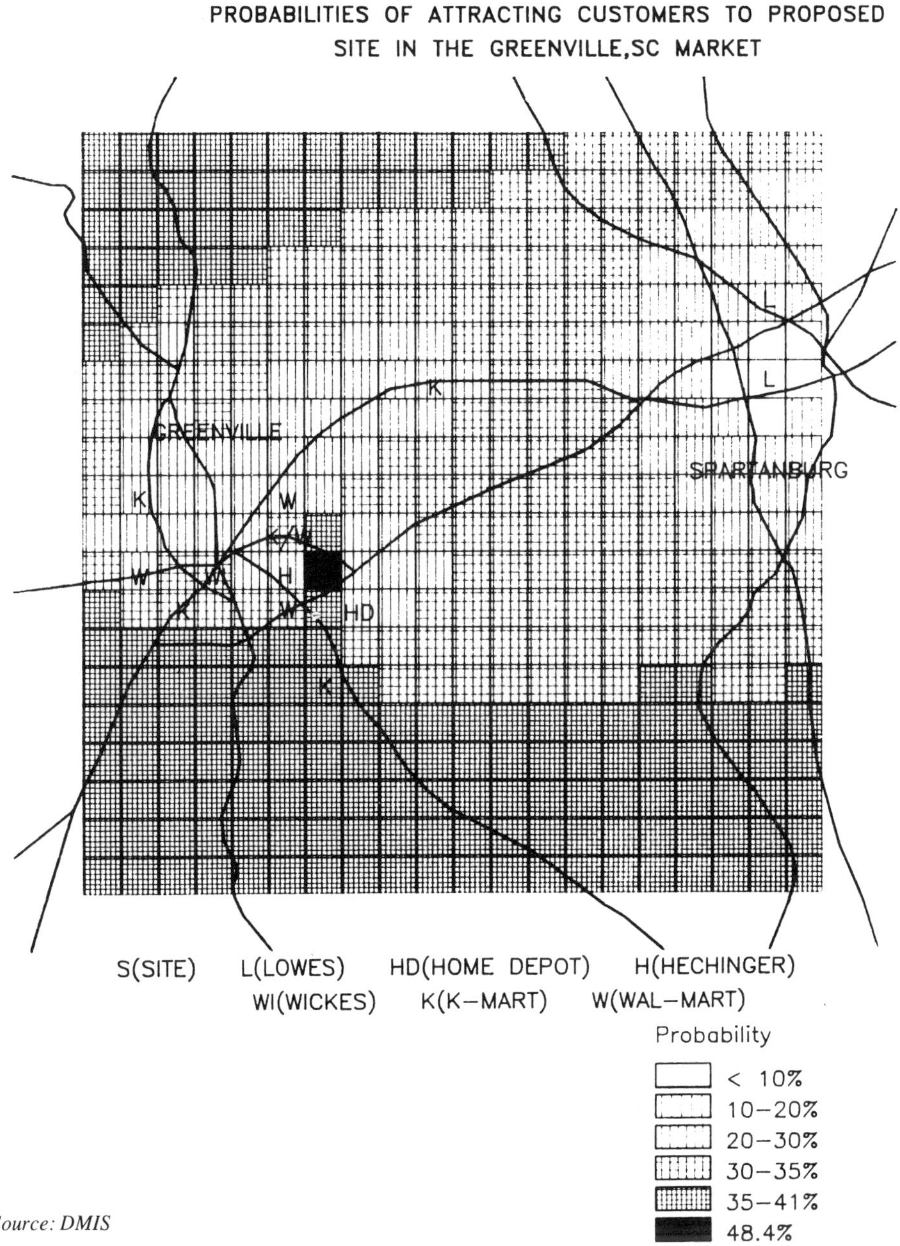

Source: DMIS

FIGURE 1 *Using the GEOCOMP Huff Gravity Model, Lowe's was able to produce a CONQUEST map displaying the probability of attracting customers to its stores in the Greenville market.*

But at which location would Lowe's be the most successful? A grid network was constructed in CONQUEST using 1 mile by 1 mile cells mapped over the Greenville market. CONQUEST then assigned the dollar potential for products sold at Lowe's to each grid cell. Once these grids and data files were developed, GEOCOMP calculated patronage probabilities for each area to determine the probabilities of attracting customers to potential sites.

Approximately 30 competitors were entered into the model based on their strength and size (for clarity, only national chains were mapped). The two possible Lowe's store sites were then independently modeled with the competition. The probabilities of attracting customers for each scenario were transferred to CONQUEST. Figure 1 illustrates the grid configuration generated by the desktop system.

THE SOLUTION

Potential store sites, competitors' locations, salesfloor sizes, and indexes based on these variables were allocated to the appropriate grid cells. It was then possible to develop a solution to the site selection problem, and Lowe's was able to pick the location that offered the greatest potential for attracting D-I-Y customers.

This case study was submitted by:

Andy Moncla and Doug Mesimer
Lowe's Companies, Inc.
Box 1111
North Wilkesboro, NC 28656

CASE STUDY

K mart

COMPANY BACKGROUND

In the 1960s and 1970s, K mart, like other national retail chains, catered to a mass market. This was done by using a merchandising or supplier-driven management style that did not require sophisticated consumer research or geodemographic analysis. However, as a more marketing-driven management style has evolved, distinguished by a focus on the consumer, K mart is increasingly relying on customer information systems to keep abreast of an ever-changing marketplace.

THE PROBLEM

In the past, K mart satisfied its trade-area demographic profiling needs by accessing decennial census data with a mainframe computer. This approach provided tract-level household information for trade areas around K mart stores. But the technique was very labor-intensive, requiring that trade areas be redrawn as K mart opened and closed stores in a market. Furthermore, the data's usefulness decreased as the census data got more and more out of date.

In an increasingly competitive marketplace, this approach had become a liability, especially in view of the potential negative consequences of a poor location decision. K mart needed a better way to analyze and select sites for its outlets.

THE SYSTEM

K mart chose Donnelley Marketing Information Services' (DMIS) CONQUEST system for its market research needs. CONQUEST provides access to Donnelley's demographic, economic, and geographic databases. (For more information about the system and vendor, consult the descriptions in Appendix 1.)

METHODOLOGY

The first step was to establish the trade area to be profiled in this case: Oakland

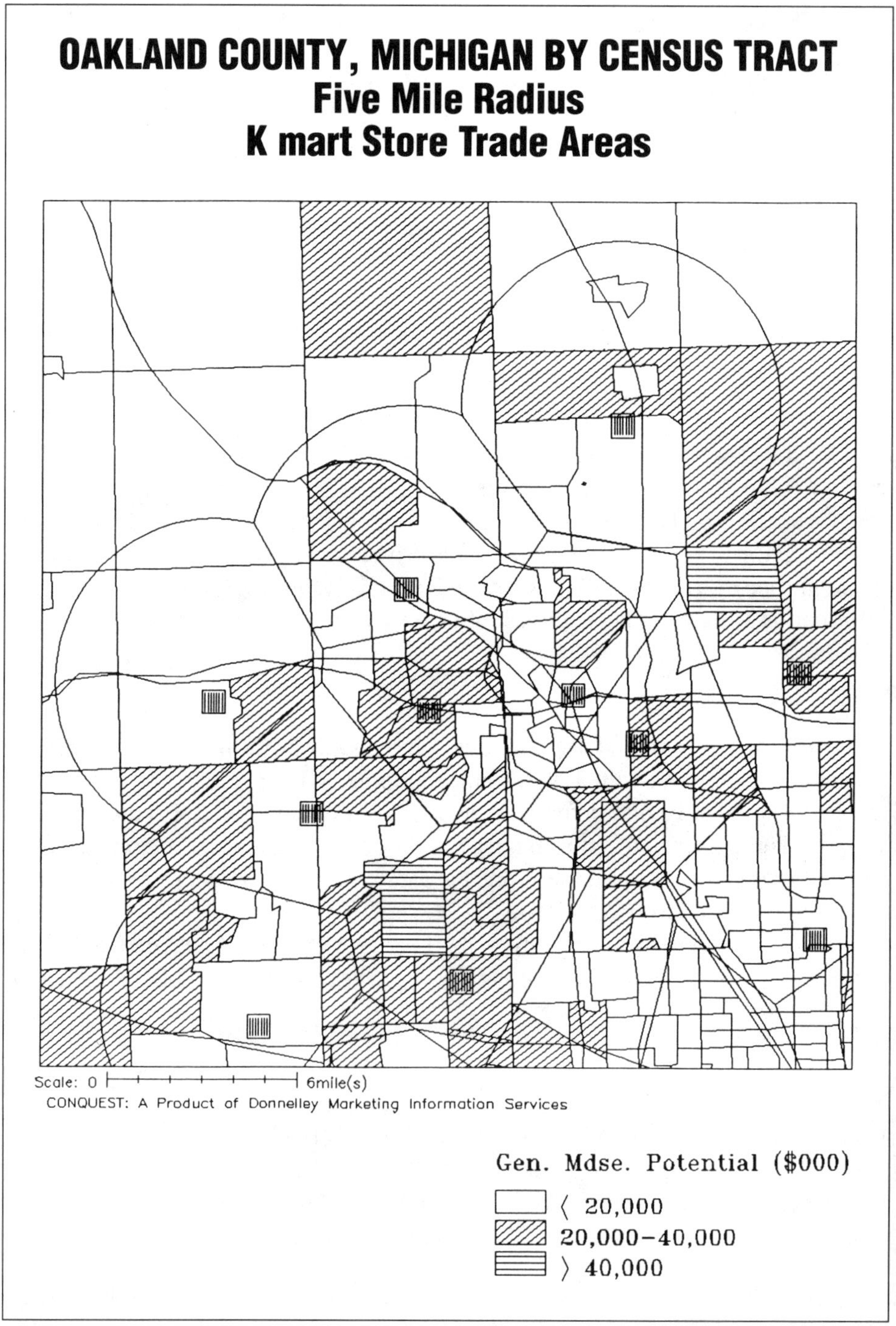

FIGURE 1 *Using a sophisticated mapping technique, CONQUEST is able to automatically tailor store trade areas to prevent double-counting of population.*

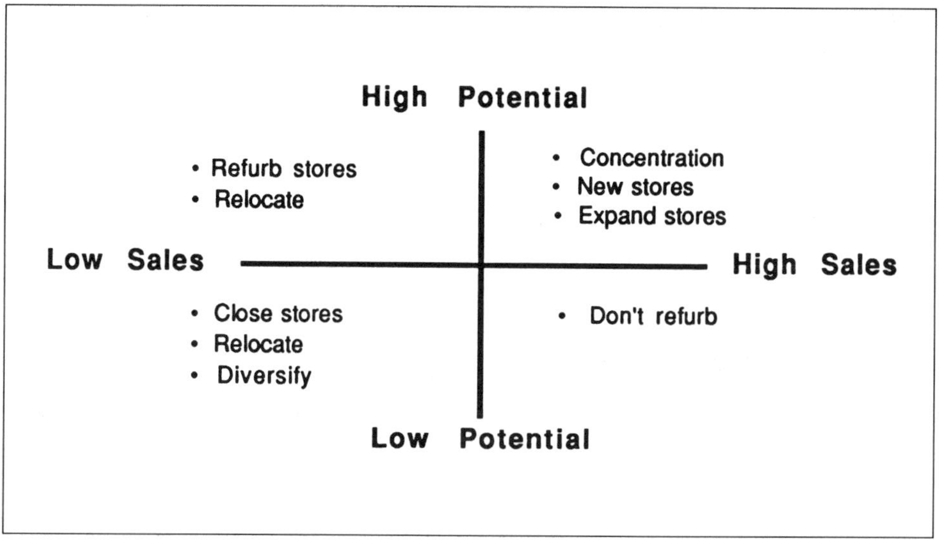

FIGURE 2 *The final product of the analysis is this figure, which helps K mart management decide what strategy to employ in each of its stores to maximize opportunities and resources.*

County, Michigan. CONQUEST generates polygon-shaped trade areas by combining a number of circular trade areas, then eliminating the overlapping portions to prevent double-counting of the population. The resulting honeycomb appearance represents a more realistic depiction of the trade areas than does a maze of interlocking rings. While trade areas can be custom-defined if desired, this approach works satisfactorily in many markets. Since K mart stores are so prevalent, consumers often base their patronage decision on the basis of which store is geographically closest.

An analysis of these maps reveals which markets are over- and under-penetrated. Most important, they help market analysts pinpoint areas to be targeted. Since consumer markets shift over time, and mobility changes the character of neighborhoods, the "right mix" of stores today could be an imperfect network tomorrow. The ongoing nature of this analysis makes a desktop system a must.

Another CONQUEST application involves merging stores' sales data with market-potential information and plotting store performance against potential with a quadrant framework that identifies the most logical strategic alternatives. (See Figure 2.) Depending upon the quadrant in which a store falls, a store (or department) could be a candidate for refurbishment, expansion, or even closure.

THE SOLUTION

With desktop marketing, K mart has not only been able to respond more quickly to demographic profiling requests, but has been proactive in selecting the best sites to locate new stores and expand existing ones. It also has provided marketing and real-estate support for subsidiary specialty operations in such diverse fields as office supplies, sporting goods, bookstores, and home-improvement centers.

This case study was submitted by:

Ronald Gellish, General Manager
Strategic Market Planning
K mart International Headquarters
3100 West Big Beaver Road
Troy, MI 48084

CASE STUDY

Far North Mall

COMPANY BACKGROUND

Far North Mall, a small community-based shopping center in Canada, was experiencing very poor sales due to low traffic just eight months after opening. Although the mall was not as visible as a large center on a major artery, management did feel there were certain advantages to a smaller community mall. The mall's management realized it was crucial to re-evaluate the center's present marketing strategies.

THE PROBLEM

Management identified two major concerns impacting sales: 1) a failure to acquire repeat business or customer loyalty, and 2) a poor location with regard to major traffic arteries. However, the mall did offer convenient parking, ease of shopping, and overall convenience due to its straightforward layout. The management realized that these factors were important to promote, but they did not seem to be a drawing card for the market they were presently targeting. Essentially, they needed answers to these questions:

- Who are our existing customers?
- Are these customers coming from inside or outside the primary trading area?
- Are there similar consumers within the trade area who are being overlooked?

THE SYSTEM

The mall managers chose the CONQUEST/Canada system from Compusearch, a menu-driven desktop marketing system tailored for the Canadian market. Of particular use was the system's LIFESTYLES WORKSTATION market segmentation system. (For more information about the system and vendor, consult the descriptions in Appendix 1.)

METHODOLOGY

The mall managers decided to conduct a customer-origin study that identified the exact shape and size of the center's trading area. They profiled the mall's customers by classifying them into unique consumer segments, each with its own demographic and consumer expenditure characteristics. The profiles indicated that over half of the mall shoppers were young, two-income families with children and mortgages. This group represented a totally different market with more diverse discretionary income than the groups that had been targeted. Prior to the profile, mall management had targeted all of its advertising and promotional efforts toward upscale and affluent households.

Once this information was digested, mall management was ready to establish a new marketing direction by implementing the following strategies:

- Target nearby, middle-class, young families using direct mail.
- Ensure frequent advertising (this group tends to be very busy and requires constant reminders).
- Continue promoting the convenience features of a smaller mall, as this is important to a young family "on the go."
- Design a calendar of family-related cross-promotions.
- Offer weekend theme promotions for children, such as "a festival of clowns."
- Re-evaluate the merchant mix.
- Merchandise those items most demanded by this group.

THE SOLUTION

Six months after these strategies were implemented, overall traffic and sales had increased significantly. At this time, Far North Mall conducted a second customer-origin study. This profile showed a high concentration of middle-class young families, younger working couples, and a few upscale, high-income, older families with teenagers. This profile also indicated that the trade area had grown, because the mall was now attracting a greater number of young families from outside the primary trading area.

By defining its target consumer, Far North Mall was able to successfully build mall traffic. Understanding customer characteristics allowed the mall's marketing strategies to fit rather than fight with the needs of the target market. The most encouraging results of the research revealed that by making the most of a location, it is possible to expand a primary trading area without being on a major street or highway.

This case study was submitted by:

Kelly Woodcock
Compusearch Market and Social Research, Ltd.
330 Front Street West, Suite 100
Toronto, Ontario, Canada M5V 3B7

This study is based on an actual case, but due to the proprietary nature of the topic, fictitious names are used to maintain confidentiality with the company and its personnel.

CASE STUDY

Consumer Appliances, Inc.

COMPANY BACKGROUND

Consumer Appliances, Inc., a national retailer of consumer electronics and appliances with more than 200 stores in 30 major markets, was embarking on a new promotional campaign. In keeping with its policy, the company worked closely with its suppliers in developing advertising campaigns.

THE PROBLEM

To improve its efficiency and increase its ability to work more closely with manufacturers on targeted promotions, the retailer needed to identify its customer base more accurately, assess market potential, evaluate store locations, and estimate market share. Traditional sources of market intelligence and media usage information were not providing the necessary solutions.

THE SYSTEM

Consumer Appliances selected the OASYS system. Developed by National Demographics & Lifestyles (NDL), OASYS is a PC-based system providing consumer and market data nationwide. The system's ability to interface demographic data, expenditure data, and lifestyle characteristics lent itself to the challenges facing the retailer. OASYS also allows users to incorporate their own data. (For more information about the system and vendor, consult the descriptions in Appendix 1.)

METHODOLOGY

To analyze store locations, the retailer and NDL developed a quality index, a scoring system based on five key factors determining the potential value of a consumer: (1) age, (2) income level, (3) homeownership, (4) credit-card usage, and (5) specific lifestyle characteristics. OASYS then identified those zip codes in the retailer's general marketing areas that showed heavier concentrations of consumers who exhibited the desired characteristics. Figure 1 illustrates the distribution of the quality index by zip code.

To verify the validity of the index, the retailer tested one of its markets to see if the sales figures from given trade areas corresponded to the quality index for the zip codes in those areas. "We found a very strong positive relationship between the expected potential of the area and the dollars per household from that area," reported the retailer's director of planning.

Convinced of the dependability of the scoring system, the retailer realized it could turn the process around for site selection. By looking at an area where a store did not yet exist and determining the quality index for that area, the retailer was able to make a "reasonable prediction" about how well a store might do there.

In addition, the retailer used the scoring system to examine existing markets zip code by zip code, to see how well the market was being covered. "It's a bit like

FIGURE 1 *Using OASYS, Consumer Appliances was able to score the geography around its store with a composite index of key characteristics.*

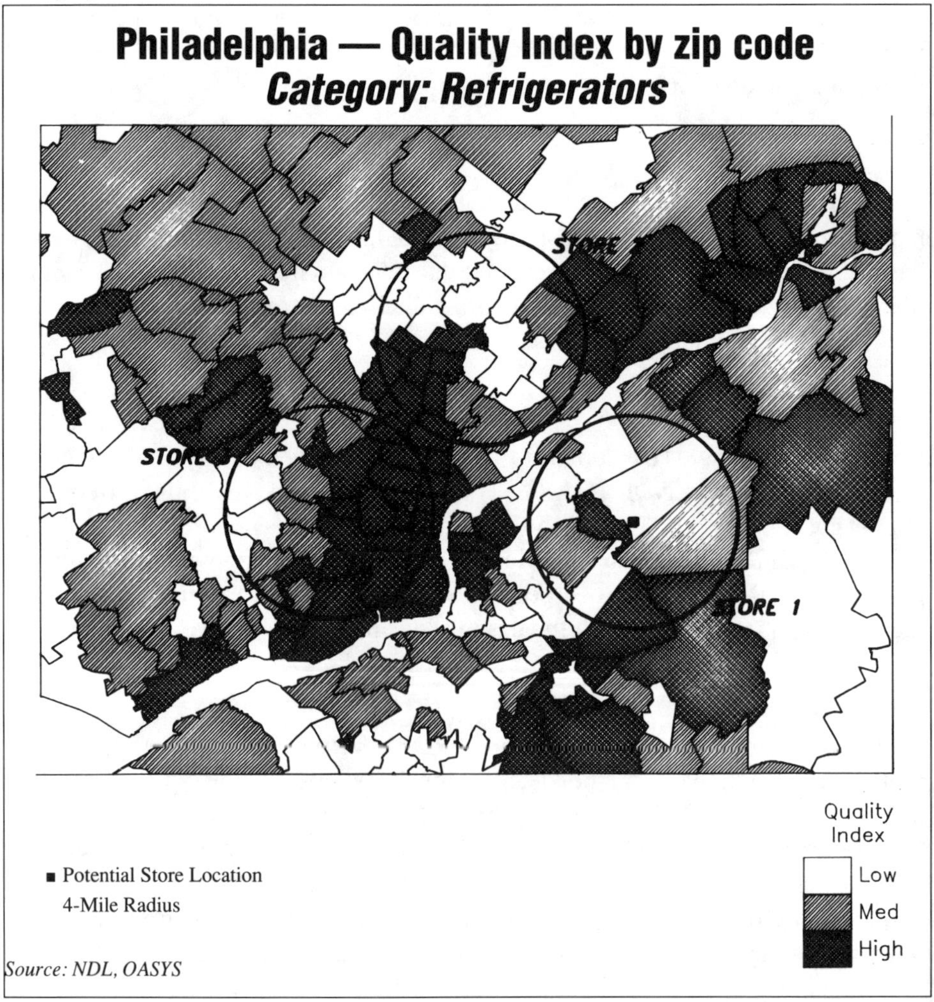

prospecting for oil with a geological map, and highlighting the areas that appear to have high potential for us but where we're not now getting high penetration," the planning director explained. The map may indicate the need to open, close, or move a store to optimize the retailer's coverage of the marketplace. "This is not an exact science, but it gives you more information about what you're doing or proposing to do. It helps you make better-educated guesses."

SOLUTION

Consumer Appliances is now using OASYS to predict consumer expenditure levels for different product categories by zip code. In the second phase of their working relationship, NDL and the retailer are using OASYS applications for target marketing. By examining internal sales transaction data, OASYS can provide profiles of the retailer's customers on three dimensions: (1) product, (2) brand, and (3) geography. "This will give us a much better definition of our target customers, enabling us to reach them more efficiently through improved media planning," says the retailer's planning director. The information is also helping the retailer launch new product categories, optimize product mix, and target promotional efforts for specialized product categories.

This case study was submitted by:

Nancy Solomon
Marketing Communications
National Demographics & Lifestyles, Inc.
1621 Eighteenth Street
Denver, CO 80202-1211

This study is based on an actual case, but due to the proprietary nature of the topic, fictitious names are used to maintain confidentiality with the company and its personnel.

6

Financial Services and Insurance

The fastest-growing user group for desktop marketing systems has been the financial services industry, and banks have been on the leading edge. Between 1978 and 1982, the financial services industry underwent massive deregulation. Deregulation made it easier to become a player in the banking arena, and the number of banks grew dramatically during the 1980s.

BANKING

The rash of new competitors meant that financial institutions expecting to survive had to get smart fast. This meant adapting desktop decision-making to the financial services environment. Financial institutions were faced with an array of demands resulting from the industry's new market orientation. They needed to select sites for branches and automatic teller machines, develop new products, and target existing products. Nonmarketing tasks, such as certifying nondiscriminatory lending policies, also required usable data.

Financial institutions were also faced with converting account information into "customer" information and transforming it into a marketing information system. They began by identifying their best customers and creating Marketing Customer Information Files (MCIFs). MCIFs distill the "internal world" of a bank's yearly or monthly customer transactions into household activity consumption reports. This enables banks to quickly discern product- and volume-specific customer purchase behavior.

Internal MCIF information then had to be linked to the external marketplace. Desktop marketing systems make it possible for a financial institution to locate and quantify customers in the marketplace that most resemble its best customers. The growing complexity of financial products placed even greater emphasis on desktop decision making. As Louis Tazioli of National Decision Systems notes, "The banking industry has marketing issues not faced by other industries, especially with the growing variety of products banks must offer. The customers for home loans, IRAs, credit cards, and ATMs have varying characteristics and needs. Without desktop market analysis capabilities, researching the needs of these disparate target groups would be next to impossible."

Today, the financial services industry suffers from overextension. There are currently 4,000 banks and more than 6,000 insurance carriers in the U.S., and industry observers expect a shakeout during the 1990s. It has already begun. According to Ed Furash, a noted industry consultant, "Price warfare has become the primary form of competition in the business." This price warfare is unlikely to abate until consolidation occurs, which Furash sees as an inevitable trend.

"Under consolidation, the institution's goal is to make itself something special in the eyes of customers so they will pay the price differential needed for profitability," says Furash. To reach the goal of institutional differentiation, financial marketers must get closer to their customers' needs. Financial service companies will increasingly use desktop systems because they are the most efficient way to develop a customer segmentation strategy. "The ultimate goal of a desktop system is to use information to segment the market to the point that the financial marketer makes the customer feel that he or she is a segment of one," says Rolland D. Johannsen of the Furash group. Indeed, this is necessary, because the financial product and the way it is delivered are seen as one in the eyes of the customer.

"California is the future," states Furash. Regional consolidation has already begun in California, where 85 percent of the state's market share is controlled by five financial services providers. California is ahead of the country in this instance because it has experienced overextended branching for a longer period of time.

Fewer than 5 percent of the industry's current users of desktop systems have successfully integrated marketing data with operations management and financial goal-setting. Given the fact that financial service providers need to be market oriented, full integration is inevitable during the 1990s.

THE INSURANCE INDUSTRY

The insurance industry is facing many of the same problems characterizing the financial services industry in general, especially increased competition and a dire need for market intelligence. Some segments of the industry, notably health insurance, have faced severe financial challenges. Relative to other financial services, however, the insurance industry remains highly regulated. This greatly limits the industry's flexibility in responding to market challenges and indicates an even greater need for desktop market analysis.

With more than 6,000 carriers in the U.S., the insurance industry is crowded by competition. Most astute insurers already know the importance of market research and the integral part that demographics play in the strategic planning process. Although the industry has grown in the past decade, most of this increase has occurred in companies that offer a diversified line of insurance packages. "We find that growth comes to companies that meet the needs of their customers," explains a vice president for marketing planning.

Many visionaries in the insurance industry predict a trend similar to that observed for banking. Successful product oligopolists will create their edge through product quality and low cost. They will leverage their delivery systems to emphasize convenience and develop brand loyalty with added service points. Successful carriers will leverage perceived superior relationship quality and value-added services.

CASE STUDY

AmSouth Bancorporation

COMPANY BACKGROUND

AmSouth Bancorporation is a bank holding company based in Birmingham, Alabama. It has assets of nearly $9 billion and 177 branch offices throughout Alabama and northwest Florida. Within AmSouth's Retail Division, the Branch Capital Management (BCM) group provides information to assist with location-based decisions.

THE PROBLEM

In conjunction with a recent product development effort, BCM surveyed AmSouth's markets to determine where there would be high demand for multiple relationship accounts. This product, targeted at recent college graduates, offers deposit and credit services in a single account. The challenge was to identify where and how to promote the product.

THE SYSTEM

AmSouth uses Donnelley Marketing Information Services' (DMIS) CONQUEST marketing information system to evaluate branch capital expenditure requests and to provide demographics that support target mailings and product management. The ability to incorporate the user's data into the system was an advantage for this project. (For more information about the system and vendor, consult the descriptions in Appendix 1.)

METHODOLOGY

To help determine the viability of the product, BCM developed a demographic overview of the target segment within AmSouth's markets. The overview provided a background against which AmSouth product management could identify high-opportunity counties for promotion and distribution of the new product. The overview divided the counties in AmSouth's market areas into quintiles based on four factors: population aged 18 to 34, new deposits, household income, and propensity to use credit products. The counties were then grouped by the frequency with which they appeared in the top quintiles when ranked on the four variables. Using CONQUEST's TargetScan and mapping modules, a summary map showed

Alabama: Population Growth, Ages 18–34, 1989–1994

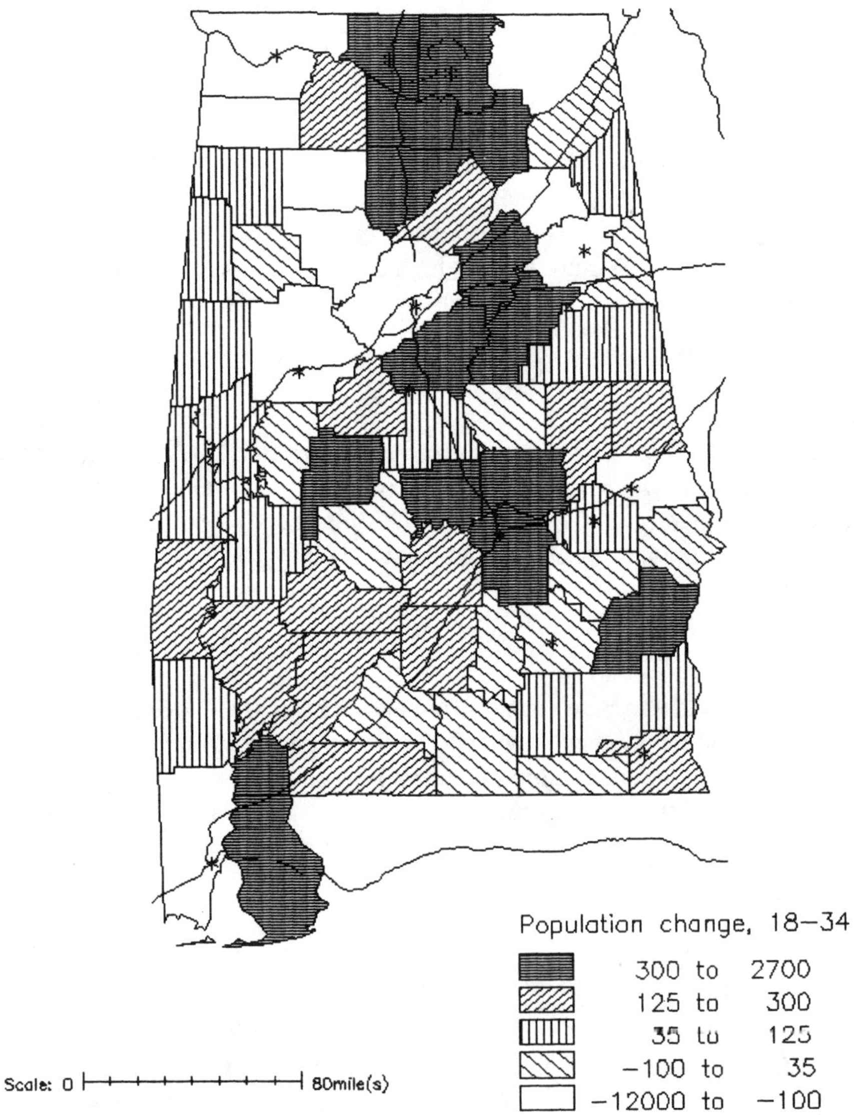

∗ = city with college enrollment of at least 2,000 students

CONQUEST: A Product of Donnelley Marketing Information Services

FIGURE 1 *AmSouth begins its analysis by mapping population growth projections for the state of Alabama overlaid with the locations of cities with high concentrations of college students.*

Alabama: Recent Graduate Market, Opportunity Rank
Based on Growth, Deposits, Income, and Credit Use

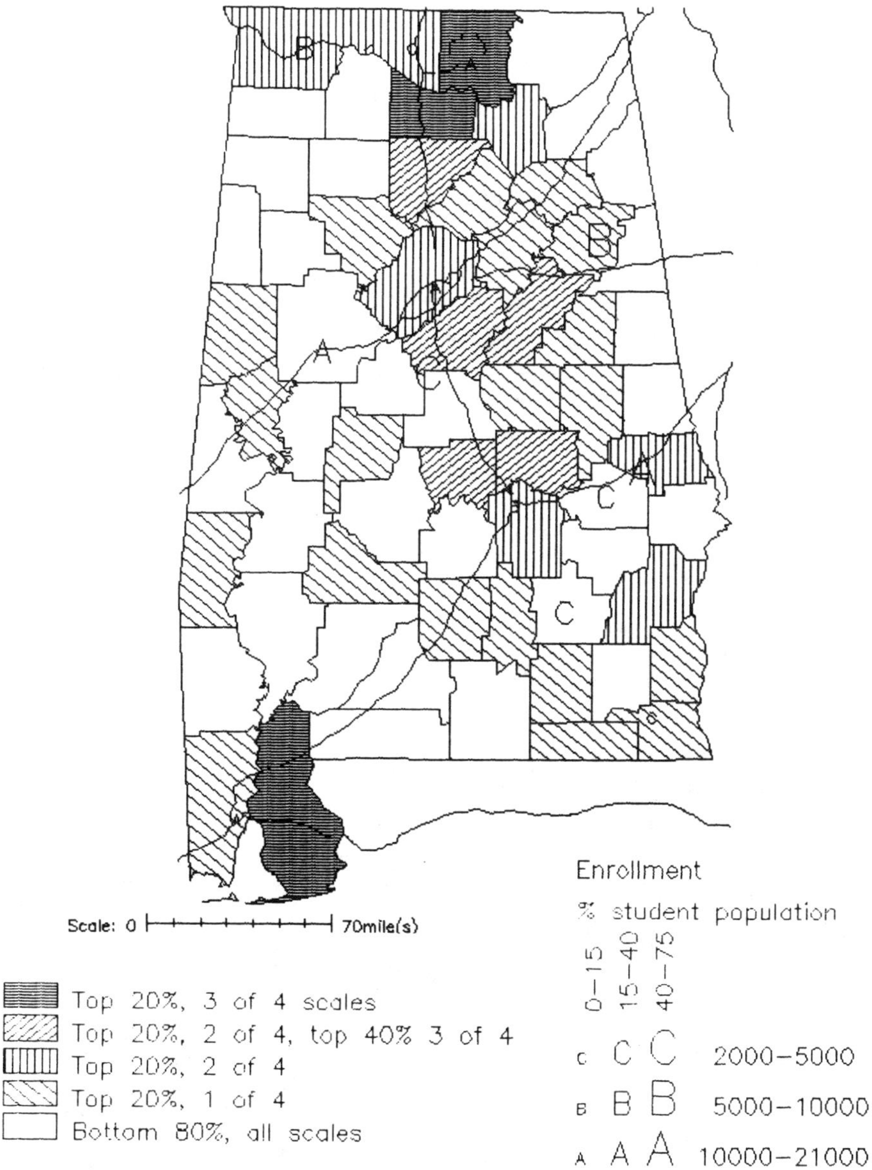

CONQUEST: A Product of Donnelley Marketing Information Services

FIGURE 2 *A custom scoring algorithm was developed using population, income, deposit, and credit-use data to determine areas of opportunity.*

each county's combined performance on the four measures. Figures 1 and 2 display population growth by county for the target age group and distribution of the recent college-graduate population.

BCM then created graphs to indicate counties with the strongest performance on the variables examined. For example, Figure 3 ranks counties by credit-card usage.

AmSouth added 1988 and 1989 total deposits for each geography to the data file using the CONQUEST FileMaster module and calculated new deposits. The resulting data file was downloaded to a Lotus spreadsheet and sorted by each of the four variables into quintiles. The spreadsheet assigned each county an Opportunity Rank, based on where it ranked for each of the four indices. These rankings were reloaded on CONQUEST and mapped.

While the maps helped AmSouth's product managers identify high-opportunity counties for the product, they could not provide a comprehensive analysis of all factors that predict product demand. Since part of AmSouth's strategy is to begin targeting college graduates while they are still in school, BCM added a reference file identifying all cities with four-year college enrollment of over 2,000 students. The reference file was converted to a symbol file that also included the total enrollment and student-to-population ratios for all cities.

FIGURE 3 *Counties were ranked for each key variable in the analysis, including credit-card usage, as shown here.*

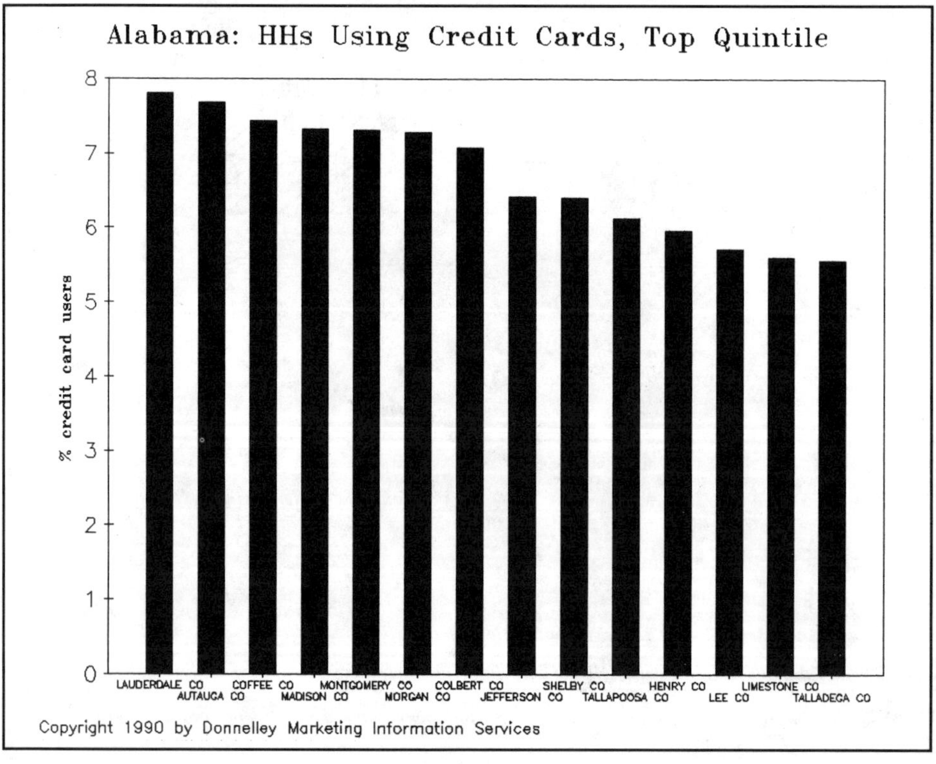

When this file was overlaid onto an Opportunity Rank map, AmSouth's product managers could easily spot high-opportunity counties and cities with high college enrollments. The size of the symbol indicated whether a city was dominated by a university or had a diverse population with a small share of students. This was important because a university-dominated city warranted a city-wide sales effort, while in other cities, branch-specific promotions might suffice.

AmSouth uses a proprietary database marketing system to develop geocoded household-level relationship data on the bank's entire customer base. BCM used CONQUEST to upload AmSouth's total number of customers in a given geography and calculate the bank's penetration in that area. Since the household file contained appended age and income estimates, BCM was able to match customers aged 18 to 34 with incomes of $25,000 to $75,000 to determine the bank's penetration for the market in designated cities and counties.

SOLUTION

Using CONQUEST, AmSouth's product managers identified potential areas for target marketing and new-product distribution. Providing product managers with a simple way to identify counties likely to have a high number of potential customers reduced the need for managers to spend time familiarizing themselves with specific demographic data for each of Alabama's 67 counties. It also provided BCM with basic information from which it could identify markets warranting further study.

This case study was submitted by:

Steve Reider, Retail Banking Officer
AmSouth Bancorporation
P.O. Box 11007
Birmingham, AL 35288

CASE STUDY

Home Savings of America

COMPANY BACKGROUND

Home Savings of America is the largest savings-and-loan institution in the U.S. It operates savings branches in 9 states and loan offices in 17 states. Home Savings is one of the nation's largest originators of mortgage loans. It is known for its conservative management style, with over 90 percent of its loan portfolio in residential home mortgages and 100 percent of its savings portfolio in retail deposits. Home Savings' financial performance is contrary to the industry as a whole. It is well capitalized, very profitable, and experiences an annual growth rate of over 15 percent. Its strategy emphasizes retail operations, streamlined products, customer service, convenient branching systems, and a stable image.

THE PROBLEM

For years, television stations have sold media spots based on program ratings using broad demographic groups. With no effective alternative, advertising agencies have been forced to accept these ratings at face value when trying to differentiate the appropriateness of various programs for their clients. With no way to measure differences between a client's customer profile and a broad demographic group, an agency is most likely to emphasize the effectiveness of its creative development rather than the value of its media buying, which is what Home Savings wanted to evaluate.

THE SYSTEM

In recent years, Home Savings has developed customer profiles using the ClusterPLUS geodemographic segmentation system developed by Donnelley Marketing Information Services (DMIS) as part of its CONQUEST market analysis system. CONQUEST is a PC-based geodemographic marketing system that contains a variety of databases, including television audience ratings data from A.C. Nielsen, which is a sister Dun & Bradstreet subsidiary to DMIS. (For more information about the system and vendor, consult the descriptions in Appendix 1.)

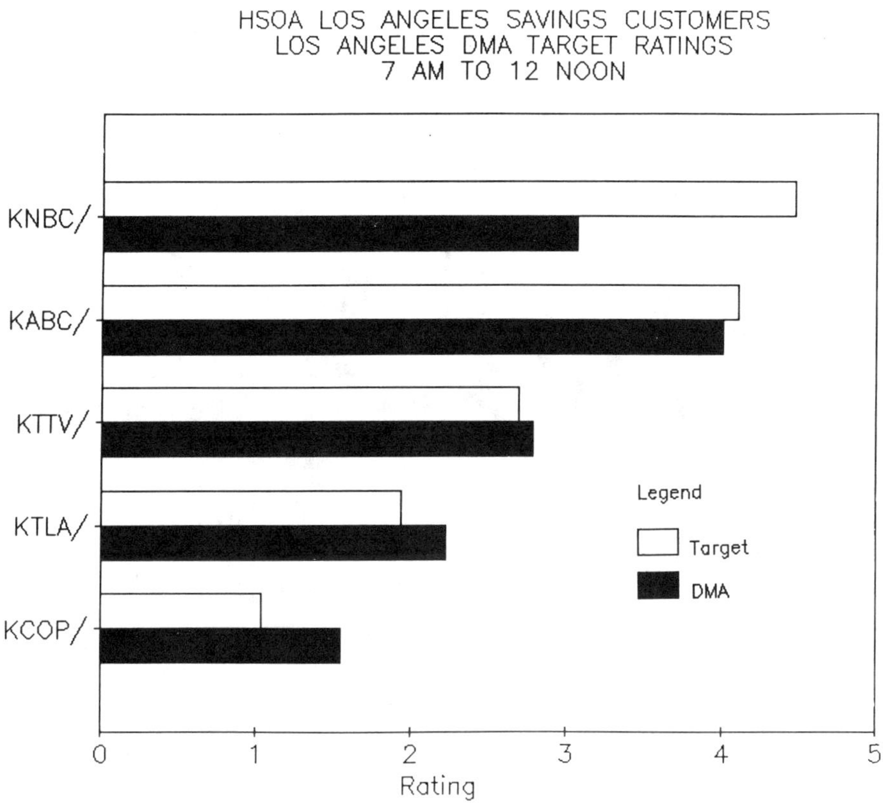

Source: 1990 TV/CONQUEST, Nielsen Media Research and Donnelley Marketing Information Services

FIGURE 1 *Targeting ratings with ClusterPLUS enables Home Savings to identify significant differences in media use between a targeted and general audience.*

METHODOLOGY

Home Savings measured differences in the ratings of various television stations using ClusterPLUS profiles of its best customers in the Los Angeles and San Francisco DMAs (Nielsen's Designated Market Areas). At the same time, it compared ratings based on a targeted audience (i.e., a custom grouping of clusters) and those for a general audience (i.e., the broad demographic group presently used for media buying). (See Figure 1.)

The target clusters were identified as those with the highest percentage of customers. Then the cluster groups with the highest relative incidence of customers (i.e., those accounting for at least 50 percent of all customers) were selected as the target audience. Figure 2 shows penetration rates by cluster for the Los Angeles DMA.

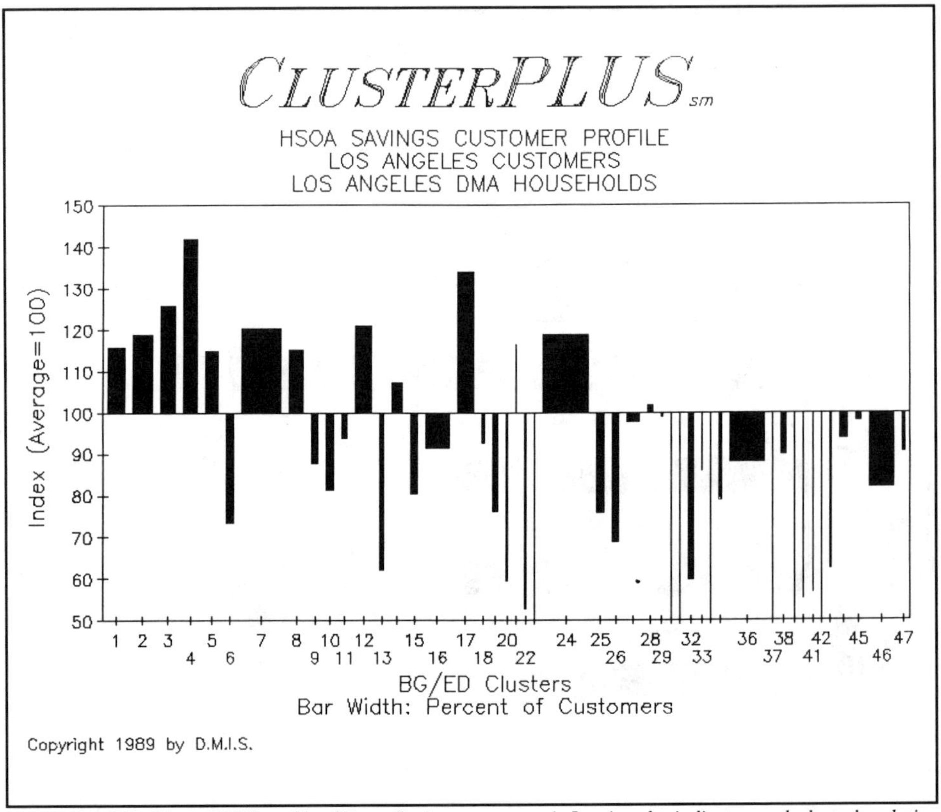

FIGURE 2 *This ClusterPLUS profile of Home Savings customers in Los Angeles indicates each cluster's relative propensity to be a customer (height), as well as its share of the total market (width).*

Media buyers for Home Savings could now use this comparison to support their negotiations with television stations. Actual media buys also can be matched with their corresponding ratings for general and targeted audiences to give clients some indication of how effective past advertising has been. Figure 3 demonstrates how the data can also be mapped to show the geographic distribution of the examined attributes.

In using targeted audience ratings as a guide for future media purchases, the question remains as to how accurate past ratings data are in forecasting future ratings. By matching media purchases with corresponding ratings data, Home Savings was able to show that past general audience data could predict current ratings within 1 percent of the actual ratings. In contrast, targeted audience data indicated what current ratings would be within 2.5 percent of the actual ratings.

THE SOLUTION

Although targeted audience ratings proved a less reliable indicator of future ratings,

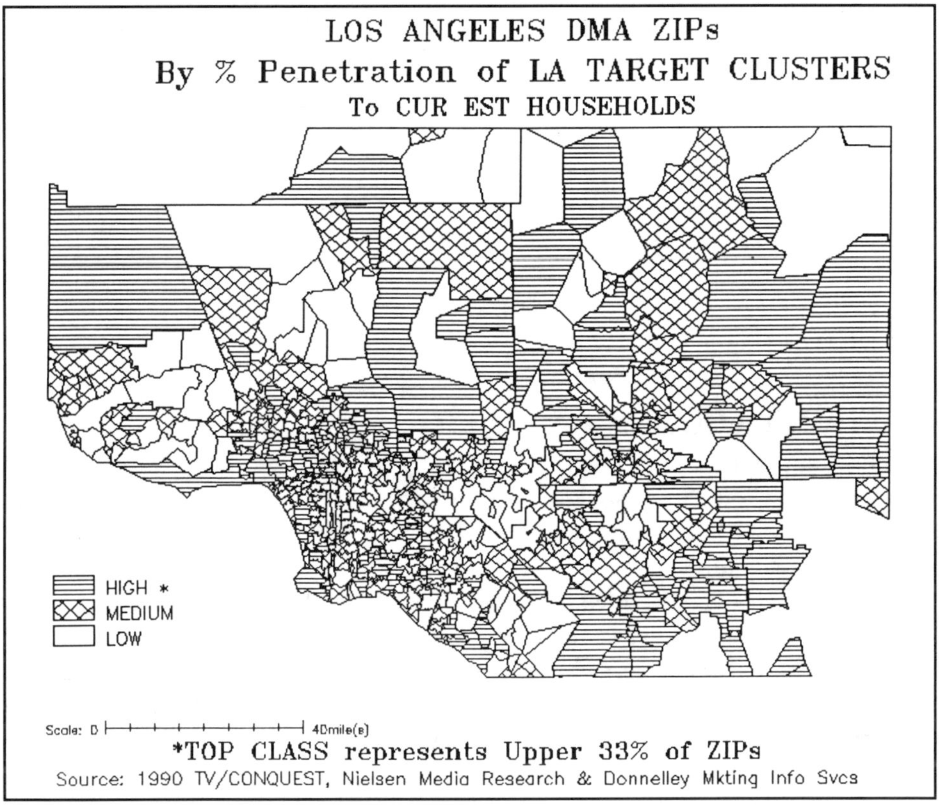

FIGURE 3 *Identifying a target audience has many applications beyond media planning. Here the market area is mapped at the zip-code level to show neighborhoods with the largest concentrations of Home Savings target customers.*

the application of the targeted audience ratings also showed that Home Savings achieved 5 percent higher aggregate ratings points during the quarter than indicated by the general audience ratings. Thus, the trade-off is whether a 1.5 percent reduction in ratings estimation accuracy is worth achieving a 5 percent increase in the effectiveness of future advertising. In any case, Home Savings felt more confident in its ability to reach its target audience.

This case study was submitted by:

Robert H. Shaw
Manager of National Operations Research
Home Savings of America
4900 Rivergrade Road
Irwindale, CA 91706

CASE STUDY

South Gulf Savings and Loan

COMPANY BACKGROUND

South Gulf Savings and Loan (South Gulf) is a full-service savings-and-loan institution located throughout most of the Southwestern United States. It has branches in the greater Houston area, with others situated in cities such as Albuquerque, Dallas, San Antonio, and Tulsa.

With assets of approximately $5 billion, South Gulf's business consists primarily of residential real-estate lending, retail and wholesale deposit services, and mortgage-backed securities and mutual funds. Recently, the marketing team at South Gulf became interested in identifying the potential acquisition targeting opportunities within their region in an attempt to diversify its product mix and customer base. In particular, South Gulf was interested in looking at ABC Financial (ABC), also located in Houston, to identify whether or not ABC was a good candidate for acquisition.

THE PROBLEM

Marketers at South Gulf knew from past experience that they must initially consider some major factors when analyzing a financial institution for potential acquisition, including: the proximity of ABC branches to South Gulf branches, the size of the customer household base in the branch trade areas, comparative customer household characteristics for South Gulf and ABC customers, and the comparative financial products offered by South Gulf and ABC. The challenge was to obtain the necessary data and interface it in an effective and meaningful manner.

THE SYSTEM

South Gulf tackled these issues with National Decision Systems' Infomark® Desktop PC System. The MicroVision™ segmentation system provided the basis for the analysis. Other components used by South Gulf for this market research were the Financial Database and Pop-Facts® demographic database. (For more information about the system and vendor, consult the descriptions in Appendix 1.)

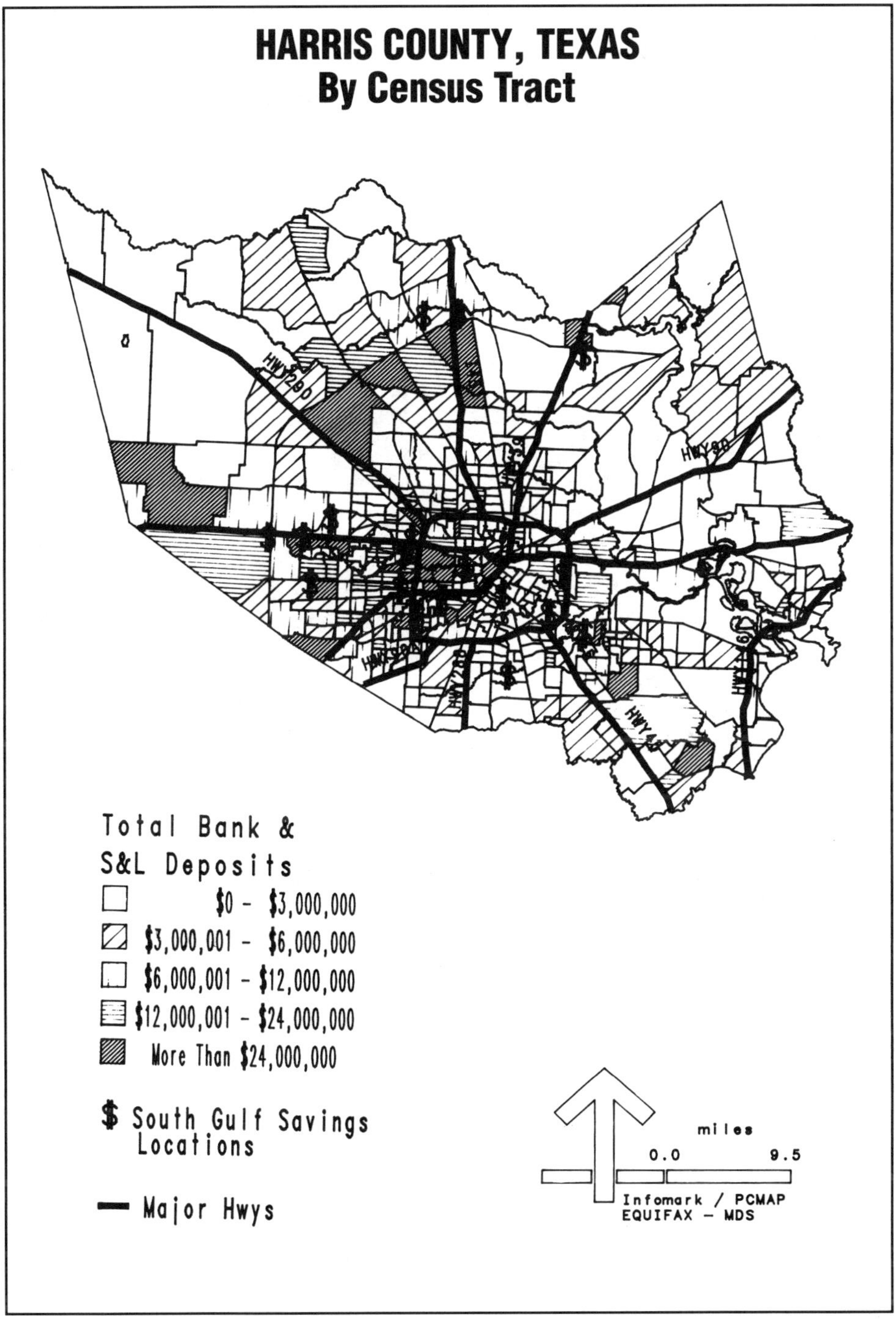

FIGURE 1 *South Gulf used Infomark to map total actual deposits for Harris County, Texas, overlaid by its branch locations.*

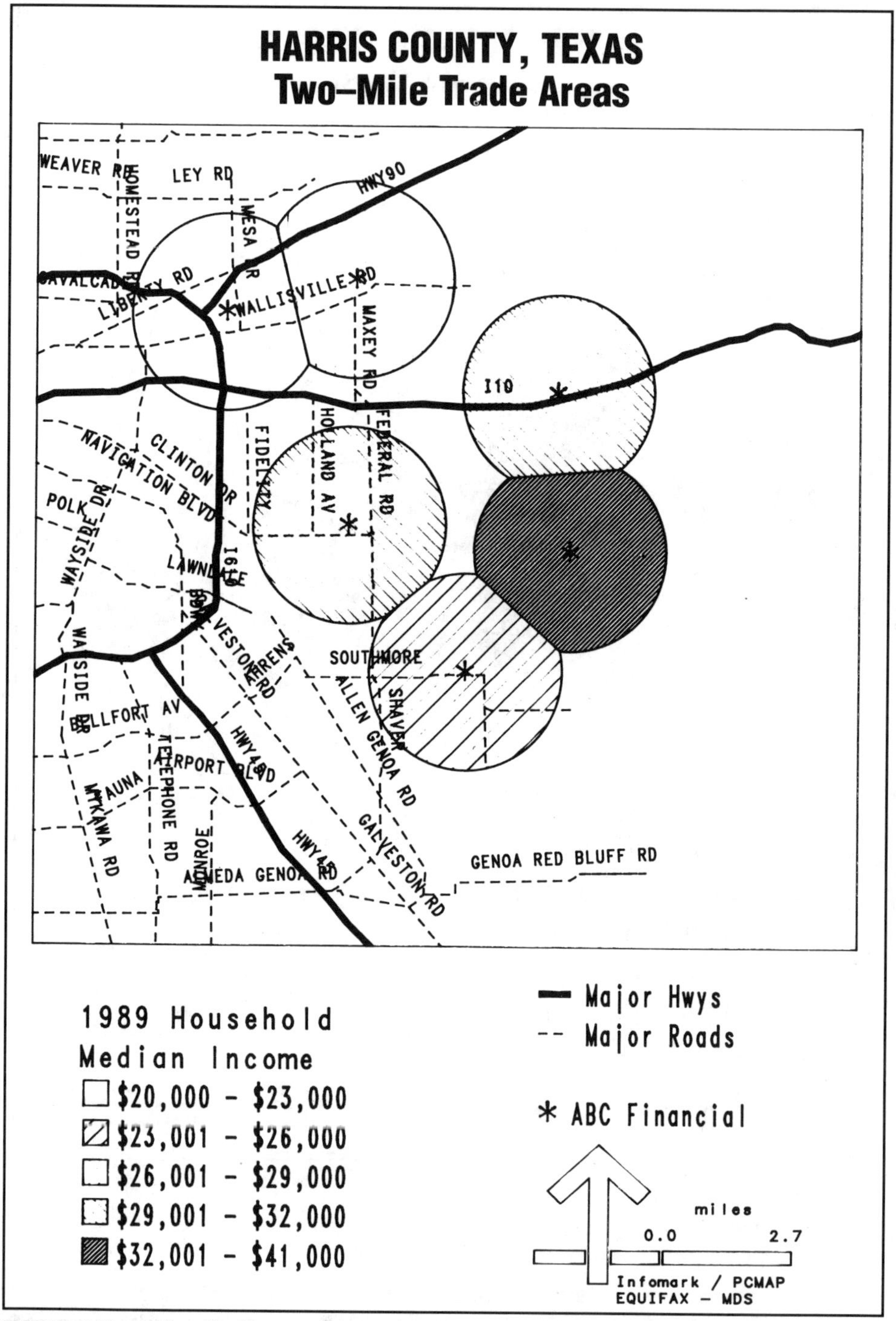

FIGURE 2 *Using Infomark's "non-overlapping trade areas" feature, South Gulf is able to determine the median incomes of households within two miles of each of its branches without double counting.*

METHODOLOGY

Since the South Gulf marketers knew that most of their vital information would come from a direct comparison of their own financial locations with ABC's locations, they aggregated their 18 branch trade areas into 1 geography and the 6 ABC branch trade areas into another geography.

The marketers first wanted a visual representation of their market area and created a census-tract map of Harris County, Texas, showing their 18 bank locations. They then accessed National Decision Systems' Financial Database and displayed aggregate bank and savings-and-loan deposits for each census tract. (See Figure 1.)

A PopFacts Summary Report for the two companies' aggregated trade areas showed that the two-mile trade areas surrounding South Gulf branches were more populated than those surrounding ABC's locations. On a per branch basis, South Gulf showed an average of 56,552 households per branch, nearly seven times the 8,282-household average for the ABC locations.

The South Gulf marketers also looked at the growth projection for trade areas surrounding their locations and the ABC branches. Although the areas surrounding the South Gulf branches grew much faster than those around the ABC branches in the 1970s, they were projected to decline almost 4 percent between 1989 and 1994, compared with a 2.5 percent decline around the ABC locations.

The marketers also looked at income estimates for ABC locations. A map showing 1989 household median income for each of the six ABC Financial locations in question pinpointed the highest median income within a two-mile trade area. (See Figure 2.)

The group then produced MicroVision Area Profile and Custom Group reports for South Gulf and ABC Financial. These reports confirmed that South Gulf's trade areas are made up predominantly of upscale segments and young singles. Figure 3 tabulates the market segments found in ABC's aggregated trade area.

ABC Financial's aggregated trade areas contained more mid-income and family segments, headed by the MicroVision segment Mainstream Families, followed by Mainstream Singles. This was important to South Gulf marketers, not only because it showed differences among customers in the ABC trade area, but because it showed a similarity between South Gulf and ABC customers. Although South Gulf is looking for evidence of diversity in customer segments on which to base its decision about acquiring ABC, marketers noted that similar customer segments could serve to strengthen the acquisition through congruity in marketing programs.

South Gulf marketers produced another census-tract map for Harris County, where the six ABC branches were located. Only those South Gulf branches closest to the ABC branches appeared on the map, which displayed the area's share of target-market households by tract with a two-mile radius around each branch location (Figure 4). With this, the marketers could distinguish the share of target customers living in ABC trade areas in relation to the three closest South Gulf locations. It also

MICROVISION AREA PROFILE REPORT

South Gulf Savings — SITE:
Agg. Trade Areas, Harris County, Texas — COORD: 00:00.00 00:00.00

DESCRIPTION	AREA TOTALS 1989 HSHLDS.	PCT.	BASE 1989 HSHLDS.	PCT.	INDEX
MVG01 1 UPPER CRUST	57879	5.7	806277	0.9	651
MVG01 2 LAP OF LUXURY	25223	2.5	1576242	1.7	145
MVG01 3 ESTABLISHED WEALTH	56968	5.6	2503444	2.7	206
MVG01 4 MID-LIFE SUCCESS	5080	0.5	516705	0.6	89
MVG01 5 PROSPEROUS ETHNIC MIX	26749	2.6	2489446	2.7	97
MVG01 6 GOOD FAMILY LIFE	102	0.0	1330794	1.4	1
MVG06 7 COMFORTABLE TIMES	3895	0.4	737148	0.8	48
MVG04 8 MOVERS AND SHAKERS	111515	11.0	2340082	2.5	432
MVG03 9 BUILDING A HOME LIFE	1022	0.1	552066	0.6	17
MVG02 10 HOME SWEET HOME	34862	3.4	4804473	5.2	66
MVG02 11 FAMILY TIES	10219	1.0	4069233	4.4	23
MVG04 12 A GOOD STEP FORWARD	345100	33.9	1836572	2.0	1703
MVG09 13 SUCCESSFUL SINGLES	6	0.0	599168	0.6	0
MVG01 14 MIDDLE YEARS	3342	0.3	451734	0.5	67
MVG04 15 GREAT BEGINNINGS	76688	7.5	3297109	3.6	211
MVG02 16 COUNTRY HOME FAMILIES	1020	0.1	4763583	5.2	2
MVG02 17 STARS AND STRIPES	5817	0.6	1626064	1.8	32
MVG02 18 WHITE PICKET FENCE	14951	1.5	5917729	6.4	23
MVG03 19 YOUNG AND CAREFREE	2915	0.3	559390	0.6	47
MVG06 20 SOCIAL SECURITY	4877	0.5	1416477	1.5	31
MVG06 21 SUNSET YEARS	2539	0.2	473496	0.5	49
MVG02 22 AGING AMERICA	4941	0.5	2458113	2.7	18
MVG02 23 SETTLED IN	11568	1.1	4520178	4.9	23
MVG08 24 METRO MINORITY FAMILIES	13988	1.4	1715460	1.9	74
MVG03 25 BEDROCK AMERICA	4098	0.4	2860794	3.1	13
MVG07 26 MATURE YEARS	715	0.1	1703331	1.8	4
MVG05 27 MIDDLE OF THE ROAD	874	0.1	318607	0.3	25
MVG03 28 BUILDING A FAMILY	3199	0.3	1349656	1.5	21
MVG05 29 ESTABLISHING ROOTS	959	0.1	405102	0.4	21
MVG06 30 RETIREMENT AGE	4034	0.4	934937	1.0	39
MVG06 31 GOLDEN TIMES	343	0.0	794242	0.9	4
MVG04 32 METRO SINGLES	1884	0.2	2279941	2.5	7
MVG07 33 LIVING OFF THE LAND	43	0.0	2338190	2.5	0
MVG04 34 BOOKS AND NEW RECRUITS	2952	0.3	860433	0.9	31
MVG02 35 LATE-LIFE LABORERS	358	0.0	4418395	4.8	1
MVG09 36 METRO ETHNIC MIX	216	0.0	1501916	1.6	1
MVG09 37 MOVING AHEAD MINORITIES	1411	0.1	592948	0.6	22
MVG02 38 BACK COUNTRY	0	0.0	5408473	5.9	0
MVG04 39 ON THEIR OWN	34471	3.4	3118116	3.4	100
MVG04 40 TRYING METRO TIMES	32838	3.2	2884541	3.1	103
MVG08 41 SOUTH OF THE BORDER	6146	0.6	719876	0.8	77
MVG08 42 HANGING ON	76	0.0	2076899	2.3	0
MVG08 43 LOW-INCOME BLUES	4156	0.4	345450	0.4	109

BASE DEFINITION STATE/COUNTY: UNITED STATES

Source: National Decision Systems

FIGURE 3 *MicroVision profiles of the neighborhoods around ABC branches indicate the presence of complementary segments to South Gulf's traditional customer base.*

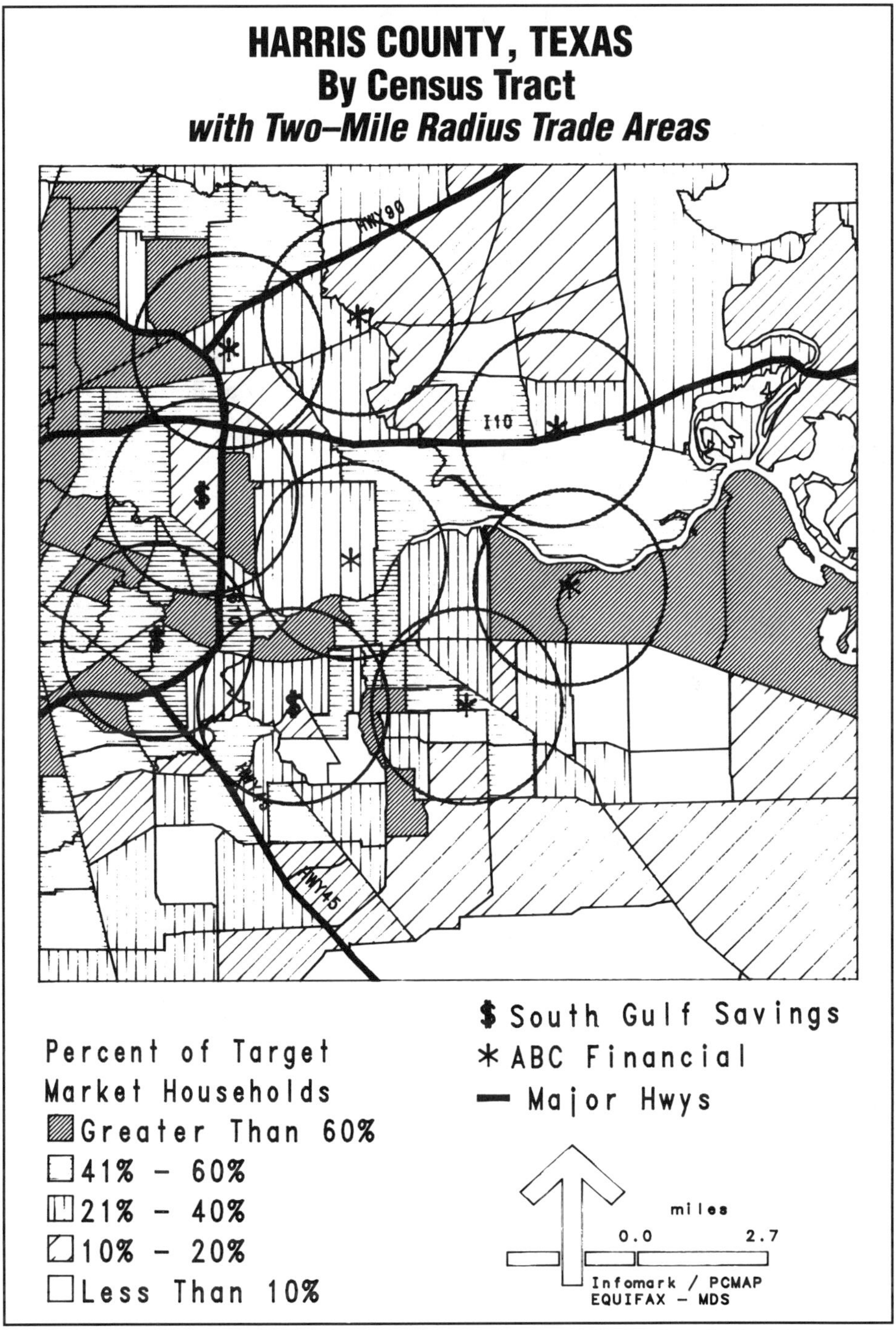

FIGURE 4 *This census-tract map shows concentrations of target households overlaid with South Gulf and ABC Financial branch locations.*

showed how much the two-mile trade areas were cannibalizing each other's business.

THE SOLUTION

Having identified the product potential for South Gulf's trade areas, the marketers looked at potential products for the ABC Financial trade areas. After adjusting on a per branch basis, South Gulf marketers discerned that ABC's trade areas had a slightly greater potential for installment loans, over three-fourths of which were auto loans.

South Gulf marketers were now ready to make a decision about acquiring the six ABC Financial locations. They determined that although the trade areas of the ABC and the South Gulf branches overlapped, cannibalization did not appear to be a significant problem. Another crucial criterion concerned the type of customers the ABC locations offered. The second map, coupled with information from the MicroVision reports, identified a large number of potential customers in the area. After final analysis, the marketers concluded that South Gulf would, in fact, benefit from acquiring the six ABC Financial branches.

This case study was submitted by:

Nancy Grebey
Manager, Banking & Finance Group
National Decision Systems
539 Encinitas Blvd.
Encinitas, CA 92024

CASE STUDY

Home Building Society/ Challenge Bank

COMPANY BACKGROUND

As in the U.S., financial institutions in Australia have been undergoing a revolution, facing proliferating services and fragmenting markets. Although the industry as a whole has been slow to respond to this change, two institutions in Australia have taken the initiative and made attempts to target their markets. Both the Home Building Society (HBS) and Challenge Bank (CB) have applied geographic information system technology in their marketing strategies.

THE PROBLEM

Marketing in financial services has traditionally been product-oriented. In recent years, this practice has fallen in disfavor as the industry has become increasingly consumer-driven. In such an environment, conservative institutions like HBS and CB have been faced with streamlining their market analysis capabilities. Implementing this new marketing attitude required an understanding of the existing market and knowledge of potential markets for different products.

THE SYSTEM

HBS and CB used the PC ARC/INFO system developed by the Environmental Systems Research Institute (ESRI). This geographic information system features map digitizing, data transfer, relational database management, graphics, geocoding, and network analysis. (For more information about the system and vendor, consult the descriptions in Appendix 1.)

METHODOLOGY

The first step in simplifying the identification of spatial trends was to map the existing customer base, accomplished by geocoding customer records based on the Western Australia Land Information System digital database. The banks' branch locations were also added to the map, classified by functions and/or characteristics such as ATMs, as were "friendly" competitor locations (ones that allow the use of another financial institution's ATM card). By overlaying the customer data with the branch data, the map showed how well existing customers were being serviced; it could suggest sites for potential ATMs or point up the need to promote friendly competitors' ATM locations.

This information was then merged with census data to determine the demographic characteristics of high- and low-performing areas. Based on this analysis, the management of HBS and CB was able to design and implement policies that strengthened current markets and allowed for the cultivation of new markets. For example, in one elderly target area, the institutions retained at least 70 percent of their existing customers by offering attractive retirement and superannuation packages. Likewise, by learning that a particular area is dominated by young well-educated professionals, they could increase their customer base by offering programs tailored to this market.

THE SOLUTION

By linking customer, branch, and demographic information with the PC ARC/INFO geographic information system, the Home Building Society and Challenge Bank were able to gain a better understanding of their existing customers and fine tune their product offerings to the appropriate targets. In addition, they were able to determine market penetration for use in planning overall marketing strategies.

This case study was prepared based on material submitted by:

Nola Roberts
ESRI-Australia
Suite 15, 476 Canterbury Road
Forest Hill 3131 Victoria
AUSTRALIA

CASE STUDY

Fleet/Norstar Financial Group

COMPANY BACKGROUND

Fleet Norstar Financial Group (F/NFG) is a $48 billion financial services company with 1,300 offices in 40 states. With such a wide network, F/NFG needed a way to effectively analyze the potential of new and existing markets. Most of the retail banking offices had become part of the organization through mergers, so there was no real methodology in place for identifying and quantifying the potential of new office sites.

THE PROBLEM

As with any organization, F/NFG needs to allocate resources carefully when looking at the potential opportunities in its market areas. However, it was already one of the largest banks in most of its markets and needed to avoid high usage areas where it already had a dominant presence. The challenge, then, was to find a straightforward, yet accurate, mechanism for profiling and evaluating existing F/NFG service areas.

THE SYSTEM

F/NFG used Claritas's Compass desktop marketing system in conjunction with its own Marketing Customer Information File (MCIF). Compass is a PC-based market analysis system that includes a variety of databases and the ability to import internal customer data. The Compass banking module includes national-level financial behavior by demographic characteristics and combines that information with the demographics of any given geography to project the financial behavior of people in an area. (For more information about the system and vendor, consult the descriptions in Appendix 1.)

METHODOLOGY

The bank combined information from its MCIF with the local product-use estimates generated by Compass to calculate market share. F/NFG could simply have focused on the areas where it had below-average share (see Figure 1), but these were not

REGIONS RANKED BY SHARE

TRACT	TOTAL $ USED IN TRACT (From Compass)	FLEET $ IN TRACT	$ SHARE IN TRACT	LOCATION
511.00	$44,780	$0	0.0%	Charlestown
506.00	$32,624	$75	0.2%	Richmond
206.03	$71,294	$3,003	4.2%	Coventry
401.03	$38,138	$1,897	5.0%	Portsmouth
131.00	$47,640	$3,059	6.4%	Glocester
127.00	$60,792	$4,058	6.7%	Greenville
117.01	$39,446	$2,762	7.0%	Lincoln
170.00	$91,299	$6,536	7.2%	Pawtucket
207.00	$39,993	$2,930	7.3%	West Coventry
117.02	$51,064	$3,896	7.6%	Lincoln Woods
114.03	$56,434	$4,375	7.8%	Cumberland
206.02	$79,194	$6,265	7.9%	Coventry
158.00	$36,329	$3,005	8.3%	Pawtucket
403.01	$49,157	$4,375	8.9%	Middletown

FIGURE 1 *By comparing Compass projections of total deposit dollars with F/NFG's actual deposits, a market-share estimate is developed for each census tract.*

necessarily high-potential areas. To identify markets with the greatest potential, F/NFG established the bank's statewide average share as a target and calculated the number of incremental dollars the bank would pick up if the business in each market area grew to a level equal to the target share. Figure 2 shows how this additional step changed the desirability of some of the markets being examined.

F/NFG was then able to use these estimates for profitability analysis, because the incremental potential methodology helped neutralize errors that might exist in a model relying on national statistics to estimate local-area product use.

THE SOLUTION

By using Compass, F/NFG was able to identify areas with high or low incremental potential and begin making some initial delivery decisions. It developed defensive strategies to protect the favorable penetration in clusters with very low incremental potential and conducted more detailed analysis in market clusters with high incremental potential. F/NFG also determined trade-area dimensions for the different kinds of facilities that could service an area (e.g., full-service branches, mini-branches, loan production offices, and ATMs) by looking at surrogate branches elsewhere in the F/NFG system, performing intercept surveys at potential sites, and even conducting license-plate customer-origin surveys at nearby competitor sites. The incremental potential for trade areas covered by different delivery options were fed into pro formas to determine which options produced the greatest return.

REGIONS RANKED BY INCREMENTAL POTENTIAL

TRACT	TOTAL $ USED IN TRACT (From Compass)	$ SHARE IN TRACT	INCREMENTAL POTENTIAL IF SHARE EQ FLEET AVG	LOCATION
206.03	$71,294	4.2%	$7,691	Coventry
170.00	$91,299	7.2%	$7,159	Pawtucket
511.00	$44,780	0.0%	$6,717	Charlestown
206.02	$79,194	7.9%	$5,614	Coventry
127.00	$60,792	6.7%	$5,061	Greenville
506.00	$32,624	0.2%	$4,818	Richmond
114.03	$56,434	7.8%	$4,090	Cumberland
131.00	$47,640	6.4%	$4,087	Glocester
401.03	$38,138	5.0%	$3,824	Portsmouth
117.02	$51,064	7.6%	$3,764	Lincoln Woods
117.01	$39,446	7.0%	$3,155	Lincoln
207.00	$39,993	7.3%	$3,069	West Coventry
403.01	$49,157	8.9%	$2,999	Middletown
158.00	$36,329	8.3%	$2,445	Pawtucket

FIGURE 2 *Because F/NFG ultimately wants to determine the tracts with the greatest potential, it created statewide averages as a benchmark and calculated the gap between its average performance and observed performance for each tract.*

This case study was submitted by:

Scott Rosa, Vice President
Fleet National Bank
111 Westminster Street
Providence, RI 02903

CASE STUDY

Community National Bank

COMPANY BACKGROUND

Community National Bank (CNB) is a major financial institution in the Midwest. It has experienced strong deposit growth over the past several years and is a leading provider of real-estate loans in its market. It considers itself a progressive and responsible institution and was intent on complying with all provisions of the Community Reinvestment Act.

THE PROBLEM

The Community Reinvestment Act requires that federal agencies supervising financial institutions assess each institution's performance in meeting the deposit and credit needs of the community it is chartered to serve. Each bank must demonstrate that the community from which it receives deposits is having its credit needs met.

In an effort to assure compliance with the Community Reinvestment Act, CNB planned to proactively determine the extent to which it was providing loans "appropriately" to the community it served. Although CNB had extensive data on its customers—both depositors and borrowers—it had no easy way to integrate these data. Furthermore, it was unable to identify the extent to which it was complying with the law.

THE SYSTEM

To assist in the analysis of its lending practices, CNB enlisted the services of DAS Information, Inc., a financial services consultant in Minneapolis. DAS, in turn, decided to use the CAM-1+ desktop system for the analysis. Developed by Datamap, CAM-1+ is a PC-based market analysis system that links demographics and client information to postal carrier routes. This information can be integrated with graphics and mapping packages. (For more information about the system and vendor, consult the descriptions in Appendix 1.)

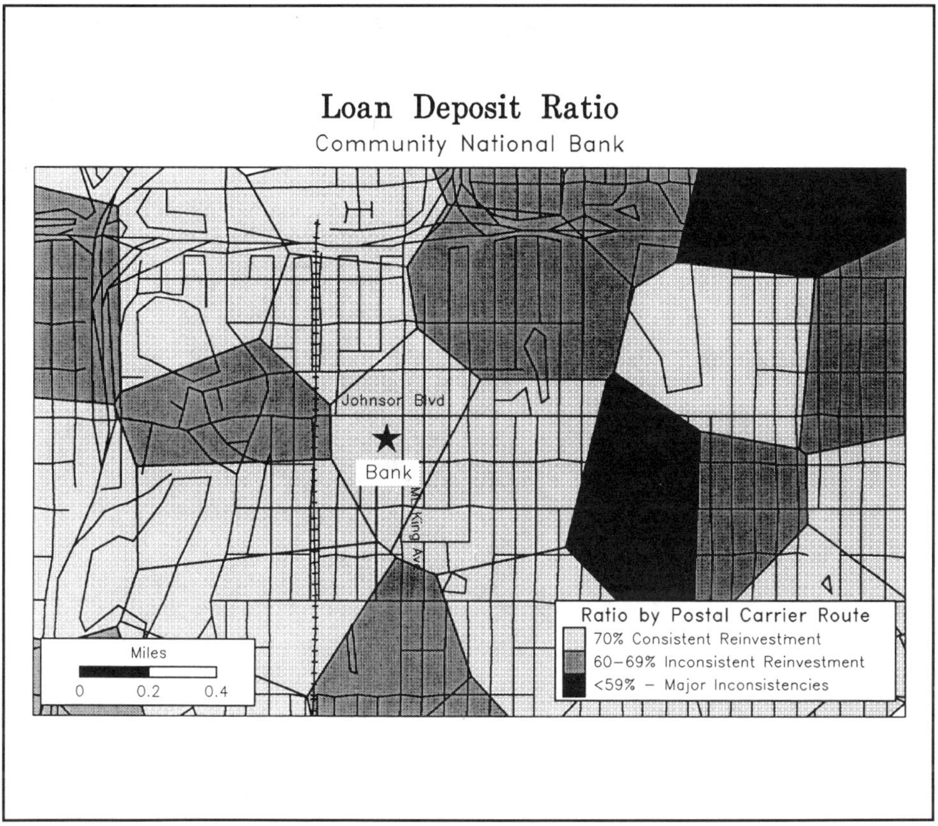

FIGURE 1 *Being able to analyze the ratio of deposits to loans is critical in demonstrating compliance with the Community Reinvestment Act. Here, Community National Bank used CAM-1+ to map these data at the postal-carrier-route level to indicate neighborhoods where compliance needed improvement.*

METHODOLOGY

The objective of the project was to match CNB's primary deposit and loan communities. Client data (complete with street address) were imported into the system to determine what constituted the bank's primary and secondary trade areas. Within these identified trade areas, the level of deposits was matched with loan activity. Using CAM-1+, it was possible to generate a loan-to-deposit ratio for these primary and secondary trade areas and, if desired, for individual carrier routes. Maps displayed the extent to which loan and deposit concentrations overlapped. Figure 1 illustrates the bank's distribution of deposits within the market area.

THE SOLUTION

Using Datamap's CAM-1+ system, DAS Information profiled the bank's depositors and borrowers. The bank was able to determine for itself the extent to which it was complying with the provisions of the Community Reinvestment Act before being audited by regulatory agencies. To the extent that discrepancies were found, CNB was able to develop programs to target areas that had, for whatever reason, a mismatch between deposits and loans.

This case study was submitted by:

Rick Byers
National Services Sales Manager
Datamap, Inc.
7525 Mitchell Rd., Suite 300
Eden Prairie, MN 55344

CASE STUDY

Mutual Life Insurance

COMPANY BACKGROUND

Mutual Life Insurance (MLI) is a life and health insurance company with 200 agencies located throughout the Denver and Boulder metropolitan areas. MLI offers term and whole life insurance, universal life, living benefit options, and annuities. For the most part, MLI is a highly successful company with long-term policyholders and a below-average rate of policy cancellations. Company pride at MLI revolves around the fact that policyholders tend to "stick with" their policies and do not move from company to company. Fewer than 10 percent of all policyholders let their policies lapse.

THE PROBLEM

Although the overall payment rate on annual premiums is very good, some agencies show a markedly higher lapse rate (one office had an 18 percent lapse rate). Management wanted to determine if there was a problem with the agents in these offices and whether or not the offices were adequately servicing their policyholders. Management was also interested in finding any similarities among lapsed policyholders. The marketing group at MLI was charged with determining what factors contributed to the higher lapse rate at some agencies.

THE SYSTEM

The marketing group decided to use National Decision Systems' Infomark Desktop PC System for this project. The Infomark system is a menu-driven software package with census data and the MicroVision geocoding and segmentation component. By incorporating its own customer files, the marketing group hoped to explain the situation it was facing. (For more information about the system and vendor, consult the descriptions in Appendix 1.)

METHODOLOGY

In examining the agencies' records, the marketing team concluded that 21 of the 200 agencies had lapse rates above 10 percent and focused the initial analysis on those

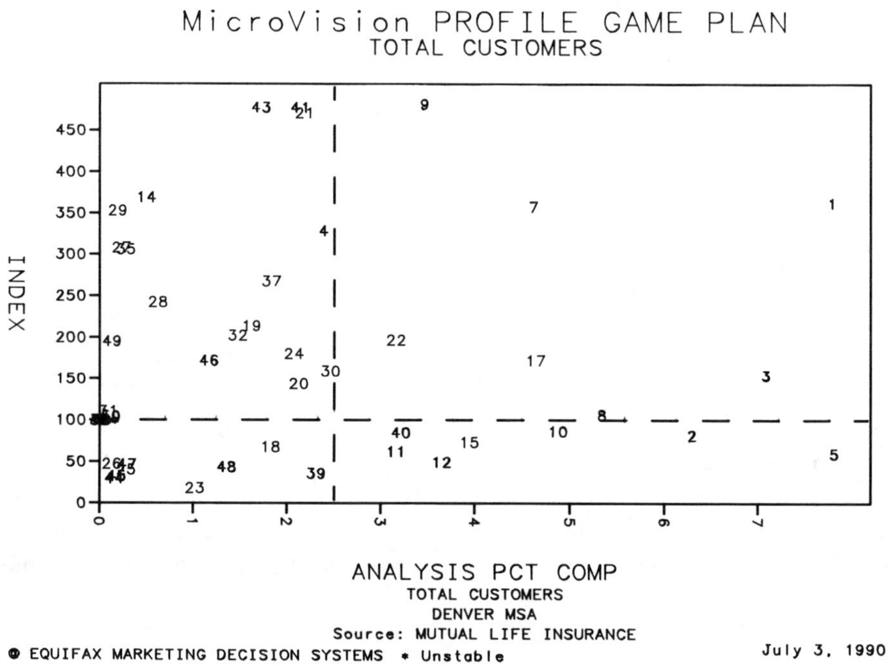

FIGURE 1 *This MicroVision profile of MLI's customer base indicates each segment's propensity to be a customer (index), as well as its size (total customers).*

agencies. The first step was a locational analysis to determine if the areas in which these agencies were located contained high-risk customers.

MLI first created a MicroVision profile of all its customers, which revealed the types of households it attracted overall (Figure 1). The researchers then created a profile of lapsed policyholders to pinpoint the types of households that may be more likely than average to let their insurance policies lapse.

MLI marketers noted that customers came from just about every socioeconomic class. However, by using a bivariate analysis module ("Game Plan"), they identified some definite distinguishing characteristics associated with their core customer segments.

MLI's core segments accounted for 31 percent of its customer base, but only 13 percent of all U.S. households. MLI marketers noticed that their core segments tended to be more affluent than average, and with the exception of the "Comfortable Times" cluster, to be more family-oriented. This did not surprise the marketers at MLI, because these segments tend to have more responsibilities and more to lose if not insured.

After comparing the lapsed customer profile to the total customer profile, MLI

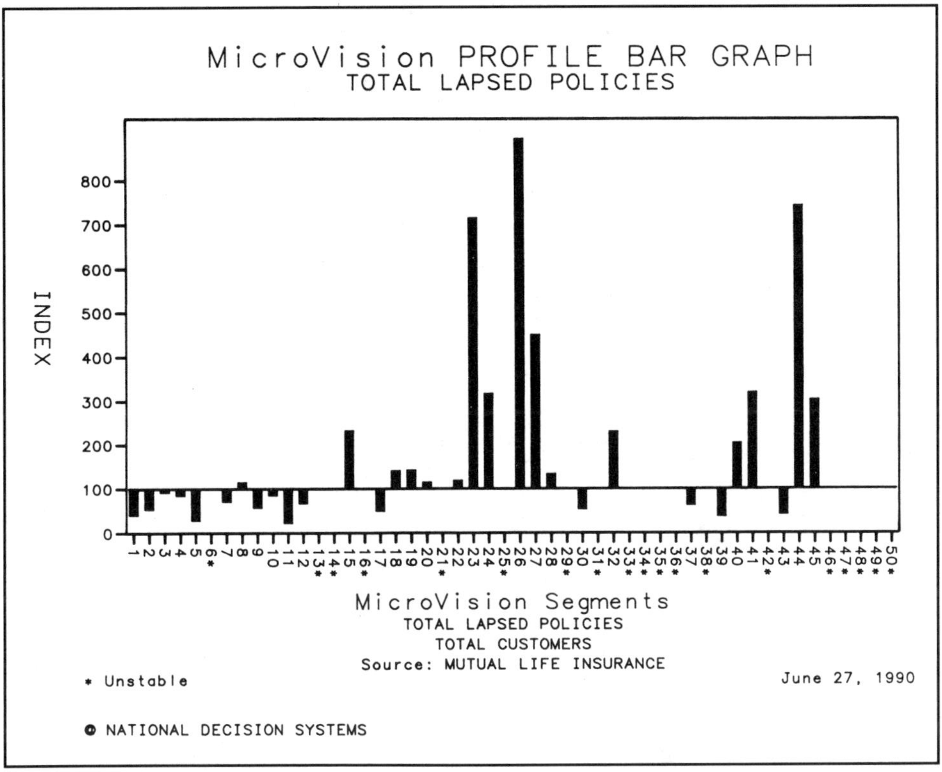

FIGURE 2 *This bar chart compares the propensity of each segment to lapse using the total customer profile as a base for comparison. Clearly, there is a handful of segments (23, 24, 26, 27, and 44) that have very high tendencies to let their policies lapse.*

marketers concluded that lapsed customers tended to be more downscale than average (Figure 2).

Once the MLI marketing team had identified core customer segments for overall and lapsed policies, it looked at the MicroVision composition of households in the 21 high-lapse trade areas. For example, the one-mile trade area around Agency X showed a high concentration of segment 24 (Metro Minority Families), one of the core lapsed policy segments.

Using the lapsed-policyholder profiles, the researchers produced market-potential estimates for trade areas to determine the MicroVision Market Index (the propensity of a market area to have lapsed policies). This provided a benchmark of what to expect in a market based on actual policyholder information. Agency X's trade area even turned out to be inhabited by segments with high-lapse propensities. Figure 3 depicts lapsed-policy rates within the trade area of Agency X.

Although this was one valid explanation for the agency's high lapse rate, the marketers wanted to identify other factors that could be contributing to the low performance of this particular agency.

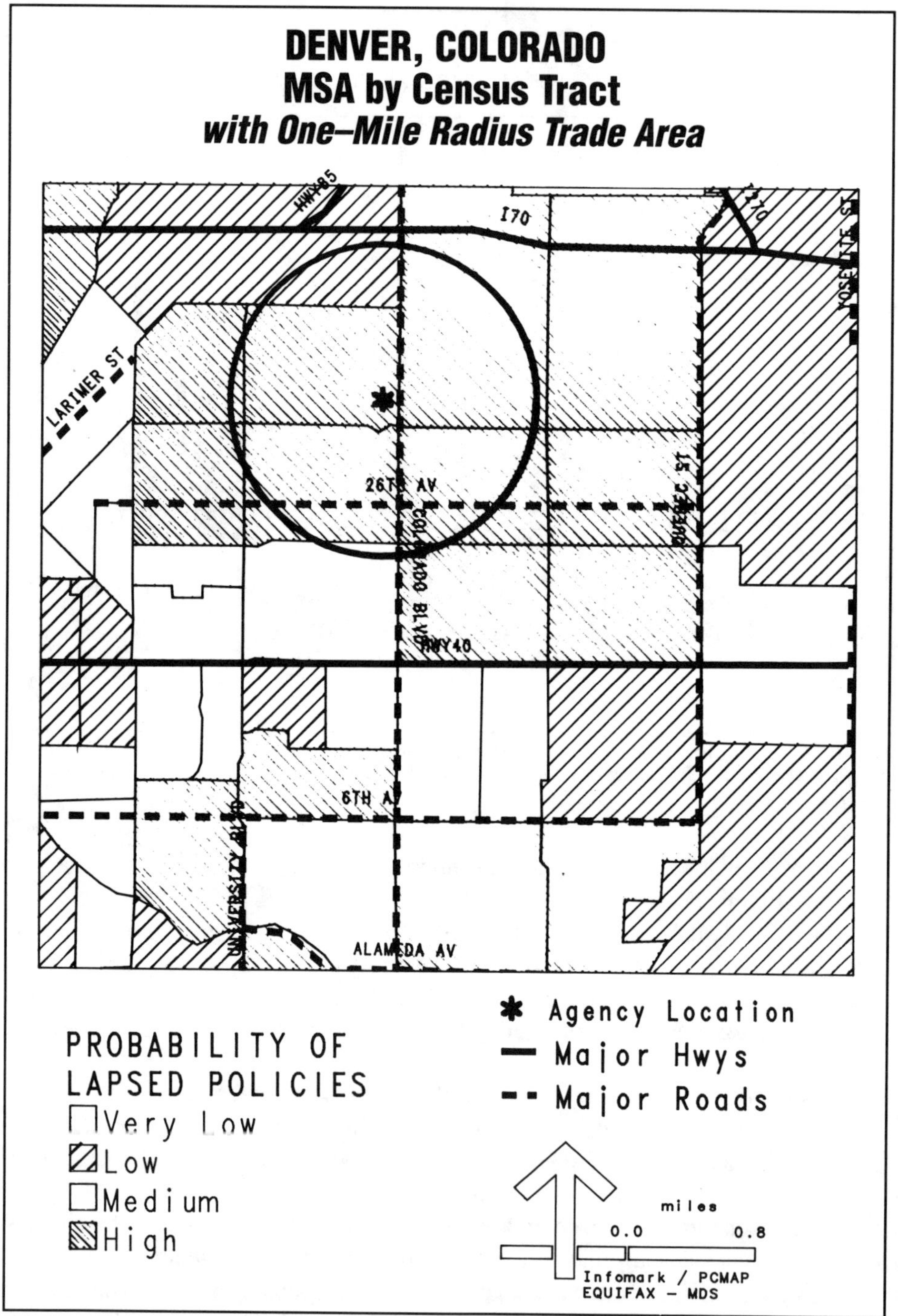

FIGURE 3 *Using Infomark, MLI is able to produce maps that identify agencies in neighborhoods with a high probability of lapsed policies.*

A MicroVision Cross Profile Correlation Report displayed the rank-order correlation of a primary profile against all profiles of a particular category (e.g., financial ranking). The profile correlations were ranked from high to low, highlighting those profiles that are similar to the primary profile under examination.

THE SOLUTION

Using the Infomark system, Mutual Life Insurance was able to evaluate the 21 agency locations with higher-than-average rates of lapsed policies. In the case of Agency X, MLI marketers were able to pinpoint some of the factors contributing to the agency's lapse rate. Armed with this knowledge, MLI hopes to cultivate lapsed segments by targeting them for other products and services.

This case study was submitted by:

Bob Nascenzi
Manager, Insurance/Investment
National Decision Systems
539 Encinitas Blvd.
Encinitas, CA 92024

7

Health-Care Industry

Since World War II, the health-care industry has been the fastest-growing sector of the U.S. economy. Characterized as a "cottage industry" as recently as the 1960s, the health-care system has expanded dramatically in the past three decades. Today, it is a mammoth institution with more than 7,000 hospitals, 16,000 nursing homes, and an estimated 300,000 independent clinics providing physician care. The health-services industry continues to expand faster than the rest of the economy and accounted for approximately 12 percent of the gross national product in 1990. It accounts for more jobs than any other sector besides education. Unlike other industries, however, the health-care industry is highly fragmented and functions through the actions of hundreds of thousands of autonomous units. Also unlike other industries, health care has historically not been characterized by competition, and services were paid for in a manner that kept a true "market" from existing.

The health-care industry underwent a radical transformation during the 1980s. Concern over the rising cost of health care resulted in a variety of cost-containment measures. Hospitals, physicians, the government, and insurers jockeyed for position in an environment characterized by major shifts in power, decision-making, and risk. Two important developments of the 1980s relevant to desktop marketing were the realizations that hospitals were in the "health-care" business and not just the "hospital" business, and that health care was, in fact, a business and not a charity or community service. These realizations were prompted in part by the introduction, for the first time, of competition. Faced with overcapacity, declining utilization, and declining reimbursement for services, health-care providers were forced to compete for their share of a "shrinking" market. The total market was actually not shrinking, but changes in consumer preferences and practices were shifting business away from traditional sources of care, particularly hospitals. This new competition forced health-care providers to shift from a product orientation to a market orientation, and opened the doors for a variety of activities that can benefit from desktop marketing.

Because of the historical lack of competition, health care had lagged behind other industries in developing industry-wide market intelligence. Although the industry produces massive amounts of information, it has tended to be highly decentralized. In addition, the private and/or not-for-profit status of many providers meant that much information was not publicly available. As providers of health services came to face the demands long addressed by other industries, the lack of market intelligence became increasingly obvious.

The mushrooming demand for market data and the lack of existing mechanisms for industry market research spurred the development of a strong health-data industry. Vendors with "generic" systems adapted their systems to health care, bringing into play their massive nationwide databases. Applications from other industries, particularly the financial services industry, were adapted to health care, some with more success than others. By the mid-1980s, health-care-specific systems had been developed.

At the same time, nationwide databases became more accessible, allowing the application of national use patterns to local area issues. Consumer data were also becoming more readily available. By the late 1980s, two large-scale (100,000-household) consumer surveys were being conducted for health-data vendors, and more were in the works. Psychographic analysis, which had been developed for other industries, was reformulated for use in health care.

The challenges facing health care in the 1990s will place even greater demands on desktop marketing systems. The industry must complete the conversion to a true service mentality, with more of an "outreach" orientation than in the past. It must be able to manage massive data sets while maintaining standards of ethics and confidentiality. It must develop means of measuring "quality" and evaluating the effectiveness of products, pricing, and promotional and distribution decisions. Finally, it must address the issue of market fragmentation faced by other industries.

CASE STUDY

Community Hospital

COMPANY BACKGROUND

Community Hospital is a 220-bed provider that serves as both a community hospital and a tertiary referral center. The hospital has enjoyed an outstanding reputation for many tertiary services, particularly cardiology, which represents about 35 percent of total revenues. At present, Community Hospital is the only hospital in the county that performs open-heart surgery.

THE PROBLEM

Community Hospital saw a marked decline in its cardiology market share over a six-month period. The decline was attributed to the recent opening of two cardiac catheterization labs at St. Elizabeth's Hospital, a major competitor. The opening of these facilities coincided with St. Elizabeth's recruitment of a "superstar" surgeon and major promotional efforts on behalf of its cardiology program. St. Elizabeth's plan to acquire open-heart capabilities within two years posed a serious threat to Community Hospital's position as the preferred provider for cardiology services.

In light of this intensifying competition, Community Hospital management decided to proactively develop a cardiology product line. The approach consisted of a targeted consumer marketing strategy in concert with a physician development strategy. At the same time, there was pressure to maximize the return on the investment of marketing dollars. Brian Saravis, vice president of marketing, took the lead in developing this marketing initiative.

THE SYSTEM

Community Hospital chose The Sachs Group desktop market analysis system to assist in the development of a product line. The Sachs Group system includes numerous applications designed specifically for the health-care industry. Components like The Market Planner®, MPTarget™, The Physician Practice Planner®, and The Contract Planner™ all have applications for the product-line development project. The SachsGroups™ segmentation system defines 29 market segments based on household type (listed in Figure 1). (For more information about the system and vendor, consult the descriptions in Appendix 1.)

SachsGroups™

THE START GROUP

Young Single Households

1. **Scramblers**
2. **Taking Off**
3. **Action Oriented**
4. **Rustic Run**
5. **Tally Ho**

THE FUN GROUP

Young Marrieds Without Children

6. **Facing Reality**
7. **Up & At 'em**
8. **Never Been Better**

THE RUN GROUP

Young Households With Children

9. **Ready, Set, Go**
10. **Up & Coming**
11. **Need Au Pair**

THE TEAM GROUP

Middle-Aged Married With Children

12. **Trying Harder**
13. **Equal Time**
14. **Agri-Family**
15. **Modern Success**

THE ONLY GROUP

Middle-Aged Single Households With Children

16. **Oil Burners**
17. **Nurturing Kind**
18. **Living for Now**
19. **Yearning for Time**

THE MID GROUP

Middle-Aged Households Without Children

20. **Mindful of Money**
21. **Impress the Boss**
22. **Deal Me In**

THE SENIORS GROUP

Medicare Generation

23. **Second Wind**
24. **Easy Going**
25. **Nature's Way**
26. **Intense Givers**
27. **Odd-person-out**
28. **Resort Set**
29. **Season Ticket**

Source: The Sachs Group Ltd.

FIGURE 1 *The Sachs Group has developed a market segmentation system based on age and household type that is useful in health-care marketing applications.*

METHODOLOGY

Saravis followed these steps in product-line development:

1) Identify market segments that use outpatient cardiology and blood-pressure-related services and/or have previously used Community Hospital cardiology services.
2) Determine where these segments live in order to implement direct-marketing campaigns and to identify potential primary-care physician-practice sites.
3) Develop an education/screening package for cardiology-related services to attract these market segments.
4) Develop a communication strategy to deliver the appropriate message to the target audience.
5) Determine the media mix that will most cost-effectively reach these target segments.

FIGURE 2 *Using syndicated data on health-care usage, Sachs was able to determine the segments that had the greatest propensity to use cardiology services.*

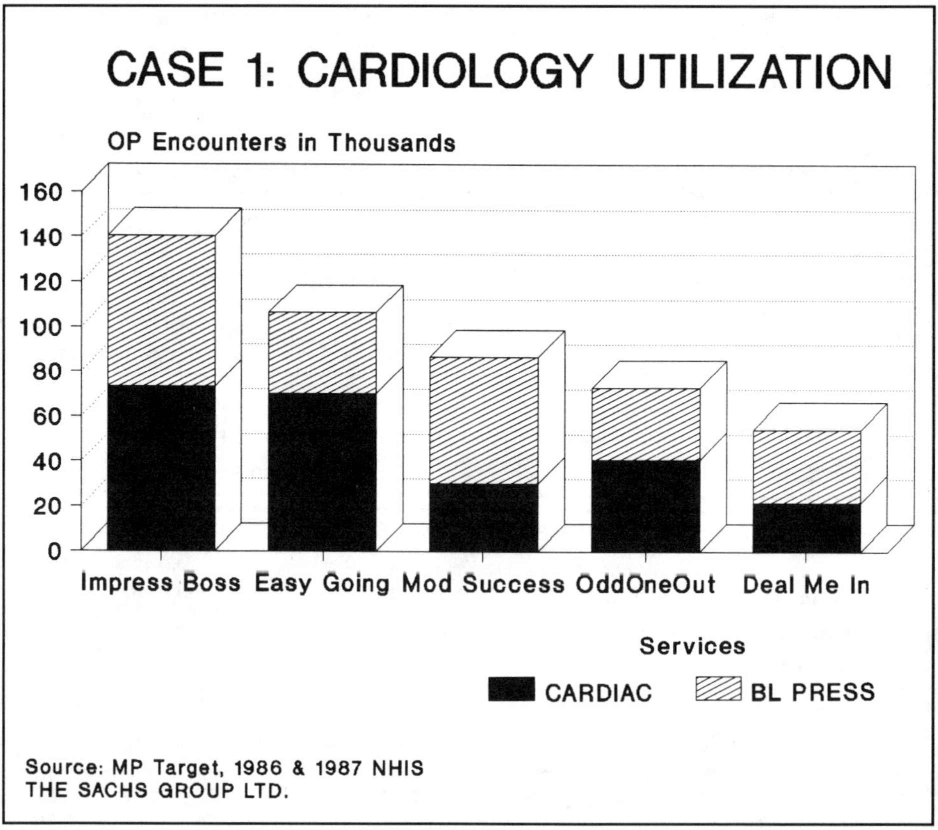

Where Do the Targets Live?

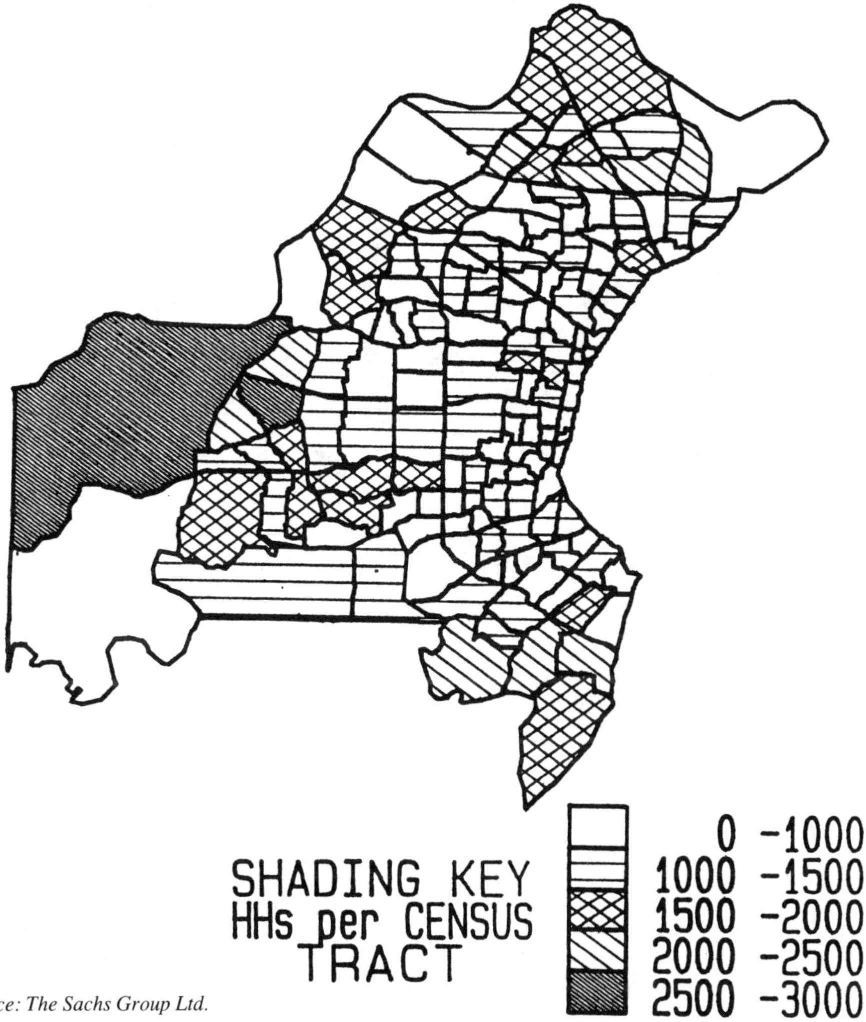

Source: The Sachs Group Ltd.

FIGURE 3 *The target segments were then mapped by census tract.*

The first step was to determine which of the SachsGroups segments were the most active users of outpatient cardiac and blood-pressure services. MP Target™ determined that "Modern Success" and "Impress the Boss" households were the top users of blood-pressure services. "Impress the Boss" households were also the top users of outpatient cardiac services, along with "Easy Going" households. (See Figure 2.) "Modern Success" households are high-income, mature families; "Impress the Boss" households are middle-income, middle-aged households without

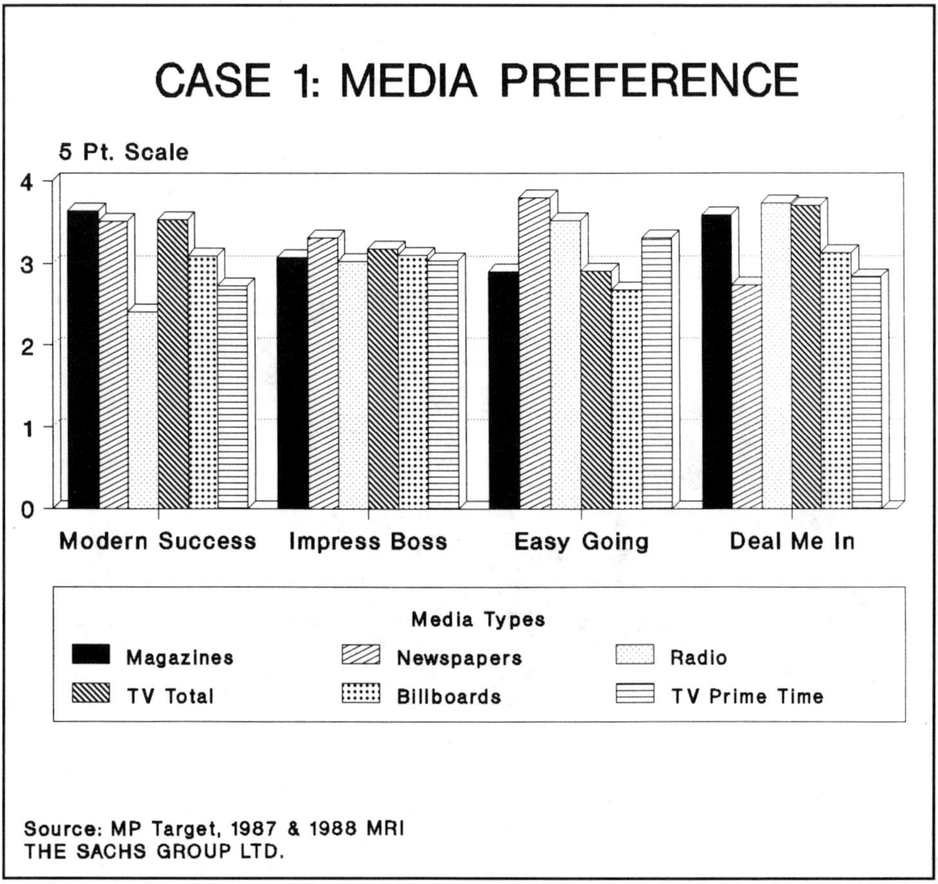

FIGURE 4 *Syndicated media-use data were incorporated to determine the most efficient means of reaching the target audience.*

children; and "Easy Going" households are senior couples with moderate incomes.

The next step was to determine where the target segments lived. With this information, the hospital could choose appropriate locations for one-day screening programs to promote trial use of Community's services and provide an additional point of access into new markets. In addition, the director of physician relations needed information to guide her in locating potential sites for primary-care physician practices.

Saravis evaluated potential locations at the census-tract level. A map revealed the location of target households (see Figure 3). Saravis was able to identify potential sites for screenings and physician practices, sites with both a significant number and share of target households. These "hot" census tracts were also in areas where the population was projected to grow by at least 8 percent between 1990 and 1995, about twice the average rate.

THE SOLUTION

Community Hospital was now in a position to develop a comprehensive cardiology program that would appeal to the targeted SachsGroups segments. Research revealed that these target segments valued prevention-oriented education and cardiac rehabilitation programs with a strong educational component. Saravis worked with the cardiology product-line manager to package "Healthy Heart" educational materials for the off-site screening promotion. He also worked with her to develop three distinct support and education groups for the three different phases of cardiac rehabilitation. By using the Sachs Group system, Community Hospital was able to realize considerable savings in direct-mail costs, expose many first-time users of services to the hospital under positive circumstances, build stronger relationships with referring physicians, and develop a cost-effective media mix. (See Figure 4.)

This case study was submitted by:

Lisa Frey, Product Management
MPTarget™
The Sachs Group Ltd.
1800 Sherman Avenue
Evanston, IL 60201

This study is based on an actual case, but due to the proprietary nature of the topic, fictitious names are used to maintain confidentiality with company and its personnel.

CASE STUDY

St. Mary's Hospital

COMPANY BACKGROUND

St. Mary's Hospital is a medium-sized facility located in the Midwest. It has a strong medical staff development program but is located in a metropolitan area that is considered to have a surplus of physicians. Its objective was to strengthen its medical staff to solidify its primary-care presence in the North Metro market, one of the more competitive markets in the metro area.

THE PROBLEM

While there is a general oversupply of physicians in the metro area, St. Mary's administrators felt that certain market opportunities still existed. The vice president of physician services and the chief executive officer of St. Mary's Hospital were convinced that there were benefits to recruiting and placing a family practitioner in that community.

In the past, planners at St. Mary's had used GMENAC (Graduate Medical Education National Advisory Committee) "ideal" physician-to-population ratios as a basis for determining physician demand. Using these guidelines, they identified an apparent oversupply of 75 family practitioners in the hospital's market area. St. Mary's planners, however, began to question this approach as it seemed outdated and oversimplified. It made no distinction based on the age and sex composition of the market, nor did the information reflect differences in physician specialty preferences between urban and rural markets. St. Mary's needed a system that would provide more meaningful physician demand data.

THE SYSTEM

St. Mary's chose The Sachs Group desktop market analysis system, designed specifically for the health-care industry. The SachsGroups™ system includes numerous applications and databases developed especially for health care. The Market Planner and Physician Practice Planner® applications are useful for such a project. (For more information about the system and vendor, consult the descriptions in Appendix 1.)

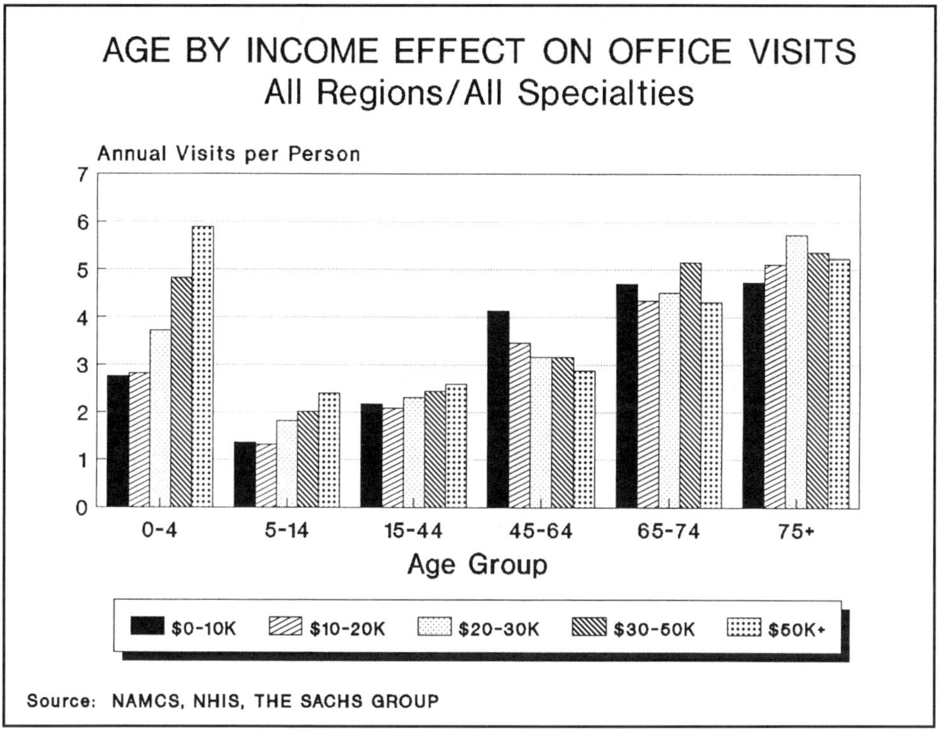

FIGURE 1 *This graph indicates that household income has a dramatic effect on the average number of office visits by age segment.*

THE METHODOLOGY

The Physician Practice Planner module of the system provided a comprehensive analysis of the market's physician needs. The Physician Practice Planner models take into account not only the age and sex distribution of local areas, but also the race, income, and rural/urban characteristics of the local market. Figure 1 charts the number of expected physician visits by age and income for the entire market.

The Physician Practice Planner models vary by region of the country and illustrate urban and rural differences. These variations are applied to local demographic characteristics in a hospital's market. The analysts selected the midwestern rural model to evaluate targeted zip codes in the North Metro market. The analysis indicated a clear shortage of general and family practitioners in this North market area (see Figure 2).

The physician being recruited was impressed with the documented need for his services and conceded that a competitor of St. Mary's had been trying to convince him to set up practice in its facilities. In response, St. Mary's produced a map indicating the large number of general and family practitioners within a four-mile radius of the competitor's site (see Figure 3). It was apparent to the physician that his opportunities would be greater at St. Mary's.

THE PHYSICIAN PRACTICE PLANNER Standard Report

PROJECTION SUMMARY BY SPECIALTY:
VISIT DEMAND/SURPLUS/DEFICIT, PHYSICIAN SUPPLY/PRODUCTIVITY/NEED

REPORT 1 - FOR NORTH MARKET ONLY

	Physicians	Pop. Visit Volume Phy.
Allergy & Immunology	2	11,182
Card. Diseases	3	7,680
Card. Surgery	0	1,286
Dermatology	3	21,370
Emergency Medicine	1	4,571
Gastroenterology	4	2,008
General&Family Prac.	17	253,291
General Surgery	11	15,965
Gynecology	0	1,795
Internal Medicine	27	63,870
Neurology	1	4,277
Neurological Surgery	0	2,372
Obst. & Gynecology	10	48,069
Oncology	2	3,280
Ophthalmology	5	33,370
Orthopedic Surgery	5	29,227
Other Specialties	0	1,882
Otolaryngology	5	9,305
Psychiatry	5	19,233
Pediatrics	15	93,487
Phy. & Occup. Medicine	0	2,873
Plastic Surgery	2	6,984
Ped. Subspecialties	1	2,292
Pulmonary Diseases	0	571
Rheumatology	1	3,419
Surg. Subspecialties	0	2,215
Urology	0	10,488
Total	120	656,362

Data Sources: National Health Interview Survey, 1987-8
National Ambulatory Care Survey, 1985
BMI Physician Database, 1989
Rate Estimates: THE SACHS GROUP LTD., 1990
Markets Used: NORTH
Year: 1989
Projection File Name: BASEPROJ
Visit Model Used: PPVISMM

FIGURE 2 *By applying the Sachs Group's Physician Practice Planner demand model to its North Metro Market, St. Mary's was able to identify areas of opportunity in what was thought to be an oversupplied market.*

Visit Potential	Unmet Visits	Phy. to Add
12,338	-1,156	-0
8,490	-810	-0
0	1,286	1
23,842	-2,472	-0
4,232	338	0
9,005	-6,997	-3
100,968	152,323	26
31,375	-15,410	-5
0	1,795	0
102,914	-39,044	-10
2,702	1,576	1
0	2,372	1
50,421	-2,352	-0
6,139	-2,859	-1
31,496	1,874	0
24,757	4,470	1
0	1,882	0
30,443	-21,138	-3
8,749	10,483	6
94,640	-1,153	-0
0	2,873	1
6,955	29	0
2,178	114	0
0	571	0
3,927	-508	-0
0	2,215	1
0	10,488	3
555,572	100,790	17

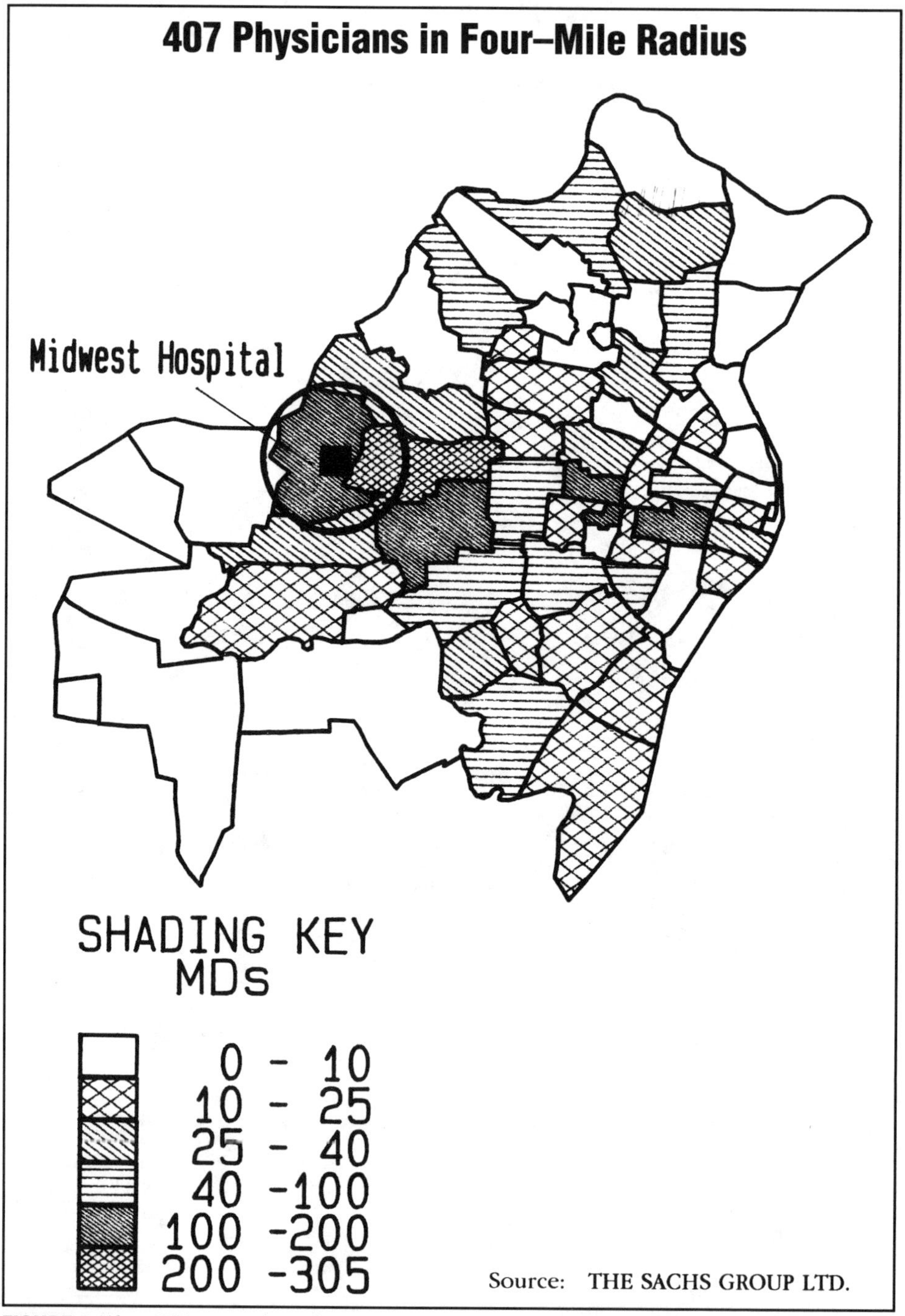

FIGURE 3 *(Above) This map indicates the oversupply of physicians around a competing hospital.*
FIGURE 4 *(Facing page) The Sachs Group's system also enables St. Mary's analysts to project diagnostic test usage in its market.*

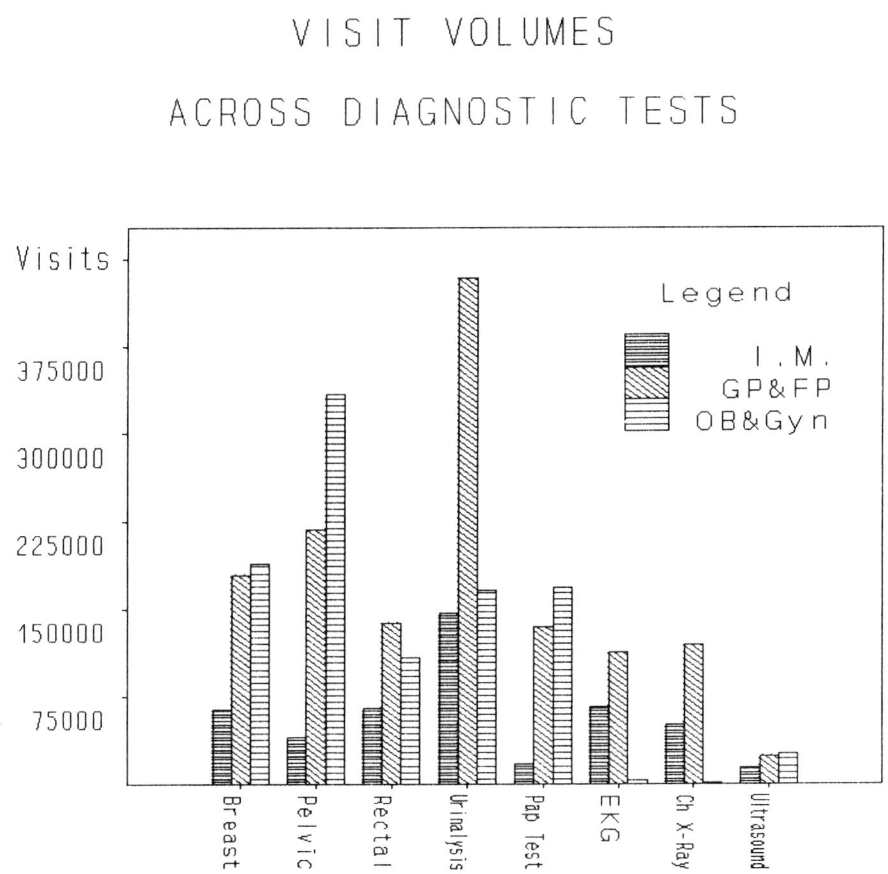

Source: The Sachs Group Ltd.

St. Mary's analysts also mapped a three-mile radius around each of two sites proposed for the physician's new practice. The area surrounding Site A had 37,238 unmet physician visits and excellent road access, while the area around Site B indicated considerably fewer unmet visits (27,863). The analysts also illustrated the expected mix of diagnostic tests that would be generated by the physician office visit demand in the market. (See Figure 4.)

THE SOLUTION

The detailed graphic presentation developed using The Sachs Group system helped convince the physician to affiliate with St. Mary's rather than its competitor. It also allowed St. Mary's to assist the physician in selecting the best possible practice site. Within eighteen months of setting up practice at the new location (Site A), the physician was providing the hospital with 36 admissions annually and referring 49 patients for admission by specialists.

This case study was submitted by:

Mary Kay Conlon
Vice President
The Sachs Group Ltd.
1800 Sherman Avenue
Evanston, IL 60201

This study is based on an actual case, but due to the proprietary nature of the topic, fictitious names are used to maintain confidentiality with the company and its personnel.

CASE STUDY

Bluegrass General Hospital

COMPANY BACKGROUND

Bluegrass General Hospital is a medium-sized hospital in Louisville, Kentucky. There is a great deal of competition among hospitals in the area. Because of this, Bluegrass General, like its competitors, is attempting to develop stronger ties with its physicians.

THE PROBLEM

The strategic planners at Bluegrass General needed data to evaluate sites for a community-wide network of ambulatory centers. They also needed to gain a competitive advantage by cultivating the loyalty of the most desirable group practices in the area in terms of productivity and location.

THE SYSTEM

Administrators at Bluegrass General called in First Research as a consultant to develop its primary-care network. First Research used CONQUEST/Health Care for its analysis. CONQUEST/Health Care is an industry-specific version of the system that includes modules such as CONQUEST Diagnosis Related Group (DRG) forecasts, which estimate potential demand for in-patient services. Developed by Donnelley Marketing Information Services (DMIS), CONQUEST is a PC-based market analysis system. (For more information about the system and vendor, consult the descriptions in Appendix 1.)

METHODOLOGY

As a first step, patient records at the street-address level were extracted from the hospital's mainframe, along with key "product-line" information such as admitting physician, reason for admission, total charges, distance to hospital, types of insurance, and length of stay. Patient records were geocoded by DMIS and integrated into CONQUEST. Patient data were aggregated by physician group and mapped to display each practice's patient dispersion (see Figure 1).

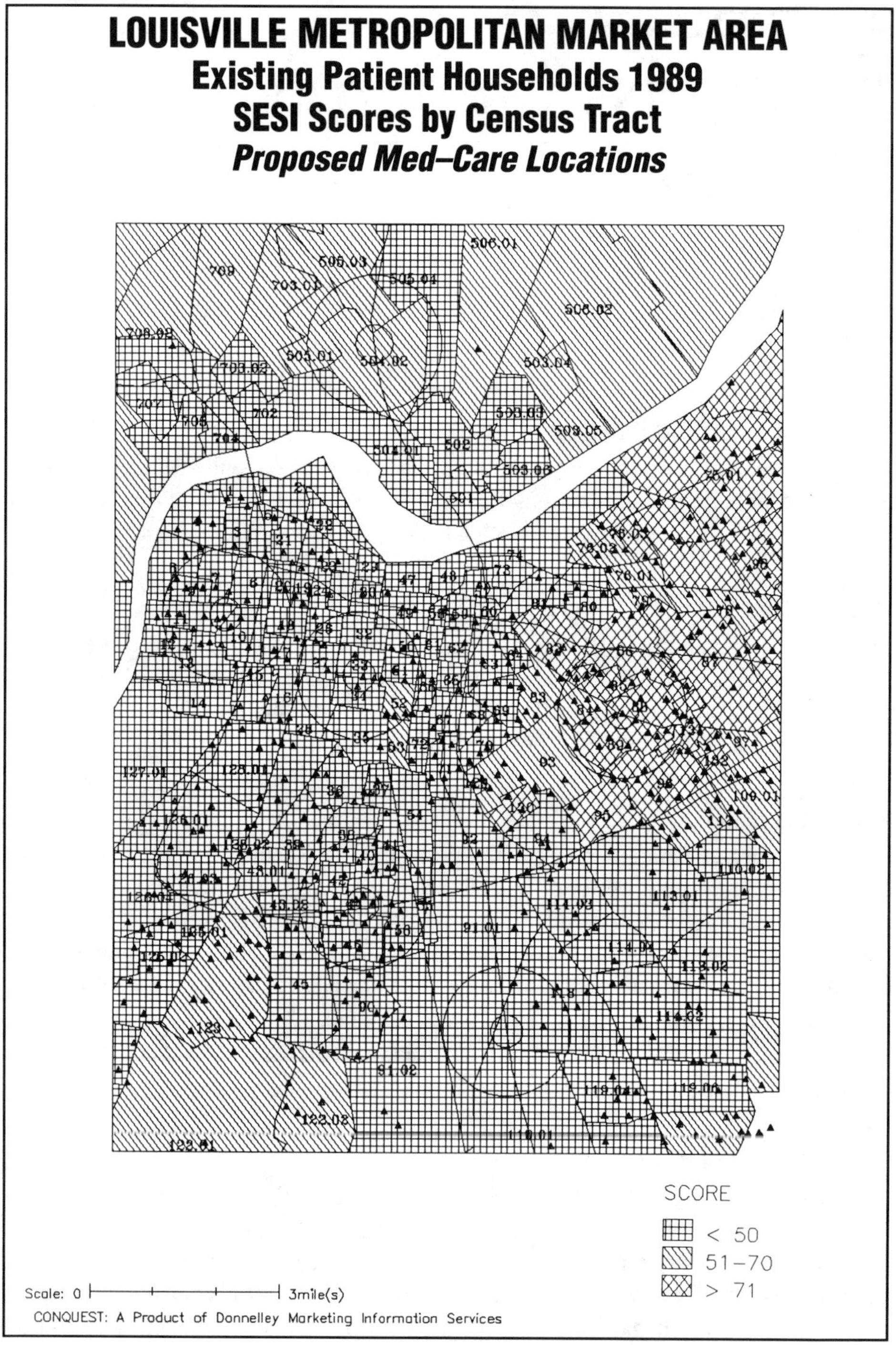

FIGURE 1 *This map displays Bluegrass General's patients by census tract.*

Donnelley Marketing Information Services
A Company of The Dun & Bradstreet Corporation

FIRST RESEARCH, INC. — AmericanProfile 11/02/90
MED-CARE SITE # 1 — ClusterPLUS Demographics

Area Composition Analysis Report

Code	Cluster Description	1990 Adult Pop	% Pop	1990 Hhlds	% Hhlds	Natl Hhld Index
S 13	Older Small Town Households	523	3.1	309	3.0	158
S 22	Older Below Avg Inc Homeowners	183	1.1	103	1.0	40
S 31	Older Low Income Couples	2814	16.6	1698	16.6	874
S 32	Low Income Single Retirees	2223	13.1	1361	13.3	950
S 33	Stable Blue Collar Workers	3750	22.2	2150	21.0	1050
S 35	Small Town Apartment Dwellers	1941	11.5	1275	12.5	658
S 37	Avg Inc Blue Collar Families	888	5.2	485	4.7	294
S 39	Low Income Blue Collar Workers	1632	9.6	1001	9.8	467
S 40	Lowest Inc Retirees-Old Homes	1778	10.5	1081	10.6	883
S 47	Lowest Inc Black Female Hd HHs	1184	7.0	757	7.4	617
Totals		16916	100.0	10220	100.0	

1. 0. 0 : Circle: 1 mile(s): 38.1837 85.7707

FIGURE 2 *A ClusterPLUS geography report for the one-mile radius around a proposed ambulatory center shows an extremely high concentration of "stable blue-collar workers."*

Next, CONQUEST's AmericanProfile module identified patient cluster segments and evaluated local practice sites. The cluster analysis indicated the characteristics of residents in the study sites. For example, Figure 2 shows that most of the population in Site 1 falls into "Working Class" clusters.

Sites were evaluated based on population change, age, sex, SESI (Socio-Economic Status Indicator), DRGs, and other variables. Comparative profiles ranked the "attractiveness" of various sites (see Figure 3).

The system generated demand estimates for in-patient hospital care by all DRGs and Major Diagnostic Categories (MDCs) and mapped growth rates of selected MDCs to reveal high-growth neighborhoods. The actual number of hospital admissions for each physician group within the target neighborhood determined each group's penetration of the local market.

Finally, the DMIS physician reference database located existing group practices. Physicians loyal to the sponsor hospital were identified to avoid conflict among hospital medical staff.

THE SOLUTION

As a result of the desktop analysis, the hospital selected 5 out of 40 group practices with which to develop closer relationships. The entire analysis was conducted without having to reveal the nature of the analysis to the physicians under study. No

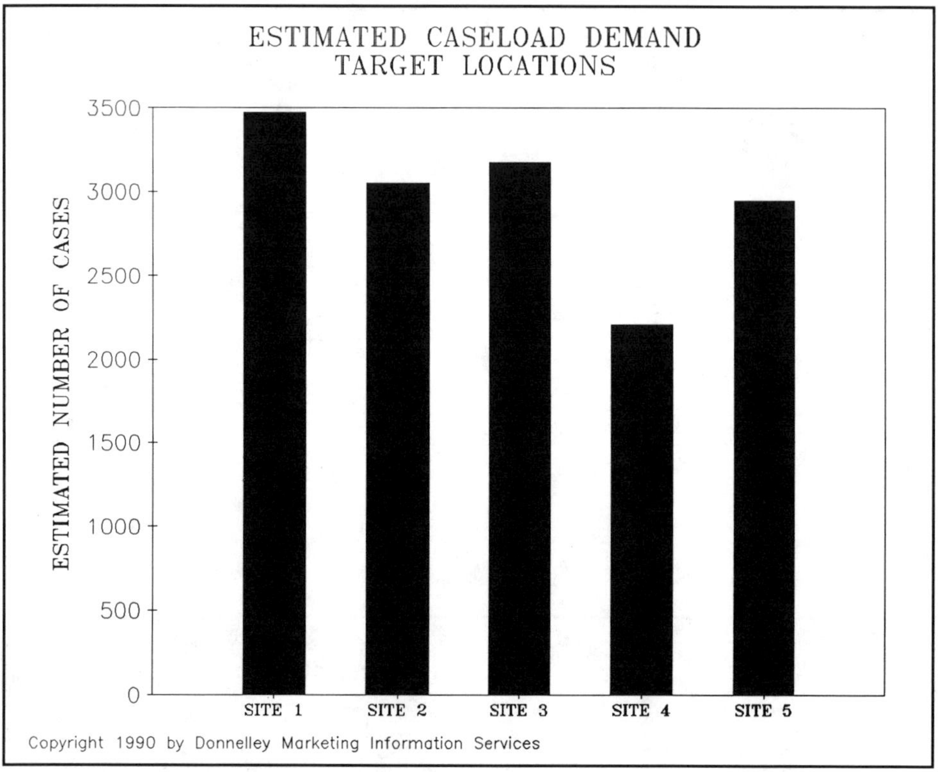

FIGURE 4 *An algorithm was developed based on population, age, sex, Socio-Economic Status Indicator (SESI), DRGs, and other variables to determine the estimated number of cases for each potential site.*

competitor was aware of the study (there are 12 other hospitals in the area), and most critical, the target practices could be "positioned" so as to negotiate the best possible outcomes.

This case study was submitted by:

William F. Davenhall, President
First Research, Inc.
9100 Shelbyville Road
Louisville, KY 40222

This study is based on an actual case, but due to the proprietary nature of the topic, fictitious names are used to maintain confidentiality with the company and its personnel.

CASE STUDY

Community General Hospital

COMPANY BACKGROUND

Community General Hospital (CGH) is located in Springfield, a medium-sized southeastern city. The hospital had the reputation for quality services. A Greater Springfield Health Care Cost and Quality Task Force (GSHCC & QTF) has been established to evaluate the efficiency and effectiveness of health-care delivery at area hospitals, and all area hospitals were concerned about the Task Force's possible findings.

THE PROBLEM

The CEO of Community General Hospital was determined to understand how CGH compared with its peers before the Task Force finished its analysis.

Mark Edmunds, vice president of strategic planning, was asked to prepare a report for the Board of Directors on the hospital in terms of patient outcomes. It was necessary to analyze Medicare discharges for CGH and nine other Springfield area hospitals in order to assess the relative quality of care of CGH.

THE SYSTEM

CGH selected The Sachs Group market analysis system with its numerous applications designed specifically for the health-care industry. Of particular use for this project was The Quality Planner™. (For more information about the system and vendor, consult the descriptions in Appendix 1.)

The Sachs Group system allowed access to Health Care Financing Administration databases for the peer group of hospitals identified by Edmunds. These data are publicly available information from Medicare discharge abstracts; they provide clinical information on diagnoses, procedures, and DRGs, as well as discharge status, patient demographics, length of stay, charges, and expected reimbursement. The Sachs Group enhances this information with data measuring severity of illness and outcome.

METHODOLOGY

Edmunds' data set used a severity-of-illness indicator on each discharge record to categorize patients into similar severity classifications across hospitals and to measure comparative "quality" via mortality rates. For this analysis, The Sachs Group used the disease-staging method available through Lexecon Health Services, Inc. to segment patients within the same DRG into one of four severity classifications.

The benefits of this disease-staging method include: (1) the ability to adjust the retrospective severity index, (2) the low cost of large disease-staging databases, and most important to Community General Hospital, (3) the ability to evaluate the quality and efficiency of identified peer institutions. The Sachs Data Services staff explained to Edmunds that The Quality Planner software can analyze any compara-

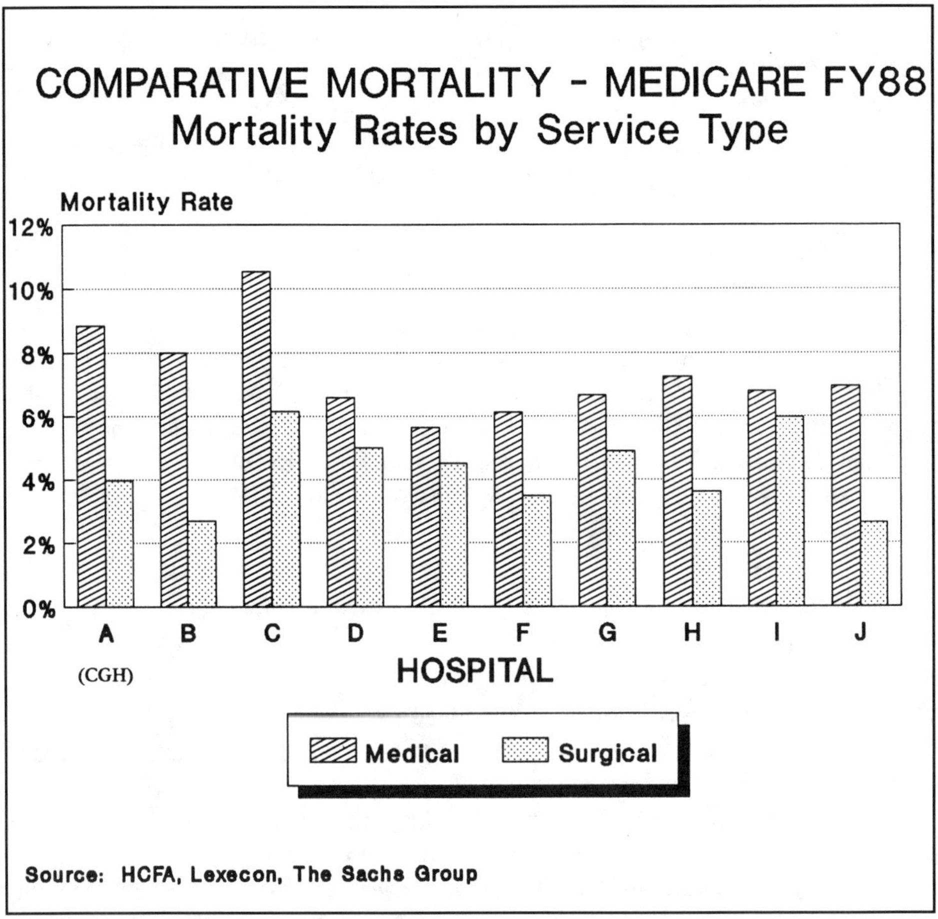

FIGURE 1 *Using the Lexecon database, CGH was able to compare its own mortality rates for specific medical and surgical procedures with those of its competitors.*

tive quality data. This is important to CGH because the state is considering a mandatory severity-of-illness system for all hospitals.

The hospital's senior planning analyst first assessed CGH's competitive position for aggregate medical and surgical product lines. He found that CGH had relatively lower mortality rates than its peer hospitals for surgical services than it did for medical services (see Figure 1).

However, CGH also had higher charges than its peer group for surgical services, as well as a longer average stay (see Figure 2).

Based on the analysis of mortality rates for Community General Hospital and the peer hospitals, certain product lines were selected for further analysis. These included general surgery, medical cardiology, medical subspecialties, neurology, oncology, thoracic surgery, and pulmonary. An in-depth mortality analysis revealed

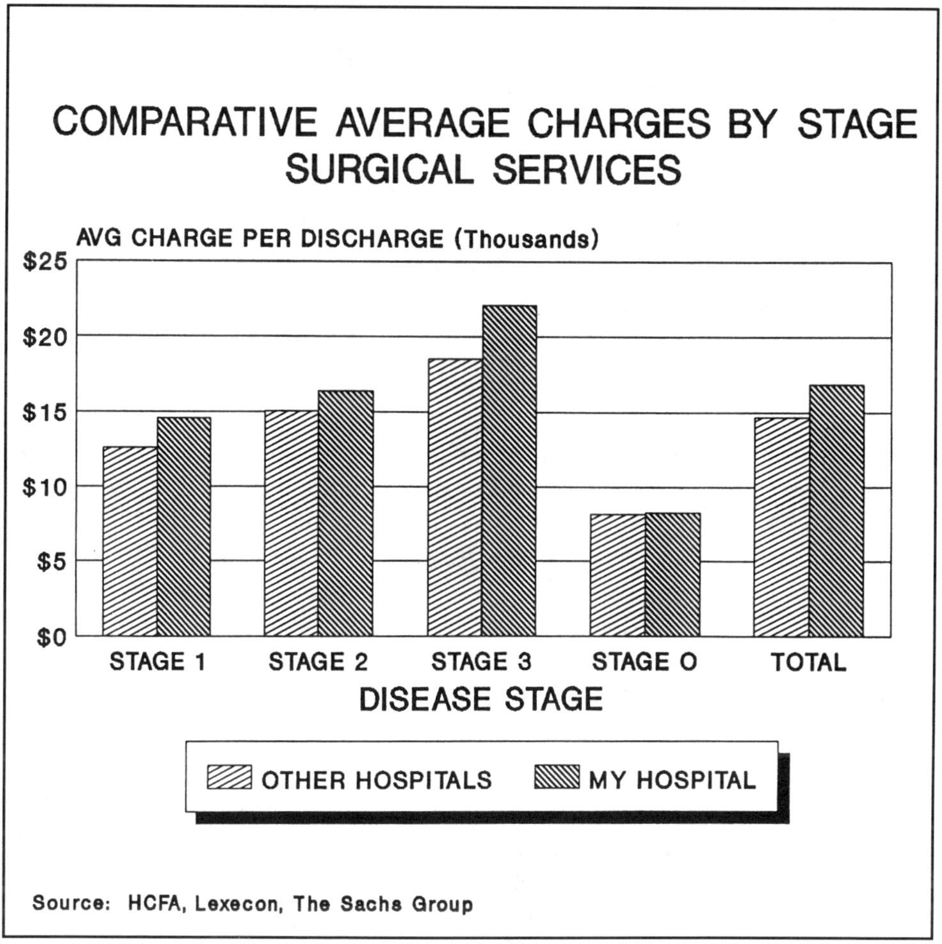

FIGURE 2 *CGH was also able to analyze its average charges against its peer group of competitors.*

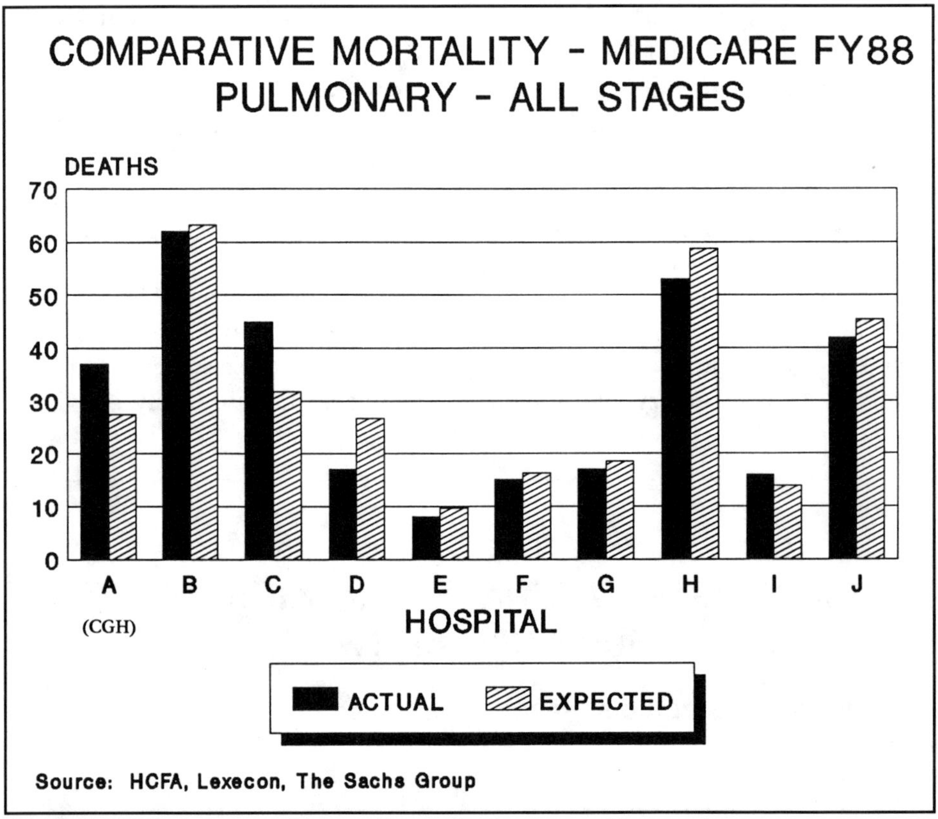

FIGURE 3 *CGH further compared its mortality rates by disease stage with expected rates.*

many important findings. For example, CGH experienced more deaths over all stages in pulmonary services than would have been expected based on the severity mix of its patients (see Figure 3). Analysis by disease stage demonstrated that CGH's mortality rates were higher than expected for Stages 1 and 2, which are "less severe," but similar to its peer group for Stage 3 or "most severe" patients.

CGH, then, appears to have more success with its most complicated cases. The next step will involve the medical staff in an analysis of patient-record information to identify patterns of care that result in better outcomes.

THE SOLUTION

The Quality Planner enabled CGH to better understand its position in the Springfield market in quality of care, preparing it to respond to the findings of the Greater Springfield Health Care Cost and Quality Task Force. It also identified areas in need of improvement. The hospital was able to present a plan of corrective action to the Task Force before the results were released to the press.

This case study was submitted by:

William Holt
Vice President
The Sachs Group Ltd.
1800 Sherman Avenue
Evanston, IL 60201

This study is based on an actual case, but due to the proprietary nature of the topic, fictitious names are used to maintain confidentiality with the company and its personnel.

CASE STUDY

Baptist Hospital

COMPANY BACKGROUND

Baptist Hospital was one of the major health-care facilities in its metropolitan area. It had long maintained market dominance with a world-class medical staff and strong financial base. Even by the mid-1980s, the development of a marketing program had not been considered. Decades of profitable operation had made the institution relatively self-sufficient until the "crunch" of the mid-1980s.

THE PROBLEM

By the late 1980s, changing reimbursement practices, stagnant demand, and increasing competition had reduced the hospital's bottom line to nearly zero. It was faced with becoming more efficient in its operation, maximizing reimbursement for the services it was performing, and identifying new sources of income. Although the hospital had occasionally received donations from grateful patients, it had never established a formal fund-raising program. As part of its program of revenue generation, the hospital created a division specifically charged with seeking donations from the community. With no existing list of donors and no experience in fund-raising, the director of the new program needed assistance in getting the philanthropy program off the ground.

THE SYSTEM

Baptist Hospital had recently acquired the MediEdge desktop market analysis system. Developed by Inforum, Inc., MediEdge is a PC-based market analysis system designed specifically for health-care applications. It has numerous resident databases and can integrate internal user data. It also provides access to the Pulse survey conducted every year by Inforum and SRl/Gallup. This survey of 100,000 households offers health-care data linked to geographic and psychographic information. (For more information about the system and vendor, consult the descriptions in Appendix 1.)

METHODOLOGY

The MediEdge system had several databases that could assist the fund-raising director in analyzing the potential for giving within the hospital's service area. The

Report 9 BGED Report on Contributors

BGED Report for
Ranked by Contrib. to Healthcare/Hospital (Desc %Across)

ZIP Code	Tract Code	Cluster Nickname	1989 Households Count	1989 Households % Down	Contrib. to Healthcare/Hospital Count	Contrib. % Down	Contrib. % Across	Index of Conc
38127	0099	Middle America	353	0.11	102	0.12	28.8	101
38127	010110	Middle America	606	0.20	174	0.20	28.8	101
38127	010120	Middle America	616	0.20	177	0.20	28.8	101
38127	010120	Middle America	47	0.02	14	0.02	28.8	101
38127	010210	Middle America	1,500	0.48	432	0.49	28.8	101
38127	010210	Middle America	711	0.23	205	0.23	28.8	101
38127	010220	Middle America	428	0.14	123	0.14	28.8	101
38118	0110	Middle America	943	0.30	271	0.31	28.8	101
38053	020220	Middle America	194	0.06	56	0.06	28.8	101
38116	022110	Middle America	1,545	0.50	445	0.50	28.8	101
38109	022410	Middle America	355	0.11	102	0.12	28.8	101
		Middle America	15,461	4.99	4,450	5.04	28.8	101
38054	020210	New Homesteaders	318	0.10	89	0.10	28.0	98
38128	020520	New Homesteaders	1,479	0.48	414	0.47	28.0	98
38128	020530	New Homesteaders	609	0.20	170	0.19	28.0	98
38053	0207	New Homesteaders	178	0.06	50	0.06	28.0	98
38017	0210	New Homesteaders	101	0.03	28	0.03	28.0	98
38028	0210	New Homesteaders	90	0.03	25	0.03	28.0	98
38134	021110	New Homesteaders	1,167	0.38	327	0.37	28.0	98
38053	020220	New Homesteaders	324	0.10	91	0.10	28.0	98
38002	0208	New Homesteaders	162	0.05	45	0.05	28.0	98
38002	0208	New Homesteaders	328	0.11	92	0.10	28.0	98
		New Homesteaders	4,756	1.54	1,331	1.51	28.0	98
38104	0025	Single City Blues	140	0.05	39	0.04	27.6	97
38104	0032	Single City Blues	349	0.11	96	0.11	27.6	97
38104	0032	Single City Blues	688	0.22	190	0.22	27.6	97
38104	0063	Single City Blues	495	0.16	137	0.15	[illegible]	
38111	0073	Single City Blues	1,141	0.37	315	[illegible]		
38111	0080	Single City Blues	613	0.20	[illegible]			
38112	0015	Single City Blues	244	0.08				
38104	0025	Single City Blues	[illegible]					
38104	0025	Single City Blues						
38104	0025	Single City Blues						
38112	0027	Single [illegible]						
38104	0031	[illegible]						
38104	[illegible]							

Source: MediEdge and Claritas.

FIGURE 1 *Based on the MediEdge Pulse survey data, Baptist was able to produce a report showing, for each census tract in its market, the potential number of households that would contribute to a hospital or health-care provider.*

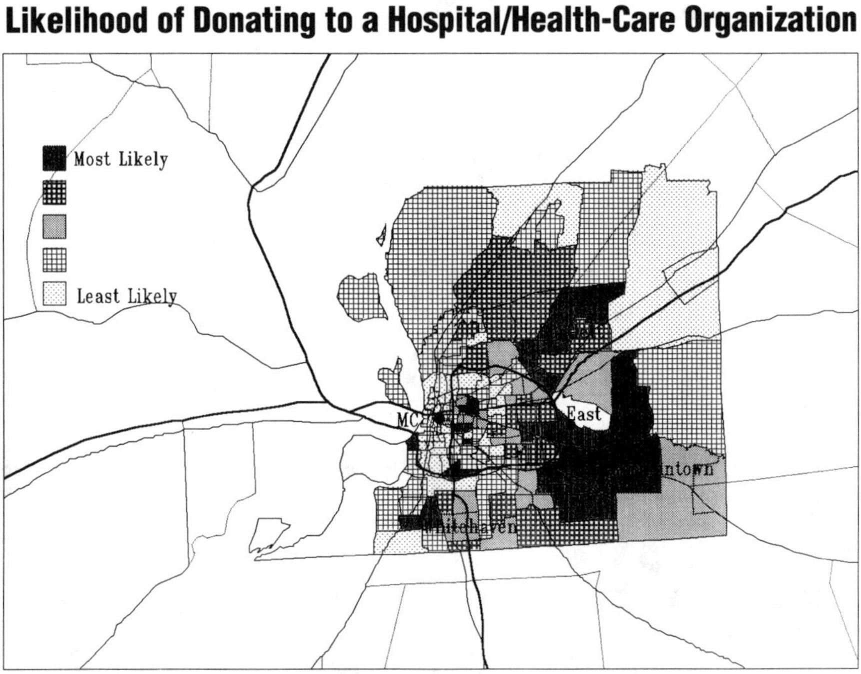

Source: MediEdge, Inforum, Inc.

FIGURE 2 *A map shows concentrations of potential donors by zip code.*

initial thrust would focus on the county in which the hospital was located and that accounted for over half of its patients. The demographic databases and PRIZM segmentation system (from Claritas Corporation) resident on MediEdge provided information to profile the county's population. More important, the Pulse survey includes data on the characteristics of health-care donors and the circumstances under which they contribute.

An initial report profiled each of the 40 PRIZM lifestyle segments in terms of their giving patterns. With this baseline information, a similar report was generated for the county under study. The MediEdge system generated a report that indicated, zip code by zip code, predominant lifestyle clusters and their respective propensity to contribute (see Figure 1). Subsequent reports indicated for each cluster the average amount contributed, the reason for the contribution, and how the contribution was solicited.

This information provided a basis for identifying the types of target groups that the hospital might want to solicit for contributions. However, it was felt that the fund-raising program would be most efficient if it was targeted more specifically to geographic areas with large concentrations of the hospital's patient base. The hospital's patient records were imported into MediEdge and geocoded to determine patients' demographic and psychographic characteristics. An index identified areas of the county with the "best" combination of residents in terms of both propensity to contribute and previous hospital use. Figure 2 indicates the likelihood of contributing to a health-care organization by zip code. Similar maps were developed to determine the distribution of the hospital's patients and the areas that scored highest on the index.

Once target areas were chosen, it was a simple matter to reexamine solicitation approaches that had been most successful with these segments of the population in the past. The MediEdge system also determined the media that would be most effective in reaching the targeted populations.

THE SOLUTION

Using the MediEdge system, a novice fund-raiser was able to quickly and effectively identify populations within the market area to be targeted for solicitation. Not only did he now know their locations, but he knew about their lifestyles, their health-care utilization patterns, their health status, and what their "hot buttons" were in terms of health-care contributions. He was able to target certain areas for personal calls, while other areas were targeted for direct-mail contact. The appropriate media mix was also determined for market-wide promotions. Not only was it possible to identify the best opportunities in terms of contributions, it was possible to eliminate those who were not likely to give and would, therefore, represent a waste of resources.

This case study was submitted by:
Richard K. Thomas
Baptist Memorial Hospital
899 Madison Avenue
Memphis, TN 38146

CASE STUDY

Southwood Hospital

COMPANY BACKGROUND

Southwood Hospital is a 400-bed facility in the Southeast. Southwood has long been recognized for its quality in-patient services and has historically demonstrated strong market penetration. Despite its strong share of the in-patient market, Southwood had never developed a strong out-patient program. By the late 1980s, it found itself losing ground in out-patient services to smaller but more innovative facilities. In its service area, it had witnessed the growth of competition among mammography service providers.

THE PROBLEM

One of the areas in which health-care competition has increased is out-patient diagnostic testing. One type of diagnostic test—mammography—has attracted more attention for several reasons. Breast cancer is a leading, but often preventable, cause of death in women, and early detection through mammography is strongly encouraged. These services are seen not only as a source of revenue for providers, but as a way to introduce women to a hospital for the first time.

Realizing that consumers could be "captured" early for out-patient services such as mammography, Southwood needed a mechanism to capitalize on the growing mammography demand. Hospital analysts realized that they had to evaluate the existing market for a mobile mammography unit in terms of market size and market share relative to competitors, location and type of facility, media approaches, and existing marketing efforts geared toward physicians.

THE SYSTEM

Southwood Hospital had recently acquired the MediEdge desktop market analysis system developed by Inforum, Inc. The MediEdge system has numerous resident databases, can integrate internal user data, and provides access to the Pulse survey conducted every year by Inforum and SRI/Gallup. (For more information about the system and vendor, consult the descriptions in Appendix 1.)

METHODOLOGY

The MediEdge system includes a "need" model for mammography services based on American Cancer Society guidelines, a "demand" model based on National

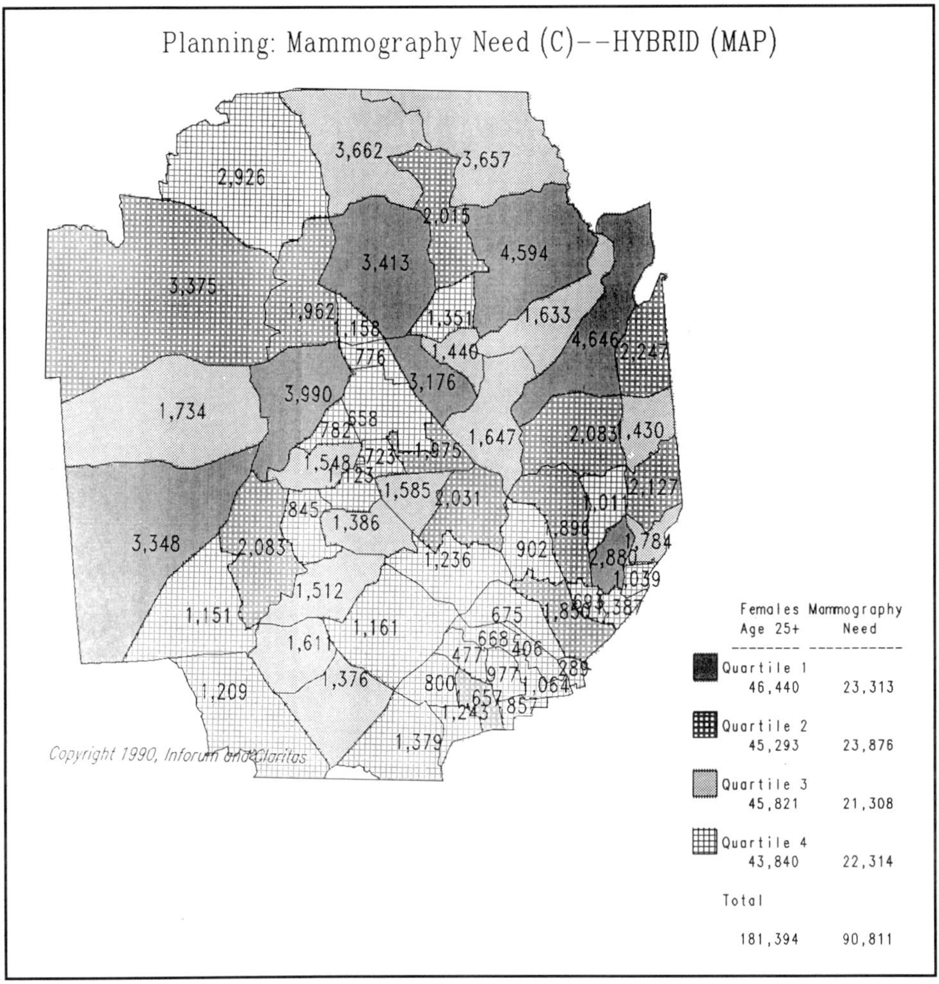

FIGURE 1 *Using several databases, MediEdge includes a demand model to determine the need for services such as mammography, mapped here for Southwood's market.*

Health Interview Survey (NHIS) historical data, and Pulse survey data that compare estimated and projected demand for mammography services at the level of geography appropriate to the service area. The analysis also makes use of a facilities database resident on the system.

The first step was to examine basic demographics of the hospital's service area to project the need for mammography services. Figure 1 shows the geographic distribution of mammography need, with actual need figures "landmarked" on the map.

Previous research had indicated that lifestyles were a strong predictor of the actual use of such services. The MediEdge system includes the Claritas PRIZM

INFORUM, Inc.
MediEdge Library -- Mammography

Media: Mammography Targets Detail - BGED

1990 BGED Report for Area: Cobb County, Georgia (Example Geography)
Where Cluster 41 is Omitted
Ranked by CLUSTER Mammography Targets (Asc),
Mammography Users (Female Resp) (Desc %Across)

BGED Code	HYBRID Tract-ZIP Geocode	Cluster Group	Cluster Nickname	Households Count	Households % Down	Mammography Users (Female Resp) Count	% Down	% Across	Index of Conc
130670304011	13067 304.01	S1	Furs & Station Wagons	948	0.45	550	0.62	50.8	120
130670304019	13067 304.01	S1	Furs & Station Wagons	1,648	0.78	899	1.02	50.8	120
130670304021	13067 304.02	S1	Furs & Station Wagons	782	0.37	484	0.55	50.8	120
130670304033	13067 304.03	S1	Furs & Station Wagons	477	0.23	271	0.31	50.8	120
130670313019	13067 313.01	S1	Furs & Station Wagons	55	0.03	40	0.04	50.8	120
131210101012	13121 101.01	S1	Furs & Station Wagons	389	0.18	207	0.23	50.8	120
131210102019	13121 102.01	S1	Furs & Station Wagons	29	0.01	19	0.02	50.8	120
131210102021	13121 102.02	S1	Furs & Station Wagons	1,129	0.54	649	0.74	50.8	120
131210102025	13121 102.02	S1	Furs & Station Wagons	558	0.26	293	0.33	50.8	120
130670303043	13067 303.04	S1	Furs & Station Wagons	1,028	0.49	560	0.64	50.8	120
130670303047	13067 303.04	S1	Furs & Station Wagons	912	0.43	547	0.62	50.8	120
131210093 4	13121 93	S4	Gray Power	416	0.20	159	0.18	48.7	115
131210095 2	13121 95	S4	Gray Power	2,246	1.06	1,103	1.25	48.7	115
131210101035	13121 101.03	S4	Gray Power	174	0.08	75	0.08	48.7	115
130670309 5	13067 309	S4	Gray Power	557	0.26	242	0.27	48.7	115
131210100 2	13121 100	S4	Gray Power	1,134	0.54	495	0.56	48.7	115
131210100 3	13121 100	S4	Gray Power	1,122	0.53	514	0.58	48.7	115
130670302028	13067 302.02	T1	God's Country	955	0.45	476	0.54	45.7	108
130670302031	13067 302.03	T1	God's Country	298	0.14	144	0.16	45.7	108
130670302038	13067 302.03	T1	God's Country	252	0.12	149	0.17	45.7	108
130670303023	13067 303.02	T1	God's Country	933	0.44	495	0.56	45.7	108
130670305 2	13067 305	T1	God's Country	1,737	0.82	854	0.97	45.7	108
130670306 5	13067 306	T1	God's Country	202	0.10	170	0.19	45.7	108
131210082011	13121 82.01	U1	Black Enterprise	1,393	0.66	818	0.93	45.1	107
131210082012	13121 82.01	U1	Black Enterprise	873	0.41	542	0.61	45.1	107
130670302032	13067 302.03	S3	Young Suburbia	1,286	0.61	643	0.73	43.6	103
130670302037	13067 302.03	S3	Young Suburbia	629	0.30	294	0.33	43.6	103
130670303018	13067 303.01	S3	Young Suburbia	1,610	0.76	658	0.75	43.6	103
130670303019	13067 303.01	S3	Young Suburbia	1,042	0.49	443	0.50	43.6	103
130670303021	13067 303.02	S3	Young Suburbia	1,193	0.57	611	0.69	43.6	103
130670303038	13067 303.03	S3	Young Suburbia	464	0.22	210	0.24	43.6	103
130670305 8	13067 305	S3	Young Suburbia	1,311	0.62	592	0.67	43.6	103
130670311072	13067 311.07	S3	Young Suburbia	712	0.34	322	0.37	43.6	103
130670302027	13067 302.02	S3	Young Suburbia	1,360	0.64	691	0.78	43.6	103
130670302033	13067 302.03	S3	Young Suburbia	283	0.13	135	0.15	43.6	103
130670302036	13067 302.03	S3	Young Suburbia	237	0.11	129	0.15	43.6	103
130670303022	13067 303.02	S3	Young Suburbia	958	0.45	471	0.53	43.6	103
130670303025	13067 303.02	S3	Young Suburbia	376	0.18	214	0.24	43.6	103
130670303031	13067 303.03	S3	Young Suburbia	631	0.30	337	0.38	43.6	103
130670303032	13067 303.03	S3	Young Suburbia	618	0.29	284	0.32	43.6	103
130670303033	13067 303.03	S3	Young Suburbia	818	0.39	358	0.41	43.6	103
130670303034	13067 303.03	S3	Young Suburbia	483	0.23	224	0.25	43.6	103
130670303035	13067 303.03	S3	Young Suburbia	741	0.35	347	0.39	43.6	103
130670303036	13067 303.03	S3	Young Suburbia	459	0.22	236	0.27	43.6	103
130670303037	13067 303.03	S3	Young Suburbia	318	0.15	155	0.18	43.6	103

 Page 2

FIGURE 2 *The demand data were profiled by PRIZM segments, proven to be a strong predictor of the use of such services.*

lifestyle segmentation module, which was used to determine the psychographic makeup of the service area. Coupled with Pulse survey data, it was possible to group the population by its propensity to use mammography services. Figure 2 presents a portion of the table indicating propensity to use mammography services by lifestyle cluster. These clusters were combined into "supergroups" to develop an overview of the service area. Figure 3 depicts the service area laid out in distinct submarkets.

Once the analysts understood the target population distribution, they could call up information from the facilities database to determine the location of both potential

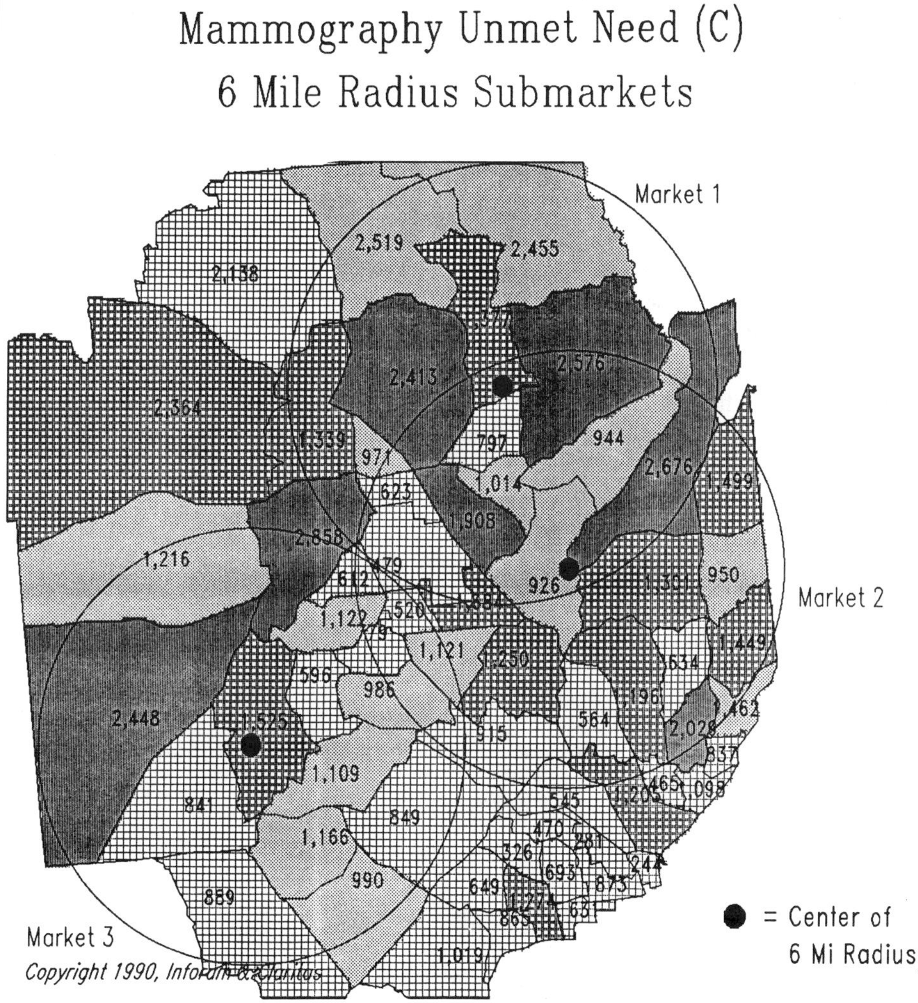

	Females Age 25+	Mammography Need	Mammography Demand	Mammography Unmet Need
Quartile 1	46,440	23,313	8,099	15,215
Quartile 2	45,293	23,876	7,700	16,177
Quartile 3	47,989	22,465	6,764	15,701
Quartile 4	41,672	21,157	5,939	15,217
Total	181,394	90,811	28,501	62,310

FIGURE 3 *This map indicates the unmet need for mammography services in Southwood's market.*

competitors and cooperative service providers. Linked with Southwood's internal records, this allowed an assessment of physician loyalty with regard to mammography services.

Once target areas were settled on, the media preferences of target-area residents were determined, and appropriate promotional campaigns developed. The MediMails component targeted individual census block groups for direct-mail marketing.

THE SOLUTION

With MediEdge, Southwood's analysts were able to identify growth areas for women most likely to demand mammography services. They were able to redirect the emphasis of the mobile unit from areas with low yield to communities where there was an unmet need for mammography services. They were also able to target physicians who did not appear to be referring an appropriate number of cases, and to determine the appropriate media approach for the most "desirable" among the target audience.

This case study was developed by:

Richard K. Thomas
Baptist Memorial Hospital
899 Madison Avenue
Memphis, TN 38146

This study is based on an actual case, but due to the proprietary nature of the topic, fictitious names are used to maintain confidentiality with the company and its personnel.

CASE STUDY

Memorial Hospital

COMPANY BACKGROUND

Memorial Hospital, part of an investor-owned chain, is located in Atlanta, Georgia. The hospital's market is characterized by declining in-patient utilization due to the substitution of new out-patient technology. This trend called for improved accuracy in forecasting expected admissions by product line, since historical patterns were not likely to hold.

THE PROBLEM

For assistant administrator Sandra Walczak, the challenge was clear. "I needed to understand how our in-patient business would be affected by these out-patient trends, both in terms of admission volumes and resulting revenues," she noted. A reliable estimate of future admissions for various diagnostic related groups (DRGs) needed to be developed to realistically plan for the hospital's future.

THE SYSTEM

Memorial chose The Sachs Group desktop market analysis system. It includes numerous applications designed specifically for the health-care industry, including The Market Planner®, The Physician Practice Planner®, The Contract Planner™, and the SachsGroups™ segmentation system. (For more information about the system and vendor, consult the descriptions in Appendix 1.)

METHODOLOGY

Walczak attended The Sachs Institute's Advanced Modeling and Forecasting Workshop, which focused on how to model "what if" scenarios about changes in in-patient utilization rates. She learned how to incorporate assumptions about changes in physician practice patterns, new technology, and managed-care penetration, all of which can influence shifts to the out-patient setting. One of the techniques available from the Sachs Institute identifies specific DRGs most likely to be affected by these factors.

FIGURES 1 AND 2 *(Below) Using sophisticated modelling techniques, Memorial analysts were able to determine which in-patient services were likely to be hardest hit by the shift to increased out-patient treatment, and how this would affect hospital admissions.*

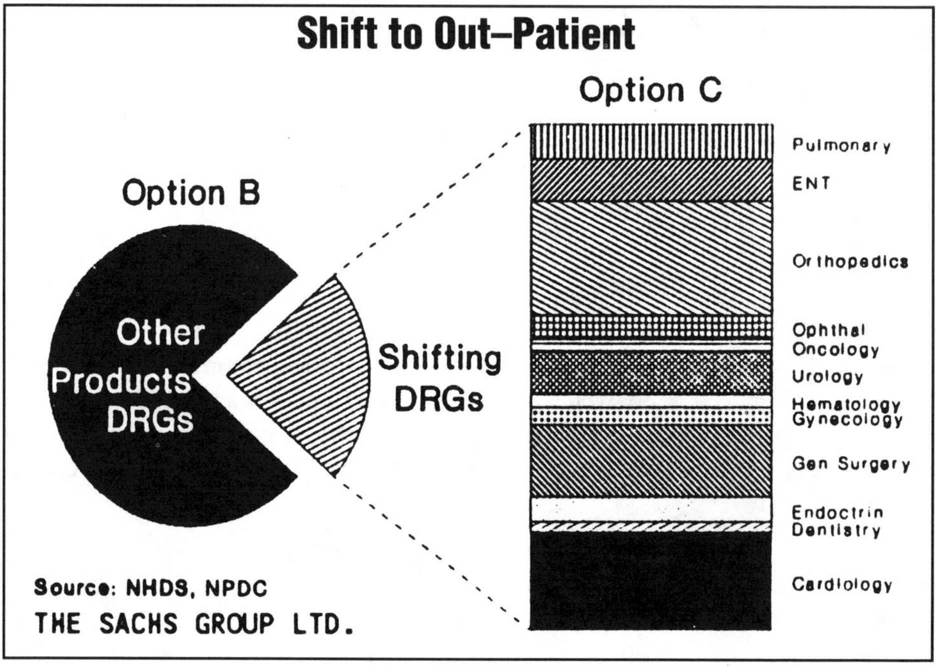

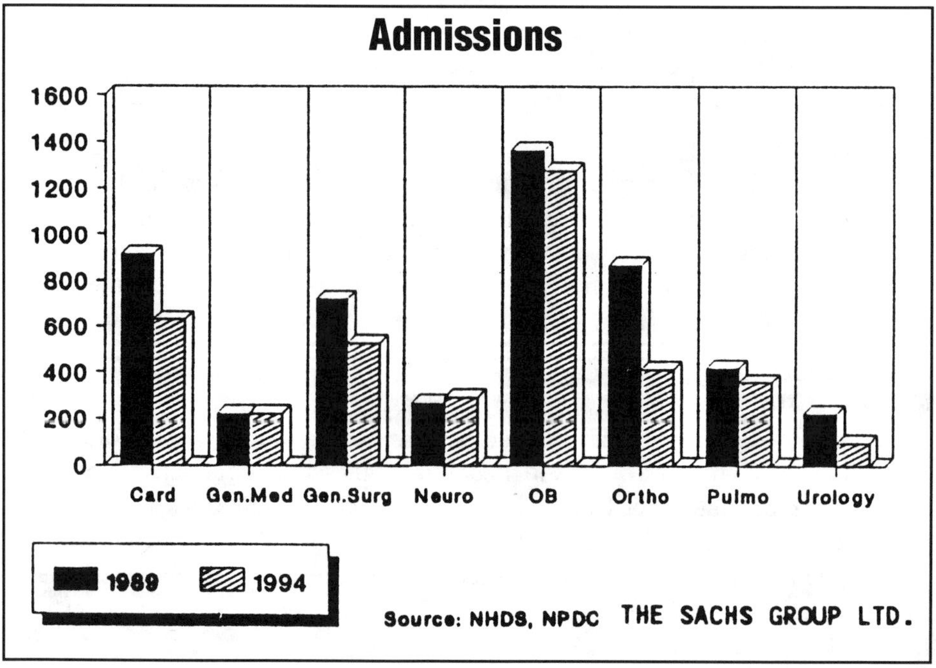

Walczak developed a utilization model that she believed would best describe her market five years from now, incorporating DRG-specific shifts. When she applied this new in-patient utilization rate to her local market, she confirmed that certain in-patient product lines would be more heavily affected by out-patient shifts. In particular, the hospital's orthopedics, general surgery, and medical cardiology services would experience the greatest impact. (See Figures 1 and 2.)

Walczak also used the modeling capabilities in The Market Planner module to project future hospital revenues and profitability. This allowed her to determine likely financial scenarios resulting from various hypothetical levels of revenues and expenses.

THE SOLUTION

As a result of this analysis, the hospital recognized the need to focus on two concurrent strategies. First, the hospital needed to aggressively pursue growth in market share compensate for the decline in market demand due to shifts to out-patient care. Second, it must expand its out-patient programs to capture shifting business. The forecasts also indicated that certain areas, such as sports medicine and cardiac rehabilitation, would be growing and presented opportunities to the hospital.

This case study was submitted by:

Kate Crane
Manager
The Sachs Group Ltd.
1800 Sherman Avenue
Evanston, IL 60201

This study is based on an actual case, but due to the proprietary nature of the topic, fictitious names are used to maintain confidentiality with the company and its personnel.

8

Automotive Industry

Domestic automobile and light-truck manufacturers have faced substantial market challenges over the past two decades. As a mature industry, it had lost touch with its consumers and, almost overnight, found its market share being gobbled up by imports for a variety of reasons involving perceived quality, affordability, and response to consumer demands.

The automotive market also experienced the "demassification" characteristic of many other consumer markets. Changes in demographics and lifestyles resulted in a large number of niche markets. As in any industry, the existence of niche markets allows smaller, more specialized and more aggressive players to erode the market share of mass marketers. American automobile manufacturers learned, almost too late, that there was no longer a mass market or loyalty for traditional brands. A highly segmented market had developed that was oriented toward specific types of vehicles.

Competition within these niche vehicle segments is fierce. Examples of expansion and competition for niche markets include sport-utility vehicles, minivans, and the affordable convertible sports car. Recent studies confirm the trend toward historical lows in brand and model loyalty in the U.S. marketplace. Richard Farrell, general manager of the Automotive Group for National Decision Systems, points out that "the automotive industry is faced with many of the planning and marketing challenges common to packaged-goods companies. These include massive product development costs, production capabilities exceeding demand, increased competition in profitable segments, saturation of marketing messages, and consumer rebate addiction. These all have a negative pressure on profitability."

These developments in the automobile industry and marketplace have created an environment that demands the use of desktop market analysis systems. As Farrell notes, "The automotive industry has been uncomfortably data rich. The manufacturers have had access to massive amounts of data on vehicle ownership, competitive sales, distribution and sales channels, and marketplace statistics. This wealth of data required the use of mainframe computers and programmers to retrieve relatively small amounts of real information in a form that managers and decision-makers could use. The emergence and acceptance of desktop marketing tools for the automotive industry closely follows the ability to distill and integrate data into an information resource easily used by the manager, planner, and analyst."

As the automobile market has become more fragmented, the need to identify and target market segments has become paramount. For auto manufacturers, this process is important on several levels. It is necessary to determine current segments within the market and understand their preferences in order to formulate marketing plans and site dealerships. In addition, manufacturers must be able to gauge the pulse of the car-buying public into the future. Not only is there an aging effect with regard to car purchases, but the long development cycle of automotive products requires a long-range understanding of future markets.

For example, the luxury-automobile market is one of the most competitive and dynamic segments in the automotive industry. Manufacturers are struggling to retain market share or, in the case of new entrants, create market share. Although luxury automobiles account for a relatively small percentage of all new-car purchases, the share of profits they represent is much greater. The competition for this market exemplifies the emphasis that must be placed on market segmentation and niche marketing.

Innovative leaders in the automotive industry have made substantial investment in and movement toward desktop support of strategic, tactical, and marketing decisions. Moving data from the mainframe to the desktop computer is a critical step for effective and responsive decision-making. The next major step for the automotive industry, Farrell concludes, will be "the integration of desktop information with better-packaged applications and, eventually, 'expert systems' to build a new generation of strategic business information tools."

CASE STUDY

Asian Motor Works

COMPANY BACKGROUND

Asian Motor Works (AMW), a major Japanese manufacturer, had become well established in the mid-size import market in the U.S. by the mid-1980s. It had captured a market share considered impossible for an import only a few years earlier. The manufacturer wanted to compete directly with the likes of Mercedes-Benz, BMW, Jaguar, and other luxury makes, and wanted to know about the specific consumer segments most likely to be its key buyers.

THE PROBLEM

Although management was convinced that a market existed for the luxury import it planned to introduce, this had to be verified. AMW had to define the luxury Japanese-car buyer well before a luxury Japanese-car niche existed. It needed to know who would purchase the new luxury Japanese nameplate—their interests, tastes, preferences, and lifestyles. AMW also had to align distribution in areas with concentrations of high-priority consumer segments.

THE SYSTEM

AMW used the VISION lifestyle segmentation system to identify the characteristics of residents in target areas. Developed by National Decision Systems, VISION is a segmentation system that divides the population into 48 lifestyle and behavioral segments and allows analysis to the census block-group level of geography. Standard VISION databases are supplemented with data from R.L. Polk, Allison Fisher, and other lifestyle and media databases. (For more information about the system and vendor, consult the descriptions in Appendix 1.)

METHODOLOGY

The first step was to develop a composite profile of the likely Japanese luxury-car buyer. Since no such vehicles yet existed, the challenge was to piece together a profile of the likely buyer for this product.

AMW merged VISION profiles from several databases to create a proxy for the types of households most likely to buy the new Japanese luxury vehicles. Data from R.L. Polk were used to develop VISION profiles of luxury-car owners within the

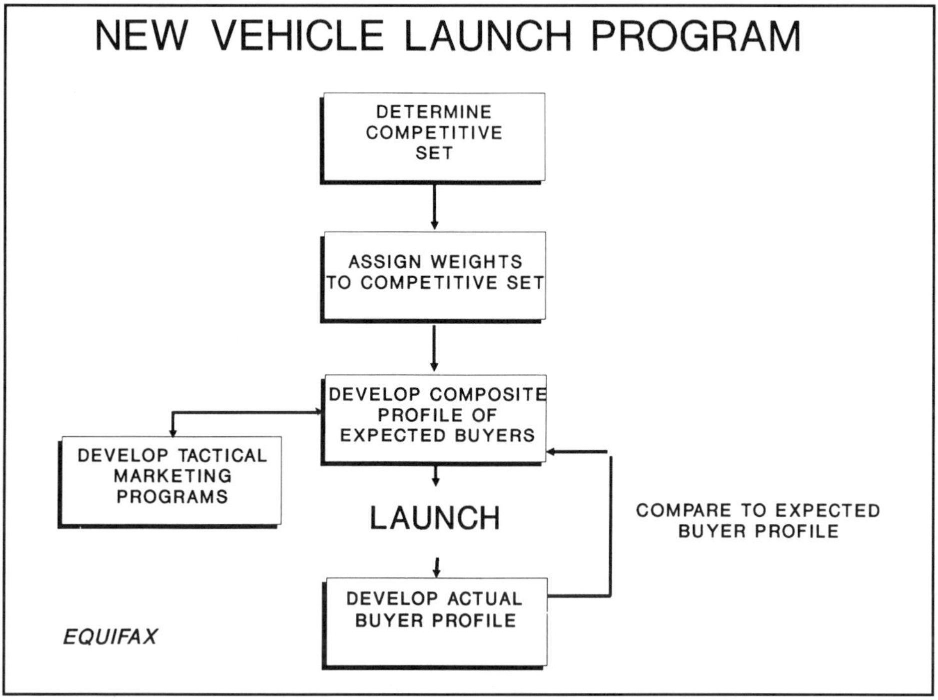

FIGURE 1 *This flow chart outlines the basic steps Asian Motor Works and NDS took to plan the New Vehicle Launch Program.*

appropriate competitive set. Data from Allison Fisher identified purchase intentions and how intentions for certain luxury makes differed by VISION segment. These data were combined with other lifestyle measures from sources such as Mediamark Research, Inc. and Simmons Market Research Bureau. Other data profiled buyers of current top-of-the-line Japanese sedans.

After a luxury-car buyer profile was developed, it was adjusted for the propensity to buy high-end Japanese sedans and to participate in key leisure activities. A final composite profile of the new Japanese luxury-car buyer was developed for two specific niches of the market—the luxury sedan niche and the near-luxury sedan niche.

Once it was established that a market for the proposed automobile existed, the next step was to plan a dealer network. The researchers rank-ordered geographic areas in terms of relative concentrations of the "core" buyer segments identified by the earlier analysis. The manufacturer was then able to appropriately locate the initial wave of dealers.

THE SOLUTION

The new Japanese nameplate quickly established itself as a major player in the luxury

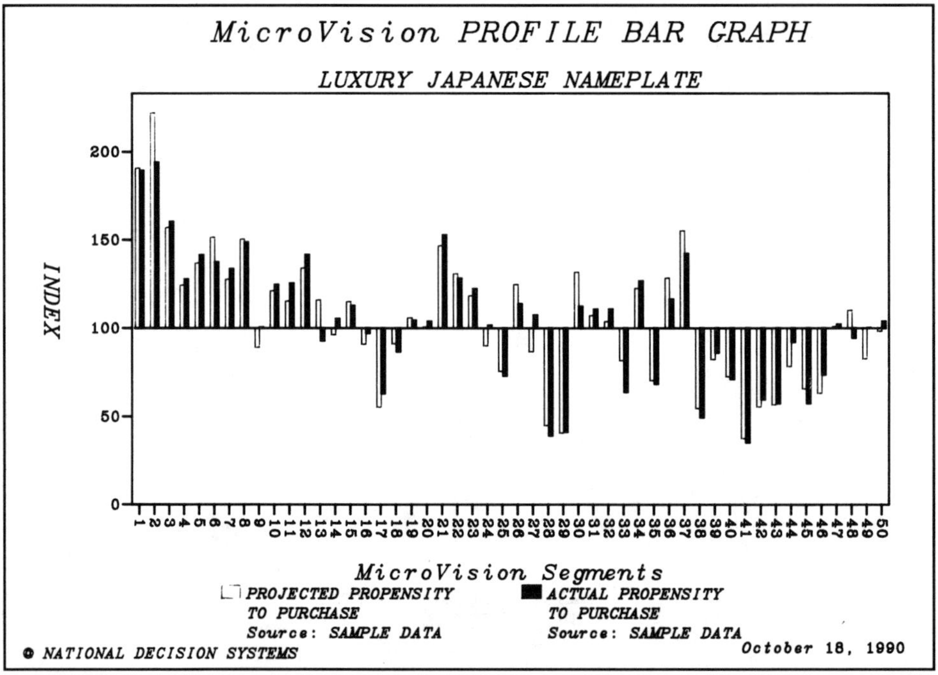

FIGURE 2 *This bar chart compares the "manufactured" cluster profile (developed two full years prior to product introduction) with the actual new luxury-car purchaser.*

automotive marketplace. It not only established strong brand equity, but outsold its closest competitor four to one. A VISION profile of actual buyers, derived from the first four months of sales, was found to be highly correlated with the expected-buyer profile. Hence, an accurate buyer profile for the luxury Japanese niche was developed more than two years before the product (or its niche) even existed. Interestingly, while the composite profile pointed to intuitively obvious high-income segments as key targets, it uncovered several "surprise" strong-buyer segments as well. (Figure 2 shows a side-by-side comparison of projected composite profile and actual buyer profile. An index of 100 indicates an average propensity to buy.)

This case study was submitted by:

Richard Farrell
Manager, Automotive
National Decision Systems
539 Encinitas Boulevard
Encinitas, CA 92024-9007

This study is based on an actual case, but due to the proprietary nature of the topic, fictitious names are used to maintain confidentiality with the company and its personnel.

CASE STUDY

Avis, Inc.

COMPANY BACKGROUND

Started by Warren Avis in 1946, Avis established the first airport automobile rental office. After going international in the 1950s, Avis expanded into auto leasing and pioneered the resale of used rental vehicles. Avis currently has 4,900 locations in 142 countries. Its 21,000 employees manage a fleet of 400,000 vehicles.

THE PROBLEM

Avis's main objective in developing desktop marketing capabilities in this particular case centered around its need to increase the sales of cars being withdrawn from its rental fleet. The research objective was to identify the most desirable market areas in which to introduce a multimedia campaign, including direct mail, radio, and telemarketing targeted at the most likely customers for rental resales.

THE SYSTEM

Avis installed the CONQUEST system in its headquarters location. CONQUEST is a PC-based geodemographic marketing system from Donnelley Marketing Information Services (DMIS) that contains a variety of databases, as well as the ClusterPLUS lifestyle segmentation system. (For more information about the system and vendor, consult the descriptions in Appendix 1.)

METHODOLOGY

The first step in addressing the issue of rental-car resales was to identify locations in eight Avis U.S. market zones. The basis for selection was the present level of resales measured against the potential for that area as determined by ClusterPLUS lifestyle segmentation analysis. Figure 1 illustrates the cluster profile for one Avis site.

The market was then segmented into two distinct target groups. Group I was the primary market, i.e., census tracts with clusters that historically indexed higher then most. Group II, the secondary market, consisted of tracts with clusters that had high usage but that indexed low relative to the general population. The clusters from each group were then analyzed against auto data for various car makes and models to establish any similarity to the fleet mix.

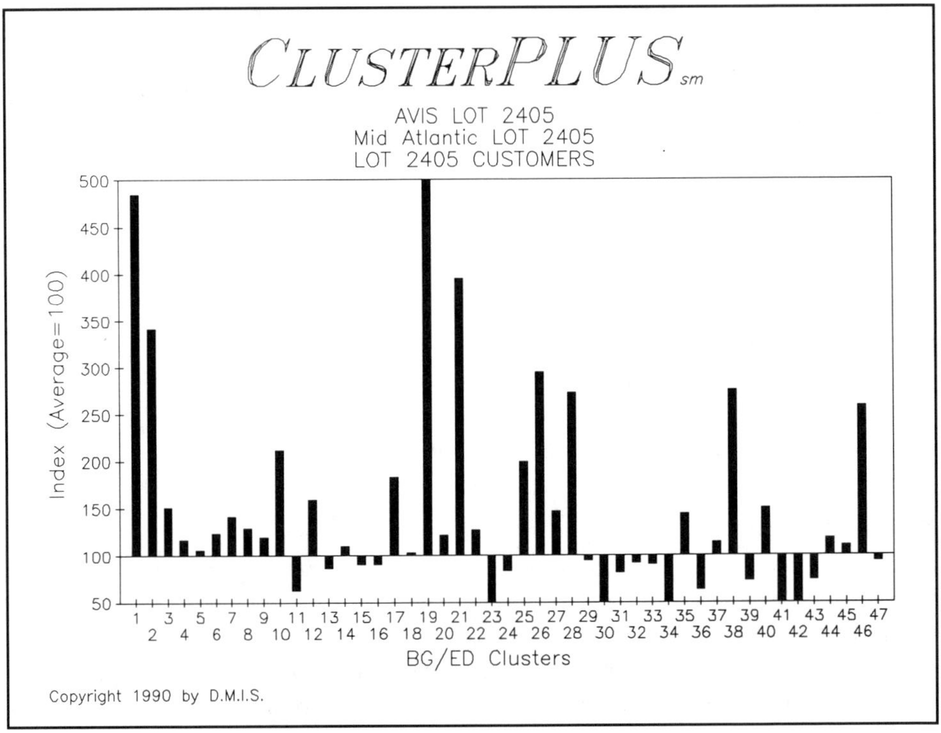

FIGURE 1 *Avis developed a ClusterPLUS profile of its Lot 2405 customers.*

The demographic characteristics of tracts in the two target areas established selection criteria for ordering names, obtained from Donnelley's residential database for the test markets. To analyze the potential of radio advertising, clusters in both the primary and secondary markets were compared with Arbitron radio usage data. Figure 2 maps the distribution of target markets for an Avis site.

THE SOLUTION

Avis designed a direct-mail piece aimed at the target group based on the characteristics of various clusters. It acquired telephone numbers from DMIS and supplied each location with a follow-up telemarketing campaign coinciding with the direct-mail piece. Avis then tracked promotion results by registering invited guests upon arrival at each location, revealing responsive geographies and target clusters. Avis also compared those who responded to the promotion with those who ended up buying cars to determine the direction for future advertising efforts.

The results of this promotion were measured by the "hard numbers" of sales and Avis's cost savings in relation to previous marketing efforts. Using CONQUEST, Avis attained a 48 percent savings in advertising costs. Before the analysis, the division-level standard was 1.05 cars sold per 1,000 mailers in programs directed

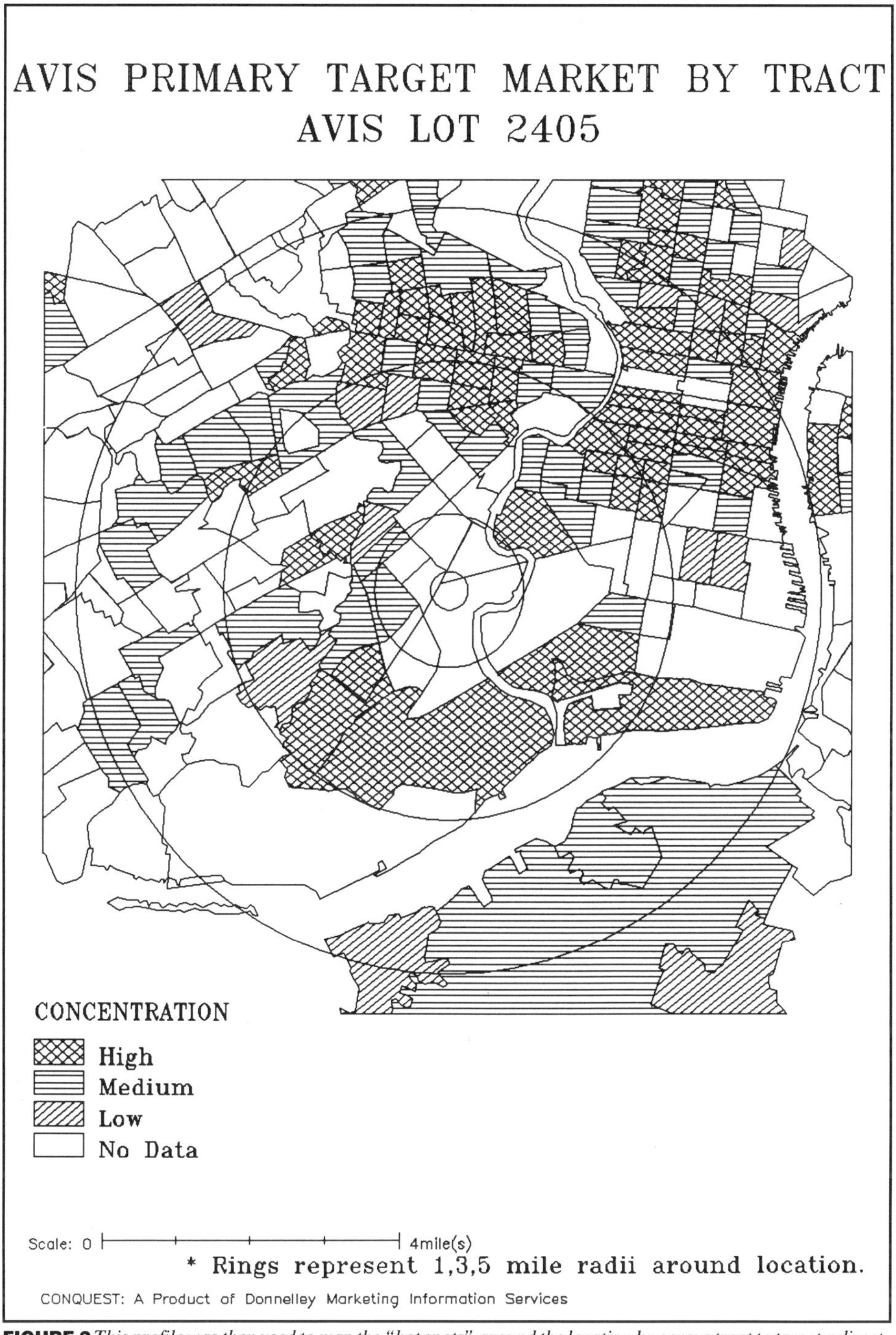

FIGURE 2 *This profile was then used to map the "hot spots" around the location by census tract to target a direct-mail campaign.*

toward an affiliated market. Through the market analysis, Avis improved its rate to 2.63 cars sold per 1,000 mailers in programs directed toward a targeted population.

This case study was submitted by:

Thomas Krieck
Director of Market Analysis
Avis World Headquarters
900 Old Country Road
Garden City, NY 11530

CASE STUDY

Isuzu Motors

COMPANY BACKGROUND

Although Isuzu Motors was not an early leader among Japanese imports, it has steadily increased its market share. Isuzu prides itself on its innovative marketing and its ability to identify trends in consumer preferences. However, prior to becoming involved in desktop market analysis, Isuzu Motors used only a demographic-based system to profile prospective new dealer locations and relocations. The information included auto registrations, and economic and age data.

THE PROBLEM

Since Isuzu was rapidly increasing its U.S. market penetration, it faced a number of new challenges. The auto manufacturer needed to profile prospective new dealer locations, relocate existing dealerships, and identify new markets for expansion. The particular issue faced here was identifying lifestyle groups to which the Trooper model appeals. Eighty-five percent of Isuzu's sales come from sport-utility vehicles. Its task was to identify lifestyle characteristics of Trooper buyers to better target marketing efforts.

THE SYSTEM

Realizing that simple demographics would not yield the sophisticated analyses needed to meet these challenges, Isuzu chose the OASYS desktop market analysis system. Developed by National Demographics and Lifestyles (NDL), OASYS provides national consumer and market data. (For more information about the system and vendor, consult the descriptions in Appendix 1.)

METHODOLOGY

Isuzu first conducted a study of the entire compact-sport-utility segment using the NDL lifestyle segmentation system. The analysis found that specific lifestyle characteristics were associated with most of the various sport vehicles. By linking lifestyle and auto registration information, Isuzu could target Trooper buyers. According to Isuzu's director of corporate planning, "We can look at an individual vehicle, an individual market segment, or even at regional differences." For example, skiing is a frequent activity for Trooper owners. The company also found

FIGURES 1 AND 2 *(Below) Using the lifestyle databases in OASYS, Isuzu can analyze its customers to better address their needs and interests. Product data can also be linked with media behavior to determine the radio formats most highly correlated with ownership of sport-utility vehicles.*

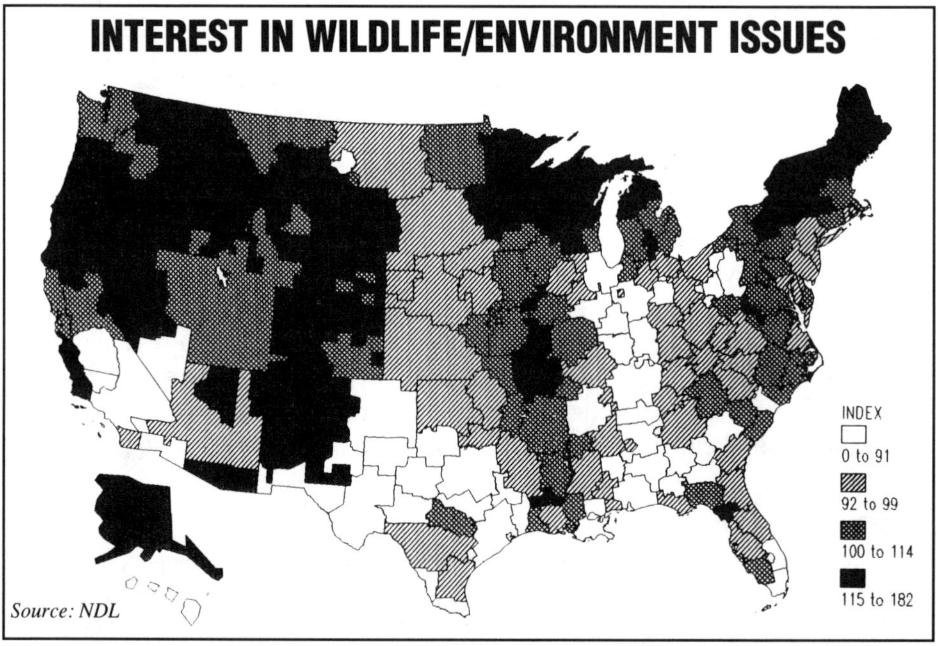

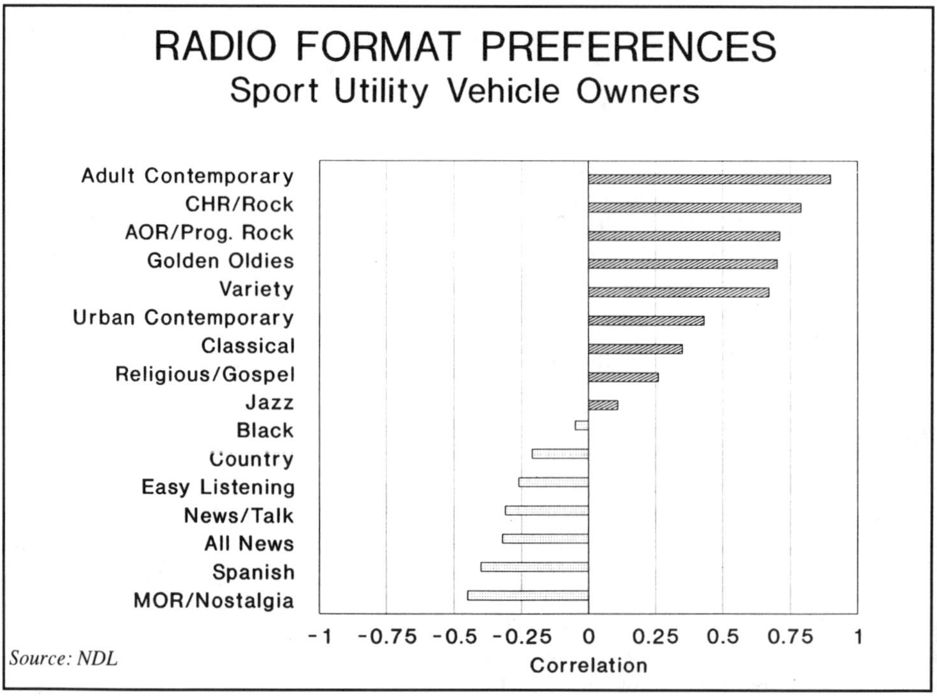

that Trooper owners are more environmentally conscious than consumers of other sport-utility vehicles (see Figure 1).

From there, Isuzu identified radio as a key promotion medium. Figure 2 indicates radio format listening preferences for sport-utility vehicle owners.

THE SOLUTION

To promote customer loyalty and attract potential customers, Isuzu sponsors ski promotions, including lift tickets and displays at ski resorts, and schedules ads in ski publications. The company has also become a major sponsor of a joint government and private sector-program to promote environmental awareness in national parks and forests.

In the first nine months of OASYS use, Isuzu completed ten major market studies. Future plans for desktop marketing center around direct mail, dealer marketing applications, and the integration of psychographic data.

This case study was submitted by:

Nancy Solomon
Marketing Communications
National Demographics & Lifestyles, Inc.
1621 Eighteenth Street
Denver, CO 80202-1211

9

Utility Industry

By the mid-1980s, the nation's utility companies had discovered marketing. "In the past, utility companies were strictly operationally driven, and 'marketing' was a dirty word," according to Bob Weyland of Temple, Baker & Stone of Lexington, Massachusetts. But after 1985, marketing became an established function in utility companies. Today, increased deregulation, competition, and alternative suppliers have made marketing an even more important component of utilities management. "The focus today is on customer service," says Jeff Knebel of Donnelley Marketing Information Services. "The consumer is much more sensitive to cost minimization and conservation, and utility companies must be responsive to these trends."

The utility industry approaches its market in a reverse manner from most other industries. The task is not to increase levels of consumption but to encourage conservation and cost-efficiency. This impetus to decrease consumption, especially at specific times, makes it necessary to know much more about the utility consumer today than in the past. As the utility industry seeks creative ways to decrease consumption, it must rely more on market research tools used in other industries.

According to John Seigman of National Decision Systems, "Utility companies want marketing information delivered to them in the way they can best use it." Indeed, the utility industry has its own organization, The Electric Power Research Institute (EPRI) of Palo Alto, California. EPRI is supported by hundreds of utility companies for the purposes of researching utility consumer attitudes and behavior. In November 1989, it commissioned a division of Booz Allen Hamilton to devise a psychographic analysis of utility consumers based on their attitudes. Called CLASSIFY, the system taps attitudes related to convenience, high-tech enthusiasm, comfort, and appearance. It is this type of desktop creativity that is helping the industry tailor its services to its customers' needs.

The utility industry now uses desktop systems in a variety of ways, including:

Load Management: All utility companies want to achieve a reduction of electric energy demand during peak periods. Load management strategies shift or reduce demand from peak times to off-peak times to reduce the capital-intensive effort of adding generators.

Economic Development: Many communities rely on their utility company to spearhead economic development programs. Indeed, the competition to attract new industries to a region is intense.

Program Development: Conservation programs are now targeting potential customers using CLASSIFY and geodemographics. The utilities industry will increasingly be positioning its programs and promotional materials to the appropriate market segments.

Consumption Analysis: Utilities are using desktop marketing systems to project household and business demand in their market areas.

With the incorporation of geocoding, street-level mapping, and sophisticated direct-mail capabilities, the utility industry is likely to become a leader in the adoption of desktop decision-making. High-tech enhancements such as satellite imaging will be particularly useful. (See page 12 for a sample satellite image from National Planning Data Corporation.)

CASE STUDY

General Utility

COMPANY BACKGROUND

General Utility (GU) is a large electric utility in the Southwest. It serves more than 1 million customers, 800,000 of whom are residential, and its service territory covers 8,500 square miles. GU is the only electric utility with franchise rights in this area, and it competes in the territory with a natural-gas supplier. Due to the varying terrain of the service area, only 60 percent of GU's customers are served by natural-gas lines. The other 40 percent must rely on electricity or alternative fuels for heating, cooking, etc. These fuels are most likely oil or propane. GU competes directly with the gas utility for these end-users and is evaluating the additional power resources it will need as its service area continues to grow at a rate of 30,000 households per year.

GU, like all utilities, has the marketing advantage of knowing who all of its customers are through its billing system. This billing system provides the base for all residential marketing efforts. Currently, GU's Demand Side Management (DSM) programs include: Home Energy Audits, Load Control for Central Air Conditioning and Electric Water Heating, High-Efficiency Heat Pumps and Central Air Conditioners Low-Interest Financing, and Time-of-Use (TOU) Rates.

Before GU implemented desktop marketing, it promoted all of its programs to all of its customers, using a general message it hoped would appeal to everyone.

THE PROBLEM

GU's marketing goals were multiple: to increase the number of participants in current DSM programs, to increase DSM program implementation options while lowering program costs, and to develop programs that would appeal to different market niches while increasing shareholder value. GU's marketing research department collects a large amount of information on its customer base, as well as territory-wide information on appliance ownership, GU advertising awareness and recall, customer satisfaction, and corporate image. GU also has individual information on electric consumption and previous program participation. The challenge was to integrate data sources and create an effective program development and implementation tool.

THE SYSTEM

To create an integrated database, GU used National Decision Systems' Infomark desktop analysis system, which includes the MicroVision targeting system. This menu-driven software package includes a demographic file with census data and selected proprietary databases. Through this system, GU has access to its integrated database as well as syndicated information such as the NDS Utility Appliance profile and the Electric Power Research Institute (EPRI) CLASSIFY-Link™ profile. (For more information about the system and vendor, consult the descriptions in Appendix 1.)

METHODOLOGY

The first step GU took was to analyze current participants in its DSM programs by appending a MicroVision code to each of its customers. These profiles showed that three low-to-moderate income segments make up over 35 percent of GU's service territory: "Home Sweet Home" (9.6 percent), "Stars and Stripes" (10.9 percent), and "On Their Own" (16.0 percent). A MicroVision game plan showed that customers most likely to be DSM customers were in higher-income groups and not in these three dominant segments. GU determined that it must develop programs or alter current offerings for these three key segments. Figure 1 depicts the cluster profile of GU's trade area.

The second step was to analyze the makeup of these three key segments. Segment 10 (Home Sweet Home) is composed of dual-income families with medium-high income levels. Segment 17 (Stars and Stripes) is composed of large families with preschoolers and middle incomes. These one-income households tend to live in mobile homes. Segment 39 (On Their Own) is made up of young singles and couples with medium-low incomes and large numbers of renters.

This evaluation allowed GU to eliminate Segment 39 from its DSM program considerations, because it knew that there are very few programs in which renters will participate. However, since this segment is GU's largest, analysis would be done to find out what types of programs would appeal to this segment.

GU then conducted an appliance makeup analysis to determine the "inventory" of household appliances by cluster. This analysis would allow GU to develop DSM programs tailored to the niche markets. Figure 2 depicts DSM potential by cluster.

The utility's next concern was how to effectively reach these customers. GU is a member of EPRI and therefore was familiar with EPRI's CLASSIFY™ model. CLASSIFY is an energy-needs-based segmentation model based on respondents' attitudes toward energy and energy use. GU linked CLASSIFY–Link with MicroVision to profile energy needs by lifestyle.

THE SOLUTION

General Utility implemented these programs with a two-pronged approach. It first sent direct-mail pieces on the targeted programs to each of its three primary

FIGURES 1 AND 2 *This MicroVision bar chart shows the segment composition of General Utility's market area. Using General Utility's customer file, a MicroVision profile was developed showing segments with the highest propensity to be Load Control customers.*

MicroVision PROFILE BAR GRAPH
GU Service Territory Makeup

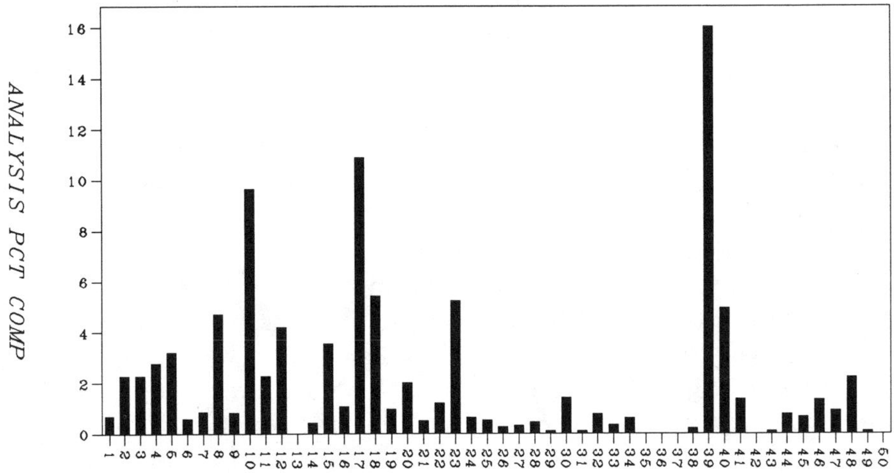

Source: National Decision Systems

MicroVision PROFILE BAR GRAPH
GU DSM Customer Propensity

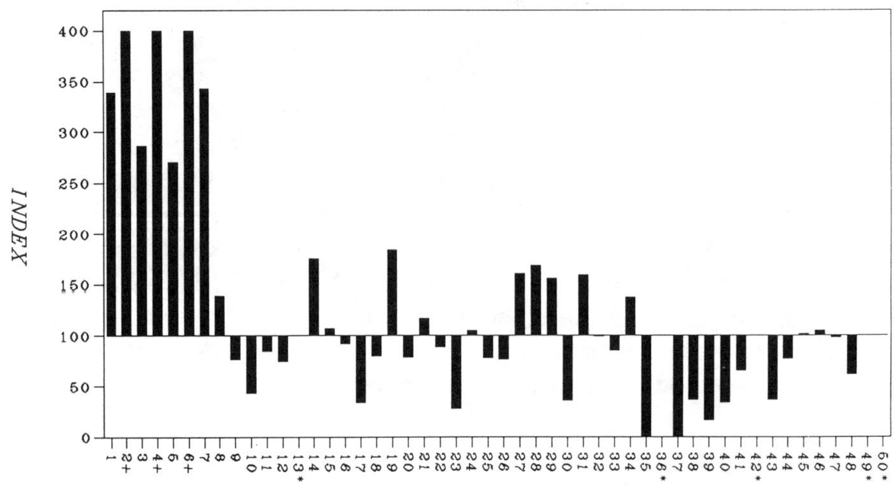

+ Exceeds Scale   * Unstable

Source: National Decision Systems

segments. The direct mail was sent first-class separately from the customer's electric bill. Each piece emphasized the key messages indicated by the CLASSIFY-Link analysis.

The second approach followed up the direct-mail effort with support messages in the targeted media for each segment. By going out into the mass media, additional segments could also participate and increase the targeted program's effectiveness.

Through this approach, GU was able to save over $175,000 in program marketing costs and increase participation levels by 3.5 times over programs run in previous years. Also, by focusing on its largest segments, GU was able to increase its overall corporate satisfaction rating by 10 percentage points.

This case study was submitted by:

John C. Siegman
Manager, Regulated Industries Group
National Decision Systems
539 Encinitas Blvd.
Encinitas, CA 92024

This study is based on an actual case, but due to the proprietary nature of the topic, fictitious names are used to maintain confidentiality with the company and its personnel.

CASE STUDY

USA Natural Gas

COMPANY BACKGROUND

USA Natural Gas (USANG) is a large natural-gas utility in the south central region of the country. It serves approximately 900,000 residential customers with a service territory covering two states and eight counties in four other states. USANG is the only natural-gas utility with franchise rights in this area.

Recent surveys have shown that the company has a more than 95 percent customer-satisfaction rating. USANG is expanding its customer-service horizons with service contract programs for natural-gas appliances, mail-order appliances, conservation items, and appliance showrooms.

THE PROBLEM

In contrast to electric companies, natural-gas companies do not have an all-inclusive list of the residents of their service area. While they know who their customers are through the customer billing file, they do not know who their noncustomers are. Electric companies, on the other hand, usually have 100 percent of the people living within their service areas as customers and can identify those who use gas for heat and hot water.

USANG faced several challenges: to increase the number of participants in service contract programs, to discover the best target market to test a mail-order program, and to determine who would be the most likely appliance shoppers at bill-paying offices.

THE SYSTEM

USANG licensed an Infomark system to do the following analysis. This menu-driven desktop system from National Decision Systems (NDS) consists of a demographic file with census data and selected proprietary databases including the MicroVision lifestyle segmentation system. (For more information about the system and vendor, consult the descriptions in Appendix 1.)

METHODOLOGY

After coding its customer file with MicroVision, the first step was to analyze USANG's service contract customers. Infomark-compatible profiles showed that

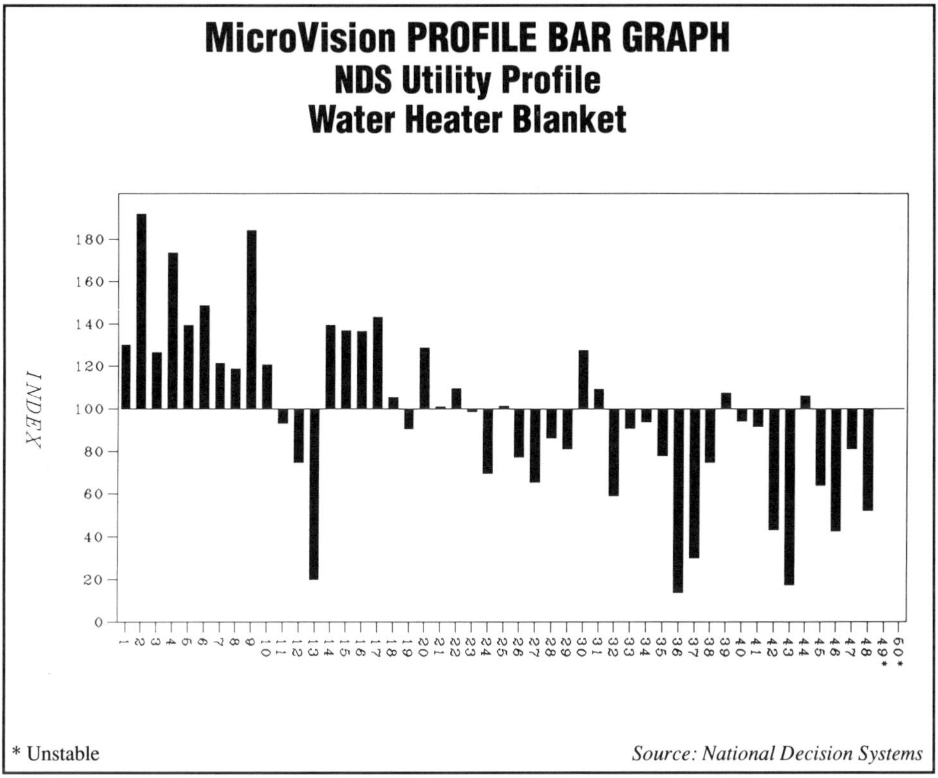

FIGURE 1 *USANG developed MicroVision profiles of its customers to determine the relative propensity to purchase certain products.*

USANG's typical service-contract customer was moderately upscale, and that it had penetrated only 17 percent of this target market (see Figure 1).

Looking at Utility and Appliance profiles available through NDS, USANG discovered that the market for conservation items was a decidedly upscale homeowner market. USANG thought that it could more effectively penetrate this type of market through its mail-order program. Once the program had become established, it could also target conservation items to more middle- and lower-income customers.

USANG explored the appliance merchandising concept profiling its in-person bill-paying customers. Over a period of two months, USANG collected information on customers who used a bill-paying office. When this information was linked to the demographic data available through the Infomark system, this group was found to be middle-to-lower income homeowners.

THE SOLUTION

As a result of the MicroVision analysis, USANG's gas service contract participation rate increased from a previously constant 11 percent to 20 percent in the first year, while lowering program promotion costs by $30,000 annually. The mail-order program produced over $200,000 in profits in its first year by targeting upscale customers. The program will now be broadened to include other MicroVision segments. USANG also opened up six new appliance sales sites as test sites in its service territory. To date, all of these sites have been profitable, and USANG plans to open six more sites in the coming year.

This case study was submitted by:

John C. Siegman
Manager, Regulated Industries Group
National Decision Systems
539 Encinitas Blvd.
Encinitas, CA 92024

This study is based on an actual case, but due to the proprietary nature of the topic, fictitious names are used to maintain confidentiality with the company and its personnel.

CASE STUDY

P&L Utility

COMPANY BACKGROUND

P&L Utility (P&L) is a medium-sized electric and gas utility in the Northwest, serving approximately 650,000 residential customers. Its service territory covers 13 counties comprising mostly urban and suburban areas. P&L is the only gas and electric utility with franchise rights in its area, and its gas service area is exactly the same as its electric service area. Since P&L generates electricity and delivers natural gas, it derives most of its contribution to profit margin from the sale of electricity. Realizing this, its communications efforts are designed to enhance its services to the customer while encouraging the end-use of electricity in off-peak periods.

Currently, the communications programs P&L has in place include: the P&L Call Us Program, the P&L Informational Program, and the P&L Low-Income Assistance Promotion.

THE PROBLEM

P&L is in a very expensive area of the country for mass-media promotions. Therefore, whenever P&L spends communications dollars to reach its residential market, it wants to be sure the message is seen by the highest percentage of the market and that the marketplace understands and relates to the message.

The company's marketers felt that if P&L could take a more targeted approach to its communications program, it could more effectively reach its residential market and save communications dollars. P&L's goals were to: increase the number of respondents to communications programs, lower the cost per respondent of these programs, and develop a better understanding of its residential customers to create more effective communications programs.

THE SYSTEM

The marketers at P&L tackled these issues with National Decision Systems' Infomark Desktop PC System. This menu-driven software package consists of a demographic file with census data and selected proprietary databases. The Infomark component of most use to P&L for this market research was the MicroVision lifestyle segmentation system. (For more information about the system and vendor, consult the descriptions in Appendix 1.)

METHODOLOGY

After coding its customer file with MicroVision, P&L created Infomark-compatible profiles for analysis. These indicated that P&L had a very upscale service area. Almost 50 percent of P&L's residential customer base is made up of MicroVision segments 1 through 15. Figure 1 depicts the cluster profile of P&L's service area.

P&L then developed profiles of the respondents to its three communications programs. These indicated that for the first two communication efforts, the Call Us and the Informational programs, customers most likely to respond were in the middle MicroVision clusters, Segments 18 through 32. For the Low-Income Assistance program, P&L found that it was underpenetrating its target market.

Next, P&L analyzed the types of general media that would more effectively reach its service area. An Infomark Cross Correlation report revealed that the most effective media for communicating the Call Us and Informational programs were newspapers and news/talk radio. By examining the respondents in the Low-Income Assistance program, P&L determined that the most effective avenue for reaching these customers was daytime television.

FIGURE 1 *This P&L customer cluster profile is ranked by size.*

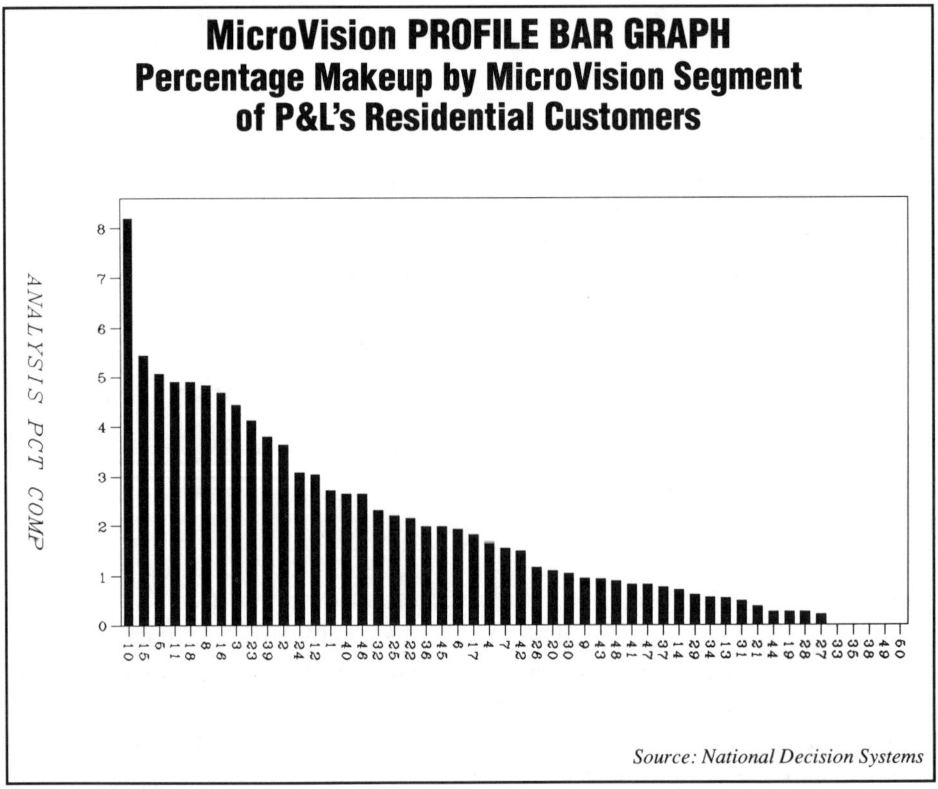

In order to develop the most effective message possible, P&L linked EPRI's CLASSIFY energy-needs-based segments with MicroVision segments. This analysis showed that for the Call Us and Informational programs, the target audience was most likely to be categorized as "Value Seekers." The messages communicated to this group were more technical in keeping with the customers' needs. For the Low-Income Assistance program, the target audience was most likely to be categorized as "Pleasure Seekers." The messages sent to this group focused on family acceptance of the decision-maker and the appeal of making smart decisions.

THE SOLUTION

By using this approach with its communications programs, P&L was able to generate a participation increase of over 17 percent in the Call Us and Informational programs, resulting in an annual cost savings of over $225,000. For the Low-Income Assistance program, P&L recorded an increase of 22 percent in actual sign-ups and a $43,000 annual decrease in program promotion costs.

This case study was submitted by:

John C. Siegman
Manager, Regulated Industries Group
National Decision Systems
539 Encinitas Blvd.
Encinitas, CA 92024

This study is based on an actual case, but due to the proprietary nature of the topic, fictitious names are used to maintain confidentiality with the company and its personnel.

10

Business-to-Business Applications

The newest application for desktop marketing systems is in business-to-business marketing. Business-to-business marketing has become increasingly competitive and is demanding more sophisticated market analysis capabilities. Developments in the business environment, not the least of which is an expanding global economy and an increase in multinational companies, are changing the manner in which business-to-business marketing is conducted. According to industry expert Dan Primavera, "There has been a substantial increase in direct marketing and telemarketing, with decreased emphasis on direct sales calls."

Because they have to pay more attention to the bottom line of marketing activities, business-to-business marketers have a critical need not only for more market information, but for information in greater detail than ever before. In response, many of the major vendors have developed business databases. To date, however, users have barely begun to exploit a fraction of the targeting efficiency that is possible.

Business-to-business marketers are beginning to learn some lessons from consumer marketers. Consumer marketers code internal files with geodemographic segmentation systems to identify the target clusters that work best in terms of profitability and market penetration. These internal data sources are linked to the external marketplace using desktop systems to locate and quantify other as-yet-unpenetrated prime customer segments. Business-to-business marketers should ultimately be able to do the same thing using Standard Industrial Codes (SICs) to segment internal files and determine which markets have been penetrated.

Given the expense of business-to business marketing, desktop applications for this area are expected to explode in the 1990s. Vendors will continue to refine their marketing solutions, and sophistication will increase as geocoding and cost-effective street-level mapping become common. According to Andy Paul of National Planning Data Corporation, "A future challenge will be to integrate syndicated survey research on [SIC] consumption propensities and volumes." Such developments will clearly enhance the utility of desktop systems for the business marketer.

CASE STUDY

Twin Cities Clothes, Inc.

COMPANY BACKGROUND

Twin Cities Clothes is a wholesale clothing distributor headquartered in the Minneapolis-St. Paul area. It distributes through its retail network a wide variety of goods, including clothing and shoes for men, women, and children. Although Twin Cities Clothes has enjoyed considerable success in the past, the growing fragmentation of the clothing market began to create significant challenges for its marketers.

THE PROBLEM

Twin Cities Clothes marketers were faced with the challenge of developing a strategy that would ensure that the right products were placed in the right outlets. A mass marketing approach was out of the question, so the marketers needed a mechanism to identify the customers (and their location) for its various products.

THE SYSTEM

Twin Cities Clothes used the Infomark desktop system to address its business-to-business marketing needs. The Infomark system, developed by National Decision Systems (NDS), is a menu-driven market analysis package that integrates its resident demographic databases with proprietary business databases and other industry data. (For more information about the system and vendor, consult the descriptions in Appendix 1.)

METHODOLOGY

Market analysts at Twin Cities Clothes began by examining market penetration for certain customer groups. Using a business database in the Infomark system, they were able to segment these customer groups by four SIC codes. Figure 1 depicts the market penetration experience of Twin Cities Clothes for key segments. Men's clothing (SIC 5611) and women's clothing (5621) are segments for which the company has a high penetration rate.

Twin Cities Clothes was fortunate in that it had maintained sales-call records that could determine profitability by SIC code. In terms of profitablity, shoe stores and men's clothing had the shortest sales cycle and the largest sales volume, resulting

FIGURES 1 AND 2 *(Below) Using Infomark's Business-Facts database and its own customer records, Twin Cities Clothes is able to determine its current market-penetration rates for key retail categories. Internal sales data were further analyzed to determine profitability by category.*

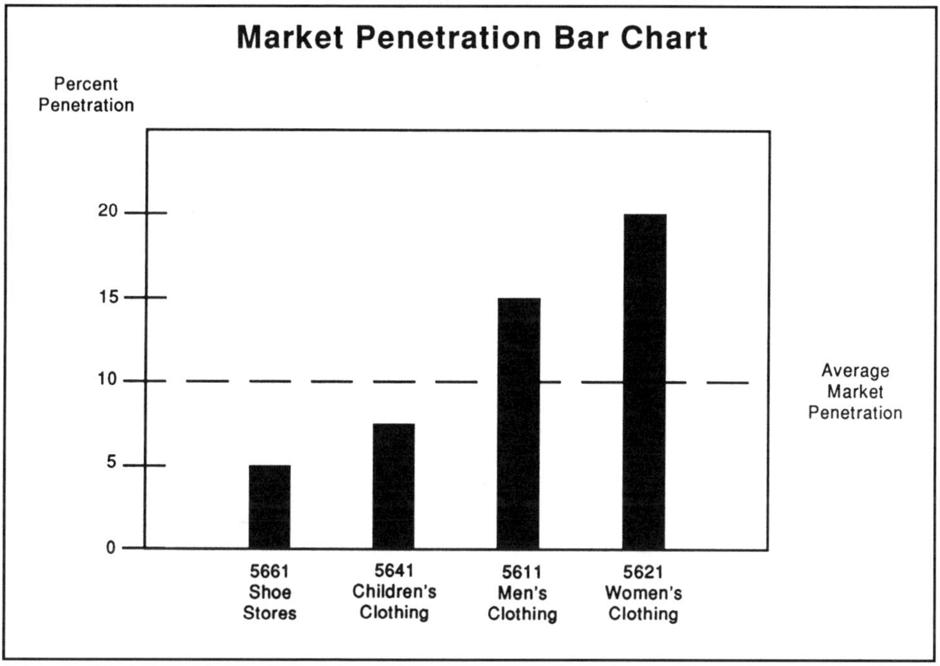

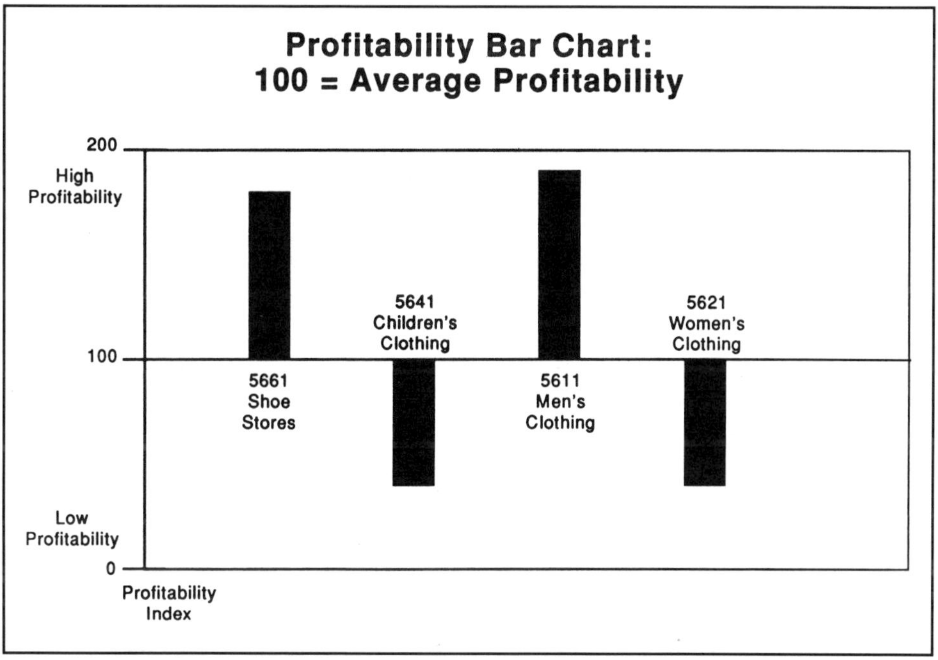

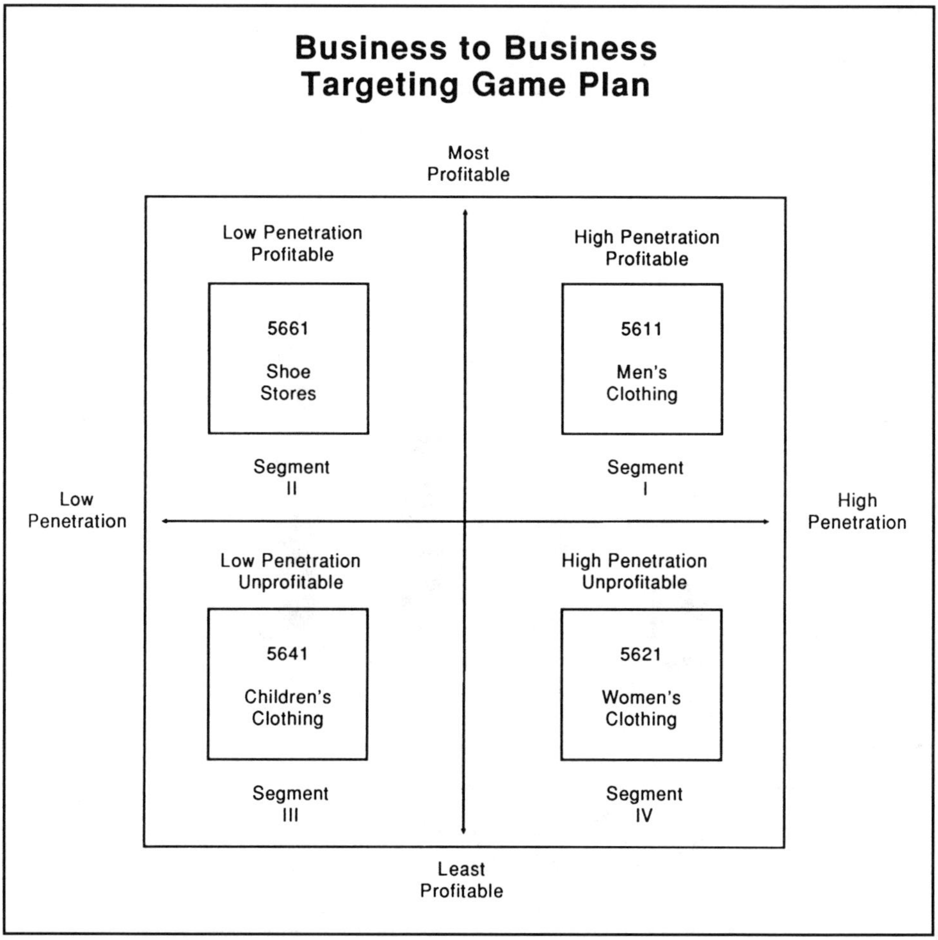

FIGURE 3 *Penetration and profitability were then combined to determine the strategic direction Twin Cities should take with each of its key customer categories.*

in the best profit "spread" potential. Average profitability for the four groups is shown in Figure 2.

Market analysts at Twin Cities Clothes found that one way to look at the available data was through a "game plan" bivariate analysis on a two-dimensional plane. When the four groups were cross-referenced by profitability and penetration, their distribution on the diagram indicated the marketing plan that was appropriate for each. Segment 1 (men's clothing) stood out as both profitable and highly penetrated (see Figure 3).

Once the most promising segment had been identified, the marketers plotted concentrations of relevant stores by zip code on a map of the company's sales territories. The marketers used the Infomark system to develop lead lists of stores complete with the prospects' names, addresses, and phone numbers (see Figures 4 and 5).

Minneapolis–St. Paul, Minnesota–Wisconsin MSA by zip code

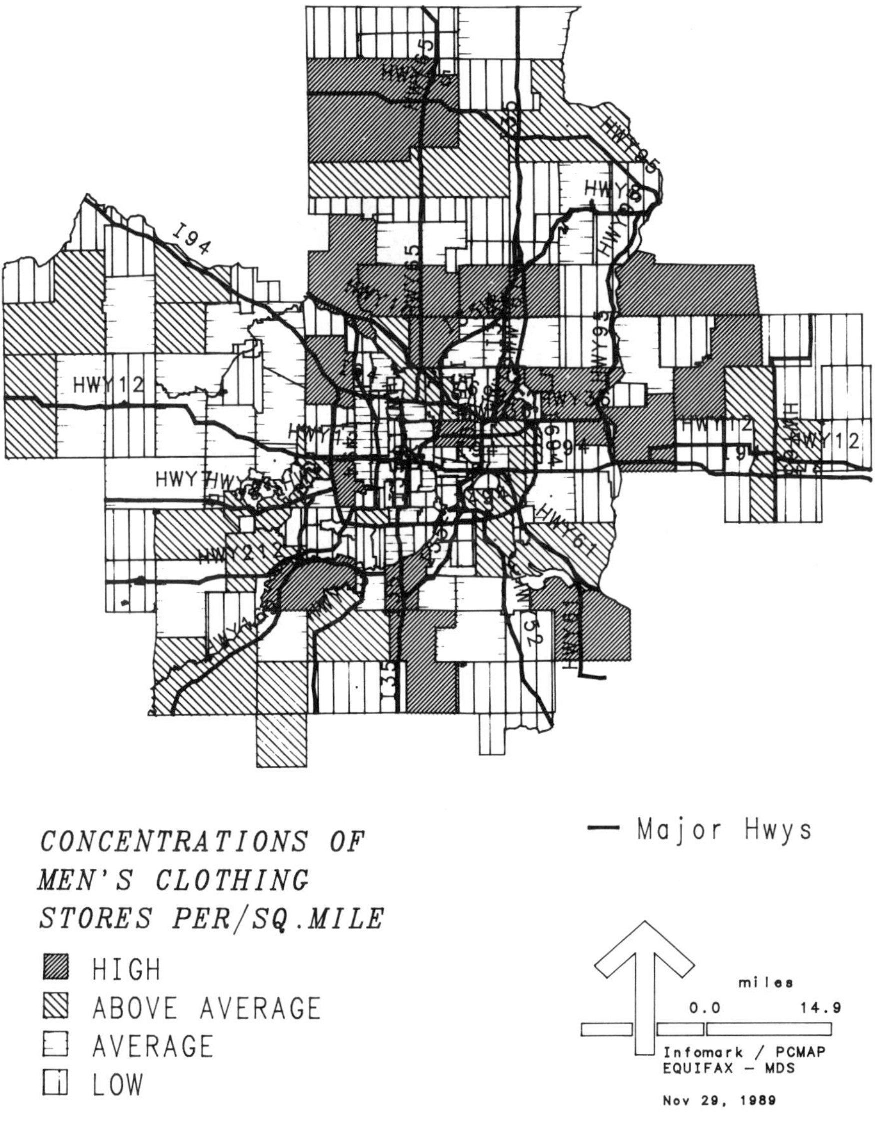

FIGURES 4 *(Above)* **AND 5** *(Following page) Each product category could then be mapped by zip code in the Minneapolis metropolitan area to determine the most efficient way to allocate marketing resources.*

Minneapolis–St. Paul, Minnesota–Wisconsin MSA by zip code *(ZOOMED AREA)*

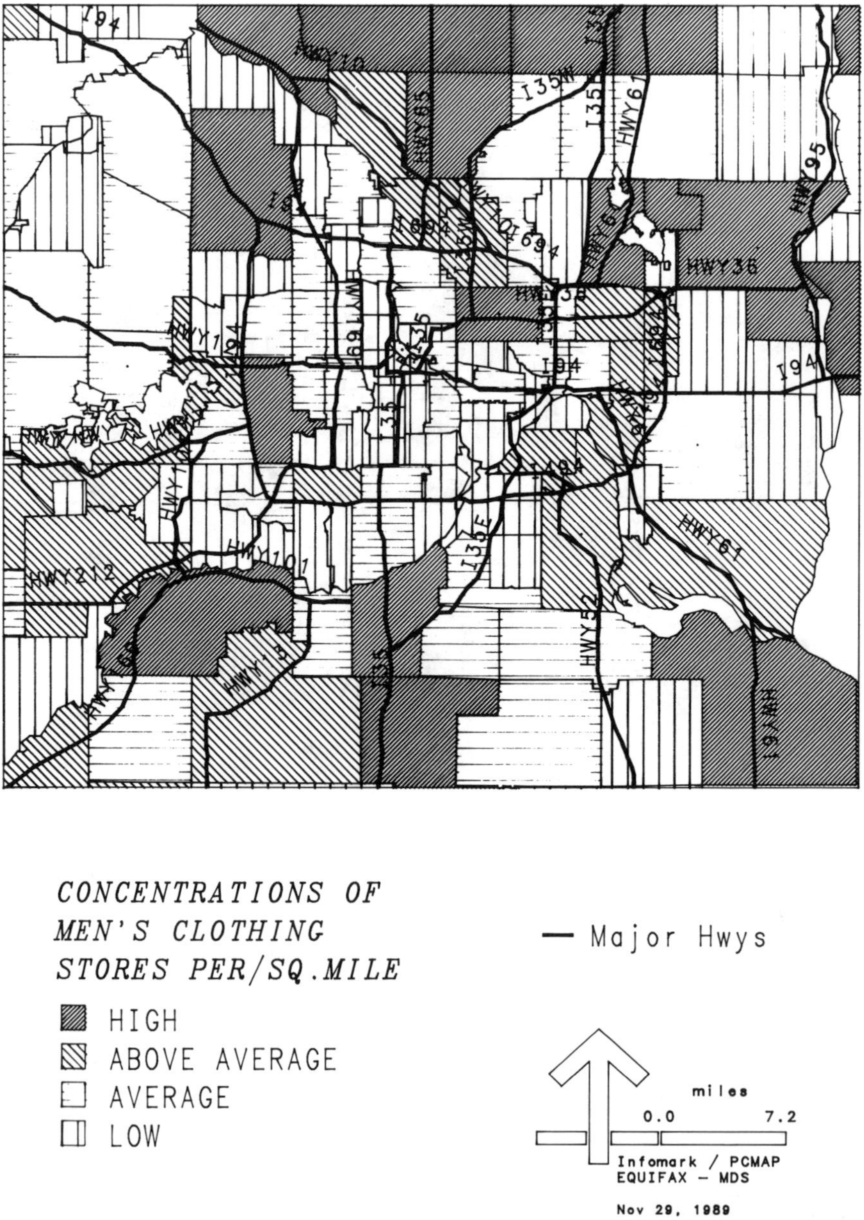

THE SOLUTION

Using the Infomark system and its business databases, Twin Cities Clothes was able to develop a much better understanding of the marketplace and the customers for its products. Instead of assuming that all stores were equal in potential, the marketers were able to identify the retail outlets with the most potential for various products. Business-to-business marketing for this user was made much more efficient by being able to target the stores with the most potential. Not only did this mean that the right products would be placed in the right outlets, but that marketing costs would be substantially reduced.

This case study was developed by:

Russell J. Kirchner
CUNA Mutual Insurance Group
5910 Mineral Point Road
Madison, WI 53701

This case study was based on an actual case, but due to the proprietary nature of the topic, fictitious names are used to maintain the confidentiality of the company and its personnel.

CASE STUDY

Action Industries

COMPANY BACKGROUND

Action Industries is a major manufacturer of recliner furniture and a subsidiary of Lane Furniture. Action requires accurate profiles of its furniture customers both nationally and by sales region. As advertising budgets have gotten tight, Action has become increasingly interested in consumer media preferences.

THE PROBLEM

An Action salesman in Texas with more than 16 years of furniture sales experience faced a serious challenge. He had been unsuccessful in his nine-month attempt to place his products in an upper-end store.

THE SYSTEM

Action Industries was already familiar with published statistics from National Demographics & Lifestyles (NDL) and became interested in the vendor's PC-based system, OASYS. The OASYS system includes a variety of consumer and market databases. The system also allows for the incorporation of internal databases with the OASYS resident databases. (For more information about the system and vendor, consult the descriptions in Appendix 1.)

METHODOLOGY

The first stage of the OASYS analysis demonstrated how demographics and lifestyles affected the company's sales, nationally and in its six sales areas. Figure 1 indicates the potential for recliner sales in the service area. Using OASYS data and his personal experience, the salesman worked with the dealer on a seasonal sales promotion and accurately predicted exactly how many recliners would sell in each category.

THE SOLUTION

The salesman now uses OASYS data to plan promotional mailings to targeted zip codes identified by income levels, buying power, and specific lifestyles. "NDL and OASYS give me more to take to a dealer," he says. "I can find out where I'm doing a good job and where I might have missed something."

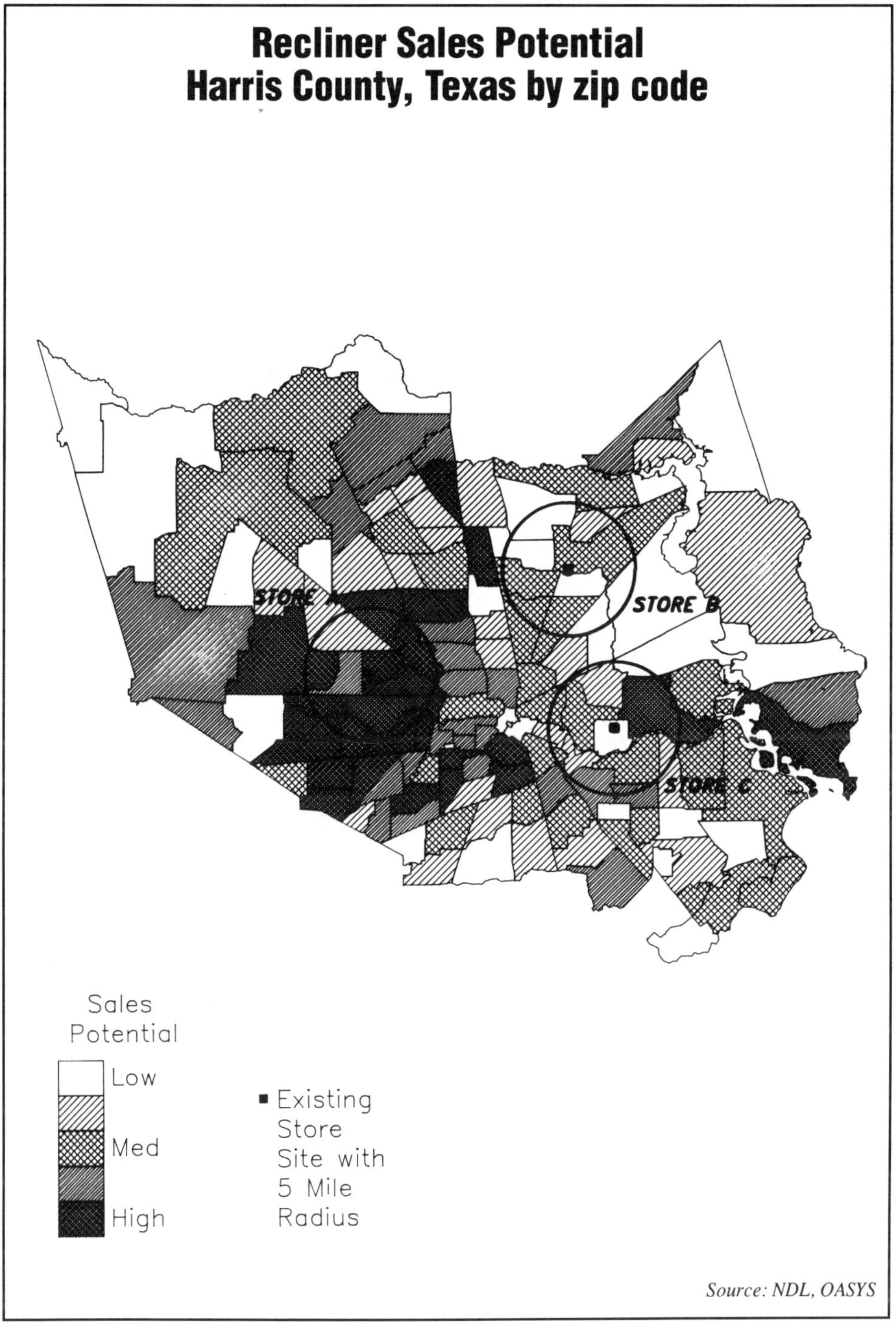

FIGURE 1 *Using OASYS profiles of consumer demand for recliners, Action Industries was able to produce maps showing the sales potential by zip code for Harris County, Texas.*

Another Action sales representative in Ohio used OASYS for one of his biggest accounts, a six-store furniture chain. In the past, Action and the retailer had shared the cost of blanketing the northern Kentucky/southwestern Ohio area with approximately 430,000 advertising circulars three times a year. After a while, the return stopped justifying the costs, and the promotion was discontinued.

On NDL's advice, the salesman asked the chain for its customers' zip codes, store by store. Each store ranked the zip codes and NDL profiled the most promising ones. Using OASYS, NDL identified those zip codes with the highest percentage of households that matched the profiles of Action customers.

Action and the chain test-delivered 53,000 circulars to the best prospects, supporting the test with newspaper ads. The number of recliners delivered into homes increased 55 percent over the previous year's promotion. Currently, Action distributes 149,000 circulars to high-potential zip codes for all six stores for every special promotion. "We save on printing and delivery costs and channel the savings into newspaper ads to improve the frequency of exposure," says the salesman. There has been a 50 to 60 percent increase in sales over all promotions from previous years.

This case study was submitted by:

Nancy Solomon
Marketing Communications
National Demographics & Lifestyles
1621 Eighteenth Street
Denver, CO 80202-1211

CASE STUDY

GE Supply Company

COMPANY BACKGROUND

GE Supply Company (GES) is a $1.1 billion+ subsidiary of General Electric Company. It specializes in the wholesale distribution of electrical apparatus and equipment. The company has more than 130 branches nationwide and a number of central warehouse locations.

THE PROBLEM

Since electrical products are sold to virtually every industry, understanding market dynamics and identifying growth opportunities is a challenge. There is a particular need to understand the characteristics of the end-users of the products. Specifically, GES wanted to identify sites for branches within the Columbus, Ohio, service area.

THE SYSTEM

GES installed the CONQUEST/Dun's BusinessLine marketing information system in its Bridgeport, Connecticut, headquarters facility. CONQUEST is a PC-based geodemographic marketing information system developed by Donnelley Marketing Information Services. BusinessLine, developed by Dun & Bradstreet, provides business listings and summary data for more than 9 million businesses. (For more information about the system and vendor, consult the descriptions in Appendix 1.)

METHODOLOGY

The objectives of the Columbus office analysis were to determine market potential, customer demographics, and existing competition, and to develop prospect lists for the field sales force. First, GES characterized the Columbus target area by examining key demographic data, including forecasts of growth. Then, it compared the target area to the Chicago base area, creating reports and maps at various geographic levels, including total market, county, and zip code.

One objective of the demographic analysis was to characterize the Columbus area by customer type (segment and SIC code), company size (number of employees), and market potential (dollar potential per employee), grouped by three market segments (Industrial, Commercial, and Contractor). Each segment was defined by specific two-digit and four-digit SIC codes. The Industrial and Commercial segments also included an employee-size criterion of 20 or more employees, while the Contractor segment included all businesses within the defined SIC codes. To determine market potential, each SIC code within the market segments was assigned a per employee dollar value ranging from \$50 to more than \$30,000. Values were based on historical company data (see Figure 1).

Using CONQUEST/Dun's BusinessLine, GES created reports and maps for each of the market segments and all segments by zip code for the Columbus and Chicago markets, and generated information using the system's BusinessLine Basics and Registry.

The objective of the competitive analysis was to develop a better understanding of where the competition was located relative to the estimated dollar market potential. This required both summary information and actual competitive information. Using BusinessLine Basics, charts and maps were created at the four-digit and six-digit SIC code levels for both areas. Also, a listing of competitive locations was

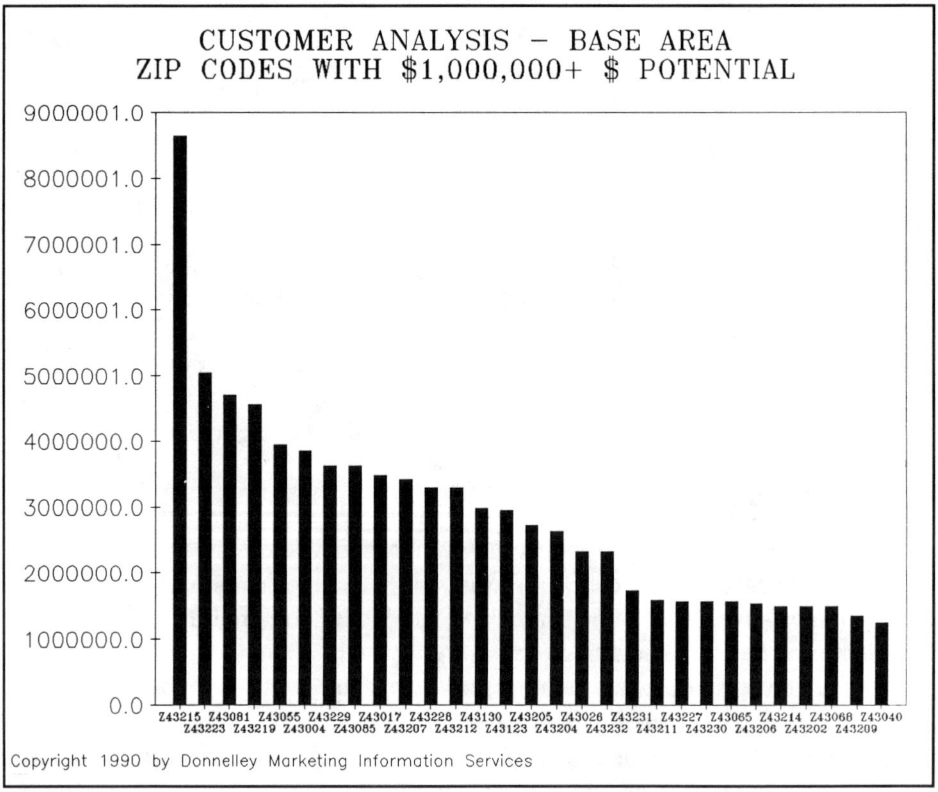

FIGURE 1 *Based on company sales data by SIC Code and the relative concentrations of key SICs in each zip code, market-potential estimates were developed for every zip in the Columbus market.*

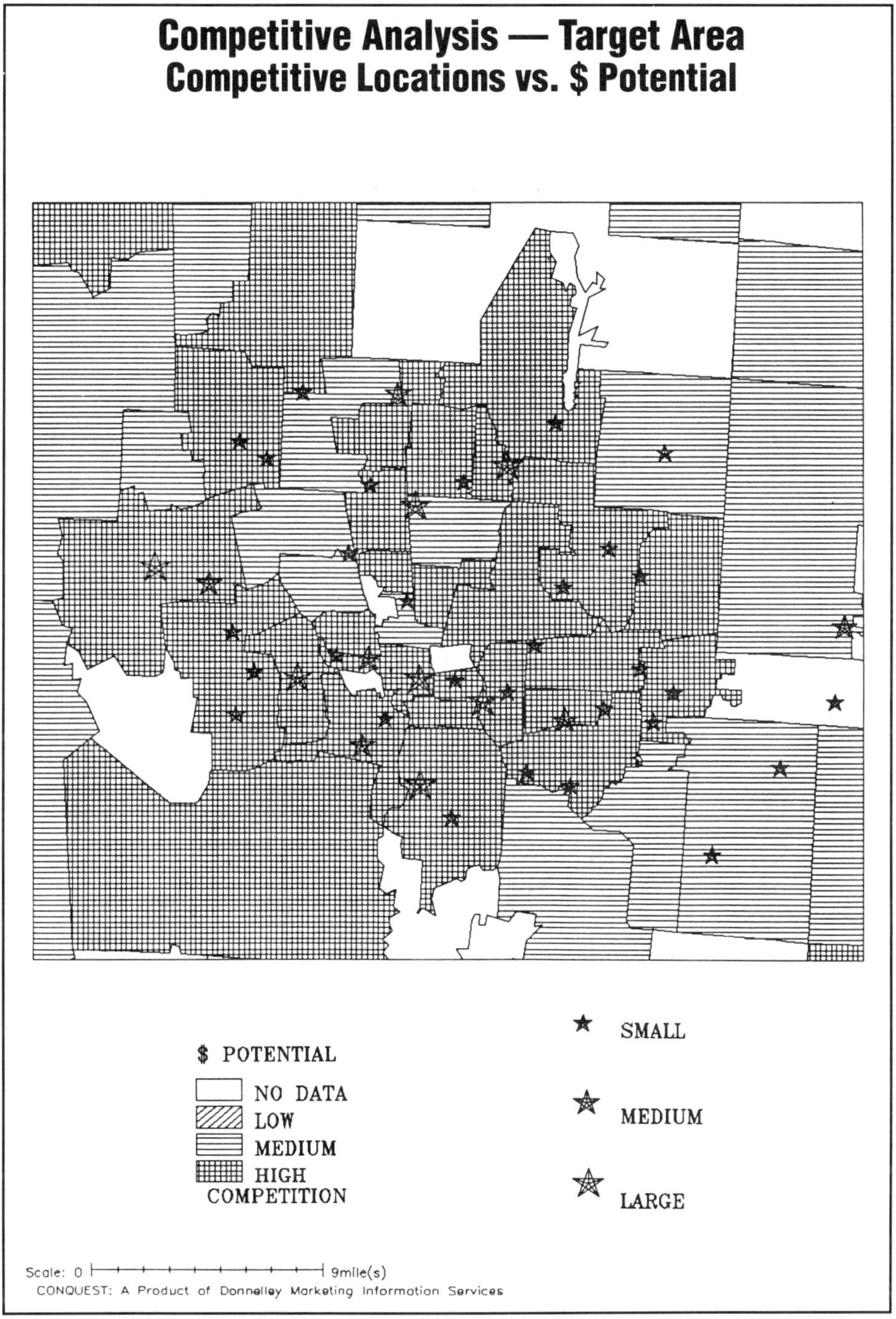

FIGURE 2 *This map locates competitors, identified by size, and overlays them on market potential for a selected area of the Columbus market.*

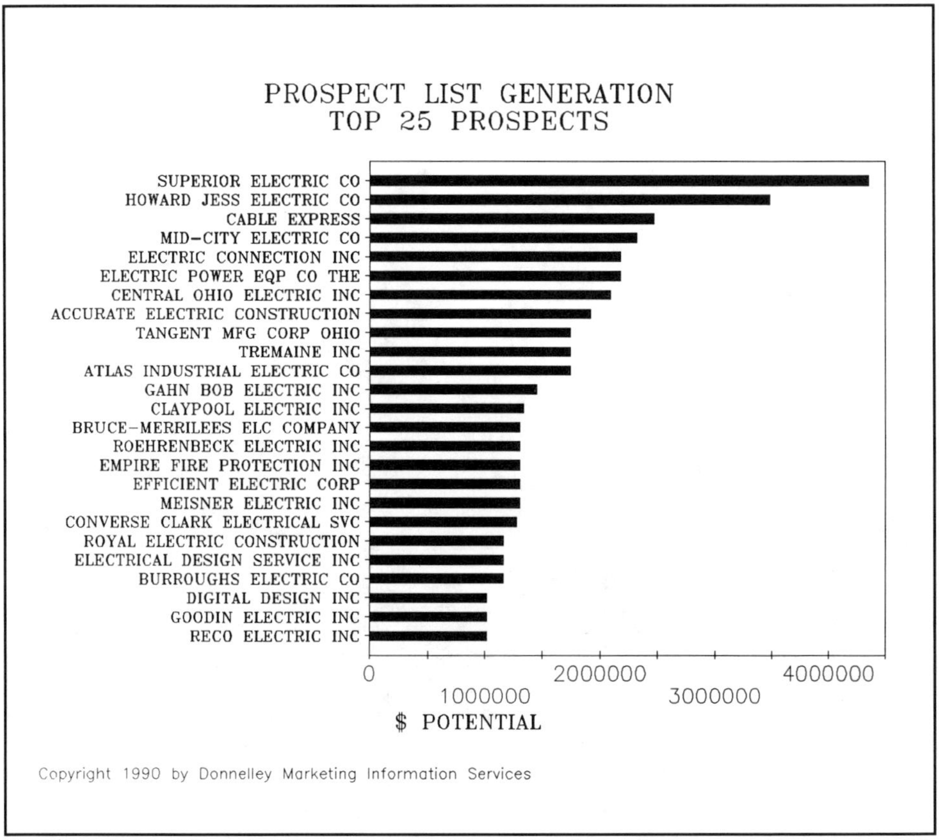

FIGURE 3 *CONQUEST enables GE to supply generate prospect lists for its sales force, ranked by dollar potential.*

generated, using BusinessLine Registry, including business name, address, sales, number of employees, SIC code, and type of location. (See Figure 2).

Finally, using BusinessLine Registry, GES created prospect lists based on dollar potential for each of the three market segments. The TargetScan module in CONQUEST assigned the required dollar-potential factor based on the prospect's SIC code and multiplied the dollar factor by number of employees to create a total dollar potential per prospect. Each segment was then ranked by dollar potential. For the Industrial segment, a listing of the top 100 prospects was generated. For both the Commercial and Contractor segments, the top 50 accounts were generated. (See Figure 3.)

THE SOLUTION

Using CONQUEST/Dun's BusinessLine, GE Supply Company was able to compare its target area to a base area and create the best prospect list available by market segment in a timely and cost-efficient manner. GE analysts could also graphically compare the characteristics of potential outlets and provide the decision support necessary for market planning.

This case study was submitted by:

Robert Brandes
Manager, Business Development
GE Supply Company
1285 Boston Avenue
Bridgeport, CT 06601

11

Other Industries

The consumer packaged-goods industry perhaps epitomizes the challenges faced by American manufacturing during the 1990s. The consumer packaged-goods industry, because of its reliance on in-store purchases, was one of the first to sense the changes that were occurring among consumers during the 1980s. The industry's sensitivity to an increasingly differentiated market has resulted in something of a revolution in marketing for firms in this field.

Consumer packaged-goods companies were among the early users of demographic data, and in the 1980s, were among the first to adopt regional marketing approaches and capitalize on psychographic analysis. Even so, the industry will probably have to move even further away from its product-line orientation than it has in the past and move even closer toward a customer orientation.

Competition in packaged goods continues unabated, and the number of brands and variety of products continues to proliferate. The disappearance of a mass market has put some national concerns at something of a disadvantage, as smaller and more targeted players begin to erode market share in regional markets and niche markets.

All the trends characterizing the consumer packaged-goods industry point to a growing need for desktop decision-making capabilities. There will be increasing emphasis on demographic and lifestyle segmentation, on regionalization, and on niche marketing. As the shift from a product orientation to a customer orientation continues, the emerging "customer segment managers" will need ready access to accurate market intelligence.

Part 2 concludes with a case study from a newly emerging high-tech industry—an online service directed specifically at consumers in their homes. What could be more fitting than to market a PC-based product using a desktop marketing system?

CASE STUDY

XYZ Foods

COMPANY BACKGROUND

XYZ Foods has long maintained a major share of the peanut-butter market in its trade area. As with other food companies, XYZ has been facing increasing competition and a reduction in marketing efficiency. In order to address these challenges, XYZ engaged Spectra Marketing, Inc., as a marketing consultant.

THE PROBLEM

XYZ Foods has maintained strong consumption patterns and loyalty among younger households with children residing in middle-to-downscale rural neighborhoods. XYZ needed to know how strong its competitors' business was in these same households and where the brand had growth opportunities. Using the Spectra Advantage System, XYZ Foods was able to separate its core franchise from the trial opportunity households and locate them by city, store, and household (see Figure 1).

THE SYSTEM

Spectra Marketing has developed a proprietary micro-marketing information system called Spectra Advantage. This PC-based system can discriminate for household purchase behavior across a 54-cell lifestyle/lifestage matrix and diagnose packaged-goods purchase behavior. The matrix can be collapsed to develop consumer marketing strategies by penetration, buying rate, loyalty, and volume consumption. Through a joint venture with Market Facts, Spectra is able to link consumer attitudes directly to the household and store. (For more information about the system and vendor, consult the descriptions in Appendix 1.)

METHODOLOGY

Spectra Advantage has been developed to address the unique consumer marketing needs of the consumer packaged-goods industry. XYZ used Advantage to analyze data for its eastern region and develop a sophisticated analysis plan. XYZ Foods compared its product with two competitive brands in terms of concentration, market penetration, buy rate, comparative pricing, and a number of other variables that distinguished the three brands. This information was cross-tabulated with data on use rates for the households in the 54 lifestyle/lifestage cells (see Figure 2).

The analysis provided a precise, customized picture of consumers who purchase the XYZ brand and competitive brands, which consumers are the heaviest users, what consumer attitudes drive this behavior, where these consumers are located and what their characteristics are, and which stores represent the greatest potential (see Figures 3 through 7). XYZ then developed consumer-based marketing strategies and linked these with tactical sales and consumer/trade promotion execution recommendations for each target (see Figure 8).

THE SOLUTION

XYZ Foods used Spectra Advantage to develop a more in-depth perspective on the market and on its competitors. The desktop system indicated the distribution of

FIGURE 1 *The Spectra Advantage System enables XYZ Foods to identify the core customers for its peanut-butter product.*

Target Demographic Profiles

	Demographic Indices	
	Core/ Loyal	Penetration/ Trial
HOH Age 25-34	155	181
HOH Age 35-44	215	186
Five+ Person HH's	209	216
Graduated From High School	87	116
Attended College	117	112
Graduated College	175	85
Professional/Manager	188	111
Skilled Blue Collar	102	177
HH Income $25-35K	96	127
HH Income $35-50K	135	114
HH Income $50-75K	164	96
HH Income $75K+	205	60

Target Consumption Profiles

Spectra Consumer Measures	Spectra Targets	
	Core/ Loyal	Penetration/ Trial
Category Development Index	135	151
% U.S. Households	21	19
% Brand Volume	36	23
Brand Pounds/HH (Consumption)	2.4	1.7
Index of Consumption	170	120
Brand HH Penetration	42	28
Index of Penetration	135	90
Brand Pounds/Buyer (Buying Rate)	5.7	6.1
Buying Rate Index	126	133

Target Lifestyle Profiles

Core/Loyal Target Lifestyle	Penetration/Trial Target Lifestyle
Own Personal Computers	Go Fresh Water Fishing
Own a Station Wagon	Heavy Renters of Video Cassettes
Belong to Health Clubs	First Time Truck Buyers
Visit Theme Parks	Do Own Home Improvements
Take Business Trips	Listen to Country Music

Target Payback

Core/Loyal Target	Penetration/Trial Target
70% efficiency versus average	11.4MM incremental pounds annually

High Opportunity Accounts

Core/Loyal Target	Penetration/Trial Target
Skaggs Supercenters, TX	Food World, AL
Giant Food, MD/VA	Kroger, IN
Lucky Stores, CA	Ingles, NC

High Opportunity Markets

Core/Loyal Target	Penetration/Trial Target
Dallas, TX	Indianapolis, IN
Detroit, MI	Charlotte, NC
Minneapolis, MN	Grand Rapids, MI
Seattle, WA	Memphis, TN

Target Strategies

Core/Loyal Target	Penetration/Trial Target
Maintain dominant brand position, guard against competition	Promote to increase trial and maintain new buyers

FIGURES 2-8 *By examining the demographic and lifestyle characteristics of the target market, XYZ was able to determine the optimal promotional mix to attract and retain new buyers.*

consumption among its loyal/core customers and verified that it did primarily appeal to middle-to-downscale families with children. XYZ was able to develop strategy alternatives based on the characteristics of its consumers relative to the consumers of other brands, and not only reduce its marketing expenditures but more effectively stock its shelves.

This case study was submitted by:
Thomas E. Dailey
Spectra Marketing, Inc.
333 West Wacker #650
Chicago, IL 60606

This case study was based on an actual case, but due to the proprietary nature of the topic, fictitious names are used to maintain the confidentiality of the company and its personnel.

CASE STUDY

PRODIGY Computer Service

COMPANY BACKGROUND

Prodigy Services Company, a joint venture of Sears and IBM, developed the PRODIGY service specifically aimed at the consumer market. This online service became commercially available in late 1988 after a year of extensive market research. During the initial study, the PRODIGY service audience and market potential were unknown. However, throughout the research phase, the market became increasingly clear. Demographic research indicated that the service should provide a wide variety of information and services in an easy-to-use friendly format for a low monthly fee.

Currently, the PRODIGY service has over 650,000 subscribers and is accessible by telephone/PC connection on a national basis. Although other online computer services are generally oriented to the business person or computer hobbyist, PRODIGY sees itself as standing alone as an online service for the consumer.

It does have competition in the form of catalog marketers. However, catalogs are expensive to produce and distribute; once printed, their product offerings can only be changed through subsequent mailings. Online systems provide greater flexibility through their immediate update capability. This capacity gives the online service a distinct advantage in responding to changing market conditions and also gives marketers a unique way to test new product offerings.

THE PROBLEM

Most companies are continually seeking alternate methods to economically reach consumers. "The American shopper is time-starved," says Russ Greenberg, program manager of market research at Prodigy. "Shoppers want convenient access to products and information about those products. And they want the ability to browse, all of which PRODIGY offers."

The need for a powerful desktop marketing system became apparent as the PRODIGY marketing plan was developed. Initially, key demographic data were fragmented into many files with differing formats. Data available at the census-tract

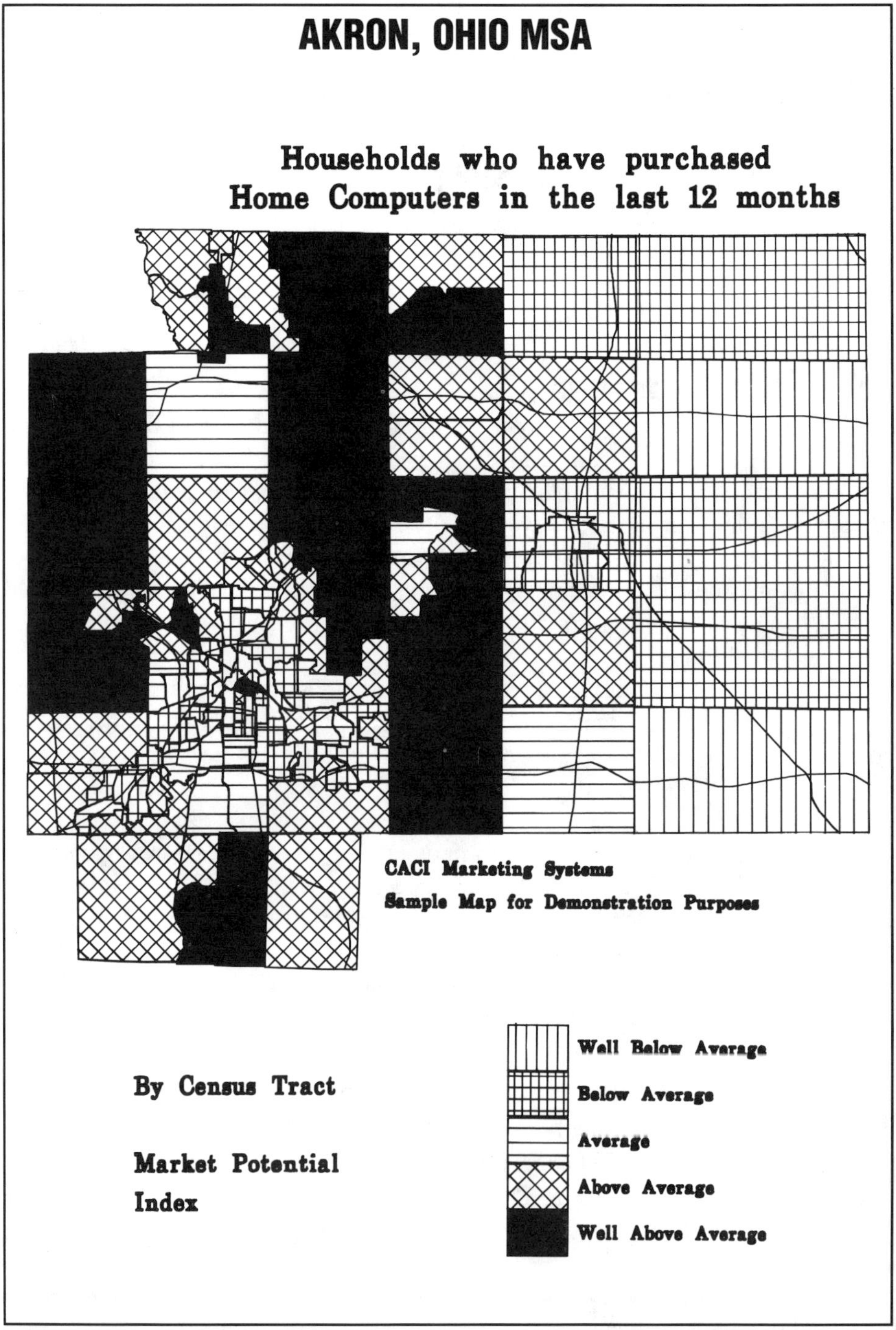

FIGURE 1 *By combining the ACORN segmentation system with syndicated survey data on home-computer purchase behavior, PRODIGY was able to determine high-potential areas for its service.*

level on the mainframe had to be overlaid with phone-exchange boundary files on a PC-based mapping system. In addition, because of the way data had to be accessed, PRODIGY was unable to examine it at both a macro and micro level.

THE SYSTEM

PRODIGY's marketers chose CACI's Insite•USA™ system, in part because they could combine their own databases with CACI's ACORN Lifestyle™ market segmentation system. (For more information about the system and vendor, consult the descriptions in Appendix 1.)

METHODOLOGY

Identifying the potential users of the PRODIGY service remained the key issue for the product's marketers. Because of the large capital investment needed to set up mini-computers in targeted cities, it was crucial to carefully analyze the many possibilities. Discovering which population segments to target, and in what cities they were most likely to live, involved linking media consumption data with the ACORN Lifestyle clusters, as well as other CACI information on banking, travel, and shopping. Figure 1 shows the geographic distribution of households that have made recent home-computer purchases.

Atlanta, Los Angeles, San Francisco, and Boston were areas selected for the initial launch of the service. Eventually, the system reached 23 Areas of Dominant Influence, and in September 1990, PRODIGY became a national network.

THE SOLUTION

The PRODIGY sales force now relies on the InSite•USA system to plan marketing promotions. By using a combination of demographic and ACORN Lifestyles data, the sales force can target the most promising neighborhoods for promotions. These take the form of participation forums in local schools and grocery stores, where potential users get experience with the PRODIGY service and operate in tandem with direct mail into the targeted neighborhood.

What is PRODIGY's mission for the future? "To increase our usage throughout the family. We want to use demographics to help us pinpoint types of families—and members within families—so everyone in a household uses our service."

This case study was submitted by:

CACI Marketing Systems
9302 Lee Highway
Fairfax, VA 22031

APPENDIX

Vendor and Product Profiles

This section describes the vendors and products featured in the case studies.* The information for this appendix was compiled from a number of different sources. Each vendor was invited to submit a description of its organization, its activities in the desktop industry, and its system. In some cases, vendors were interviewed by the authors for clarification or elaboration and particularly for information on organizational developments. The authors also contributed to these descriptions based on their familiarity and experiences with the various vendors.

The product descriptions are non-technical and include the desktop system offered by the vendor, the market segmentation system featured, and the relevant databases associated with each system. Any important applications that have been developed are noted. Industry-specific systems are indicated, along with particular industry applications and/or expertise of a vendor with a generic system. Technical information is omitted unless it was provided as an integral part of a product description. Pricing information is omitted as well since costs range widely depending on the geographic scope and databases required by each user.

No attempt has been made to evaluate the vendors beyond indicating industry developments in which they have been involved or innovations they have introduced. Every effort was made to eliminate vendor claims of superiority unless there was factual evidence to support such claims.

Ultimately, the authors had to make a number of judgment calls in terms of the final profiles. Every effort was made to make the fairest possible presentation of the vendors in terms of the issues salient to the reader.

**Only vendors that submitted case studies have been included in this appendix; this listing is not exhaustive. However, all known vendors were offered the opportunity to submit case studies for this book, and only those providing usable cases were considered for inclusion.*

CACI MARKETING SYSTEMS

9302 Lee Highway
Fairfax, VA 22031
(703) 218-4400
FAX: (703) 273-8169

CACI is an international information systems and high-technology services corporation. With sales of $150 million, CACI employ more than 1800 employees in 40 offices in eight countries. The Marketing Systems division maintains its European headquarters in London, England and its U.S. headquarters in Fairfax, Virginia.

With offices and installations throughout North America and Western Europe, a technology transfer assists clients in expanding their businesses on both sides of the Atlantic. Plans are in place to incorporate the 1990 U.S. Census and 1991 U.K. Census into the demographic databases already available.

Nearly 30,000 U.S. customers regularly use CACI's marketing information products to help them evaluate new sites, investigate market potential for product offerings, and determine customer profiles. CACI has a particularly strong presence in the retail and real estate sectors.

According to Greg Bradford, Executive Vice-President, "CACI has learned much from being a market leader in the United Kingdom. The marketing information industry in the U.S. is too product focused." In the U.K., he contends, there exists a more solution-oriented environment. CACI, according to Bradford, intends to capitalize on its strong reputation for consulting and service delivery. "The future belongs to solution deliverers," says Bradford. "Hit-and-run database selling will not be an acceptable alternative in the marketplace of the 1990s."

PRODUCTS

InSite•USA System

InSite•USA made its North American debut in the spring of 1990. Based on the British InSite system, InSite•USA is a PC-based geographic information system for state-of-the-art site location and market analysis. The easiest way to think of InSite•USA is as a "shell." Users can put many years' worth of sales volume, store characteristics, and competitive information to work without dealing with different data types and geographic areas. All geographies and datasets—census, postal, telephone exchange, shopping centers and more—are stored and retrieved based on the client's preferences. The InSite•USA system includes mapping capabilities and can be used with a digitizer.

ACORN Lifestyles Market Segmentation System

ACORN (A Classification Of Residential Neighborhoods) transforms households, survey respondents, sales records, and subscribers into social portraits for target marketing. Developed by demographers and market analysts at CACI Marketing Systems, the U.S. ACORN Lifestyles system classifies 260,000 census block groups into 44 lifestyle categories. This approach places every neighborhood in the country into a distinct cluster. The neighborhoods classified by ACORN can also be linked to data from Mediamark Research Inc., and used to infer the purchasing behavior of consumers in specific geographic areas.

OTHER RESOURCES AND DATABASES

CACI offers consultation services for customized applications, and provides a variety of demographic and market data in printed form, on diskette, and on tape. The Siteline call-in service provides reports from various databases. A series of annual publications provides a wide range of demographic data for cities, counties, and zip codes. CACI's Perfect Mail system is a precision targeting solution to direct-mail issues, and Market*Master is a database marketing system.

CLARITAS CORPORATION

201 North Union Street
Alexandria, VA 22313
(703) 683-8300

For 20 years, Claritas Corporation has helped companies identify marketing opportunities and solve marketing problems with segmentation systems, target marketing databases, and PC software systems. Founded in 1971, Claritas is headquartered in metropolitan Washington, D.C. Throughout its history, the primary mission of Claritas has been to improve client profitability through effective target marketing. Claritas considers itself an innovator in target marketing, and is a member of VNU's Consumer Marketing Information Group.

Claritas was the first U.S. company to develop and sell systems based on geodemography. The PRIZM segmentation system, created by Jonathan Robbin, the company's founder, grew in popularity in the 1980s and spurred competitors to develop similar segmentation systems.

Claritas has a strong presence in financial services and media industries. Claritas also offers an industry-specific corps of sales representatives who are considered credible experts in their respective fields. Today, Claritas provides a wide variety of target marketing services to more than 800 firms in consumer goods, financial services, media, advertising, automotive, health care, utilities, insurance, and other industries.

PRODUCTS

COMPASS Market Analysis System

The COMPASS desktop database marketing system integrates, analyzes, and maps clients' data, syndicated data, and Claritas data. COMPASS was first introduced in 1988, representing a third generation of desktop marketing software developed by Claritas. It is essentially a high-performance software platform. Its advanced macro language and data manipulation capabilities allow unlimited applications for data integration, market analysis, reports, and maps. Users can customize COMPASS by creating and storing their own applications, models, and variables. They can also work with ready-to-use applications built into the system, which is delivered on CD-ROM to ensure speed and to accommodate the growing number and size of marketing databases. To meet the unique marketing needs of various industries, Claritas has also built customized systems such as COMPASS Newspaper, COMPASS Banking, COMPASS Agency, COMPASS Cable, etc.

PRIZM Segmentation System

PRIZM helps target consumer segments by describing each neighborhood in the U.S. in terms of 40 distinct cluster types. PRIZM groups, which can be linked to a wide array of syndicated data, are based on key census variables, plus more than 100 million purchase records. PRIZM +4, which was built up from individual household data, provides PRIZM data for 9-digit zip-code areas that average as few as 12 households.

OTHER RESOURCES AND DATABASES

Claritas offers several dozen syndicated or custom databases. These include Census Bureau demographic data (up to 1,000 variables), Census Bureau TIGER street-mapping files, intersection data (latitudes and longitudes), business data for 8 million businesses, shopping centers, financial product demand (based on 130 hours of telephone interviews conducted by Claritas each day), media and purchase behavior from syndicated surveys by Mediamark Research and Simmons Market Research Bureau, retail sales potential, automobile dealers, P$YCLE segmentation, media ratings from Arbitron, Nielsen and other media ratings, bank branches, car and truck buyers, and many other databases.

COMPUSEARCH MARKET AND SOCIAL RESEARCH LTD.

330 Front Street West, Suite 1100
Toronto, Ontario, Canada M5V 3B7
(416) 348-9180

Compusearch Market and Social Research Ltd. is a market analysis firm headquartered in Toronto, with branch offices in Montreal and Vancouver. Compusearch offers the largest private database of Canadian demographic and consumer behavior information in Canada. It provides current-year estimates and two-, five-, and ten-year projections. Custom research services include site modeling and custom segmentation. Compusearch is a resource for applications that include site evaluation, market analysis, target marketing, and direct marketing.

Among the resources offered by Compusearch are: market segmentation, consumer spending categories, vehicle registrations, business statistics, and shopping center locations. The data, which are available online, in written reports, and on microcomputer software, can be accessed for any level of geography (postal, census, and custom-defined). Also available is the *Canada's Postal Markets Source* book, a reference providing key consumer and business statistics for every Forward Sortation Area in Canada.

PRODUCTS

CONQUEST/Canada Market Analysis System

CONQUEST/Canada is a menu-driven, CD-ROM-based system that produces demographic profiles for any market in Canada, both standard geography and user-defined areas. CONQUEST/Canada provides data in the form of standard or custom reports, maps, and graphics. It can integrate and analyze data from disparate sources, and export data to other packages. All of Compusearch's databases are resident in the system. Applications include trade-area analysis, site-location analysis, customer profiling, and target marketing. (CONQUEST/Canada is a version of the CONQUEST system developed by Donnelley Marketing Information Services.)

LIFESTYLES Segmentation System

Lifestyles is a market segmentation system that classifies every Canadian neighborhood into one of 70 consumer groups. Each segment has a unique demographic profile in terms of its spending patterns, financial service requirements, and media habits. This database is linked to all levels of geography (postal, census, and custom-defined), numerous mailing lists, and other media. It allows users to profile consumers and to increase the impact of direct-mail campaigns, media selection, expansion, rationalization, and other marketing programs.

OTHER RESOURCES AND DATABASES

Among the other resources available from Compusearch are consumer spending categories, vehicle registrations, business statistics, and shopping center locations. The data are available online, in written reports, and as microcomputer software, and can be accessed for any level of geography (postal, census, and custom-defined). The "Desktop Demographics" package allows access to extensive census data and can perform segmentation analysis involving up to 700 variables.

DATAMAP, INC.

7525 Mitchell Road, Suite 300
Eden Prairie, MN 55344
(612) 934-0900
FAX: (612) 934-8727

Datamap is a geographically oriented provider of desktop market analysis systems. Headquartered in Minnesota, Datamap is a publicly held organization with 20 employees. It was founded in 1975 by Grant Warfield, a geologist who was experienced in mapping natural features. Warfield felt that techniques used to make contour maps for government agencies could also be used to map population and would be commercially successful.

A growing number of clients became more interested in the databases and tabular reports than the mapping. This led to the development of the CAM-1+ (Computer Aided Mapping) desktop marketing software in 1988. Datamap also developed dealer location software in 1989 for telemarketing applications. Datamap plans to concentrate on geographic information systems (GIS) and telecommunications in the 1990s. While most GIS companies focus on land-use applications, Datamap will continue to concentrate on marketing and customer-service uses of geodemographic information. Future plans include the joint development of software and systems for several major industries.

PRODUCTS

CAM-1+ Market Analysis System

Designed for site location and evaluations, CAM-1+ can provide demographic profiles for any geographic area in the U.S. The database manager and spreadsheet program produces reports from any of over 300 metropolitan area databases, each of which contains data by zip code and postal carrier route. The system can calculate market penetration and develop "what if" scenarios.

CAM-1+ is menu-driven and has minimal hardware requirements. It can import files to create reports and is compatible with Lotus, Excel, and other spreadsheet programs, as well as the series of Atlas mapping packages from Strategic Locations Planning and other mapping capabilities, including Datamap's.

DONNELLEY MARKETING INFORMATION SERVICES

70 Seaview Ave.
P.O. Box 10250
Stamford, CT 06904
(203) 353-7000
FAX (203) 353-7276

Donnelley Marketing Information Services (DMIS) was formed in 1979 as the demographic and market research arm of Donnelley Marketing Inc., with approximately 10 employees. DMIS' purpose was to launch a new business opportunity for Dun & Bradstreet (D&B), which wanted to create the premier geodemographic company within the industry. As the field has expanded, DMIS has grown to more than 100 employees

In 1990, D&B sold Donnelley Marketing but retained the DMIS unit, which now falls under the A.C. Nielsen companies of Dun & Bradstreet. DMIS' new strategic position with Nielsen offers benefits and strategic advantages such as direct access to Nielsen data and research, segmentation tools to analyze media and product-use data, expert analytic services, and customized solutions for packaged goods and media companies, advertisers, and retailers.

Two high-growth areas for DMIS in the 1990s are expected to be the packaged-goods and retail industries. To target the packaged-goods industry, DMIS has developed a database analysis product, ScorPLUS, that provides consumer and store information for more than 35,000 grocery stores.

A major resource supporting DMIS is Donnelley Marketing's master residential file of more than 85 million unduplicated households and 120 million individuals with which DMIS can target consumers at all levels including neighborhoods, households, and individuals. DMIS claims to be the only supplier of demographic information that builds population estimates and projections using a "bottom up" census-tract approach instead of traditional top-down methods that extrapolate from higher geographic levels like counties.

PRODUCTS

CONQUEST Marketing Information System

CONQUEST was introduced in 1985 as a mainframe time-sharing arrangement. In 1986, it was the first geodemographic marketing system to use CD-ROM technology as a storage device. At this time, the system offered geographic and geometric reporting capabilities, geographic scanning, and computerized mapping at the census tract level. Databases available included demographic, retail sales and lifestyle information, all of which were stored on one optical disk.

CONQUEST was originally used by retailers and real-estate developers to assist in site selection. Over the past several years, other industries have started to use it, including financial services, utilities, telecommunications, advertising agencies, direct marketers, media, packaged goods, cable, government agencies, health care, and business-to-business marketers. Currently, CONQUEST runs on IBM-compatible machines and PS/2 models. and is compatible with most standard and popular peripherals (printers, plotters, etc.). A WINDOWS™-based system, "CONQUEST for Windows," is scheduled for release in early 1992.

ClusterPLUS Segmentation System

ClusterPLUS is a segmentation tool that classifies U.S. neighborhoods into 47 lifestyles. It provides demographic profiles, Links with syndicated data or customer files, and identifies prospects geographically by selecting names and phone numbers from the Donnelley Master Residential File of 85 million households. ClusterPLUS is available at block group, census tract, zip code, and ZIP+4 levels.

OTHER RESOURCES AND DATABASES

DMIS offers a variety of databases, including shopping centers, financial institutions, media and purchase information from Simmons and Mediamark, VALS psychographic typologies, Dun & Bradstreet business information, A.C. Nielsen local and national TV ratings data, health care, cable TV, Yellow Page directory boundaries, and more. Other system capabilities include the TV CONQUEST module for analyzing TV ratings data, the integration of street-level information from TIGER files and Donnelley Marketing's proprietary Geographic Base File (GBF), mainframe linkage to Donnelley Marketing's and Dun's Marketing Services consumer and business databases for ordering lists, and level segmentation systems.

ENVIRONMENTAL SYSTEMS RESEARCH INSTITUTE, INC.

380 New York Street
Redlands, CA 92373
(714) 793-2853

Environmental Systems Research Institute (ESRI) is a leading producer of geographic information system software. It has its international headquarters in Redlands, California, and has offices around the U.S. with 550 employees. Founded in 1969, ESRI's original objective was to introduce computing into environmental analysis with applications for planning, landscape architecture, and resource management. The company focuses on two areas: the development and support of geographic information system software and applications consulting for specific geography-related problems. ESRI software runs on minicomputers, PCs, workstations, and main frames. Its users now include people in such varied fields as urban planning, transportation, engineering, and conservation.

PRODUCTS

ARC/INFO Geographic Information System

Based on several years of experience with geographic information systems on mainframe computers, PC ARC/INFO is a PC-based geographic information system that combines interactive data management with geographic analysis. With this system, data can be spatially indexed for rapid query and management. PC ARC/INFO is designed for easy interface with mainframes and minicomputers. It has six modules and works with dBASE from Ashton-Tate Corporation. A version of ARC/INFO is available for university use.

NATIONAL DECISION SYSTEMS

539 Encinitas Boulevard
Encinitas, California 92024-9007
(619) 942-7000

National Decision Systems (NDS), a division of Equifax Marketing Decision Systems, Inc., was one of the early entrants into the desktop marketing industry, and now has over 200 employees. In July 1988, the company became a subsidiary of Equifax Inc., providing comprehensive and technologically advanced consumer information for business, industry and government. The parent company employs more than 17,000 people in 1,100 locations throughout the U.S. and Canada.

Headquartered in Encinitas, California, NDS is a leading provider of marketing information, consumer and business targeting tools, and PC-based decision support systems. The company's marketing services are used in a variety of industries across the country including retail, restaurant, real estate, financial, insurance, advertising, utilities, consumer packaged goods, automotive, and telecommunications. Applications include target marketing, customer segmentation, market analysis, site evaluation, direct marketing, sales management, and strategic business planning.

NDS claims to be the first target marketing and marketing information company to develop a customer-segmentation system containing unique consumer information and census data at the ZIP+4 level of geography.

PRODUCTS

Infomark Desktop PC System System

Infomark is an integrated desktop decision-support system with which users can produce reports, maps, and graphics of demographic, product consumption, competitive information, etc., for any geographic location in the U.S. The databases resident on Infomark provide information on demographics, business activities, consumer demand, media usage, lifestyles, and more. The system has a grid search function for locational analysis.

MicroVision Segmentation System

MicroVision is a micro-geographic consumer targeting system built at the ZIP+4 level of geography (5-15 households), combining data from the Equifax Consumer Marketing Database (ECMD) with the latest census information to classify every household in the U.S. into one of 50 market segments. MicroVision is effective for general targeting applications. MicroVision Industry-Specific combines industry survey research data with the ECMD and census information for industries such as banking, insurance, and restaurant. MicroVision-Custom incorporates a client's own information (customer files, survey data, and/or syndicated data) into a segmentation scheme designed jointly by the client and National

Decision Systems. (Note that some of the case studies in Part 2 refer to the VISION segmentation system, which was the precursor of MicroVision.)

INFORUM, INC.

53 Century Boulevard, Suite 250
Nashville, TN 37214
(615) 885-3560

Inforum, Inc., was formed in 1987 with the sole objective of developing a desktop analysis system for the health-care industry. It is a privately held corporation with more than 30 employees in 1990. In conjunction with the Claritas Corporation of Alexandria, Inforum developed the MediEdge desktop planning and information system to specifically address the needs of health-care planners and marketers. The MediEdge system was released in April of 1988 and is currently licensed by over 300 health-care institutions across the U.S.

With an exclusive health-care focus, Inforum offers demand forecasting methodologies and modeling capabilities that allow users to integrate large external data sources involving the use of precision geography. It has also developed a wide array of databases for use with its MediEdge system, including data from an annual nationwide survey of 100,000 households.

PRODUCTS

MediEdge Market Analysis System

The MediEdge system, developed exclusively for use in health care, combines planning, marketing, media analysis, consumer targeting and demographic databases with reporting and mapping software. Numerous standard applications have been developed and the system has the capability for custom applications. Extensive health-related databases on services utilization, facilities, and other aspects of the industry are resident on the system. A unique feature is the Pulse health-care consumer database, derived from an annual survey of 100,000 households. Users can incorporate customer databases and interface with vendor-provided databases, including demographic data from Claritas Corporation.

PRIZM Segmentation System

MediEdge offers access to Claritas' lifestyle cluster system, PRIZM (see the Claritas Corporation listing).

OTHER RESOURCES AND DATABASES

In addition to the standard MediEdge databases, Inforum offers optional add-on databases such as the MEDEC physician database. Inforum also has direct-mail capabilities linked to its market segmentation system. The firm provides consulting services for its users and others requiring custom research. Inforum also continues to develop new applications for its clients, including an ambulatory-care planning module.

NATIONAL DEMOGRAPHICS & LIFESTYLES INC.

1621 Eighteenth Street
Denver, CO 80202-1211
(303) 292-5000

Established in 1975, National Demographics & Lifestyles (NDL) is a leading provider of consumer database information services with more than 500 employees. NDL provides a variety of marketing services for major companies in consumer goods, financial services, publishing, direct marketing, media, and other industries. Now owned by R. L. Polk and Co., NDL has access to purchase and registration data for new and used cars and trucks. NDL is headquartered in Denver and maintains regional offices in New York and San Diego, a data entry facility in Barbados, a joint office with Polk in Toronto, and an affiliate company in the United Kingdom.

NDL collects a wide range of self-reported product- and purchase-related data and demographic, geographic, and lifestyle information that is voluntarily supplied by consumers who complete and return questionnaires packaged in packaged goods. Consumer marketers can also reach prospects with targeted mailing lists from The Lifestyle Selector, NDL's 27-million-name consumer database. The Lifestyle selector is unique since it is based on lifestyles, as opposed to geodemographic systems that are based on demographic and socioeconomic data.

In 1987, NDL rolled out its OASYS desktop product (Opportunity Analysis System). NDL also offers market profile information through OASYS, The *Lifestyle Market Analyst*, and the ZIP code analyst.

NDL plans to cement and augment the relationships it has already established. "We will continue to focus our activities on consumer durables direct marketing, and the media," says Tom Ratkovich, Group Manager of NDL's Information Products Division. NDL also intends to leverage R. L. Polk's auto registration data to strengthen its consumer behavior database.

PRODUCTS

OASYS Market Analysis System

National Demographics and Lifestyles designed OASYS (the Opportunity Analysis System) specifically for consumer marketing applications. OASYS can be used for site evaluation, media planning, market segmentation, market share analysis, new product development, and more. Through OASYS, users have access to a variety of databases including demographic databases, retail trade databases, and R. L. Polk's vehicle sales and registration databases. NDL has developed a proprietary database on consumer behavior especially for this system. Software applications include mapping and graphic display; the new 3.0 version has a graphical user interface and integrates the Census Bureau's TIGER file into the mapping capability.

OTHER RESOURCES AND DATABASES

The Lifestyle Market Analyst and *The Lifestyle ZIP Code Analyst* are annual marketing sourcebooks They are joint publications of NDL and Standard Rate & Data Service. *The Lifestyle Market Analyst,* a 1,000-page volume, provides detailed demographic, lifestyle, and consumer segment information for the nation's 209 Areas of Dominant Influence (ADIs). The information is also available on diskette.

The Lifestyle ZIP Code Analyst presents up-to-date demographic and lifestyle data about more than 25,000 zip codes from the top 25 MSAs and counties with populations of at least 35,000.

THE SACHS GROUP LTD.

1800 Sherman Avenue
Evanston, IL 60201
(708) 475-7526

The Sachs Group is a privately held corporation focusing exclusively on health care. Formed in November 1984, the company's first installations of The Market Planner were at Good Samaritan Hospital in Los Angeles and Allegheny Health System in Pittsburgh. Its client base of 250 installations includes multihospital systems, university and teaching hospitals, small community hospitals, physician group practices, medical products companies, and consultants.

The Sachs Group provides a broad range of PC-based software with data customized to the unique needs of each client organization. Each installation is managed with an ongoing program of education and user support.

The Sachs Group has developed a growing product line of specific applications or preset analyses for problems commonly faced by health-care organizations. These modules include: inpatient demand modeling, outpatient demand modeling, revenue forecasting and modeling, physician shortage/oversupply analysis, targeting services for specific market segments, comparative quality analysis, demographic analysis, media selection analysis, and managed-care-contracting risk evaluation.

Through The Sachs Institute, The Sachs Group provides a full calendar of courses for its clients. Offerings range from "how to" courses about the software to more topical courses like "Tracking Marketing Effectiveness" or "Integrating Strategic and Financial Planning." The Sachs Group has taught more than 500 hospital managers an approach to strategic decisionmaking through its regular introductory training course.

PRODUCTS

The Market Planner Market Analysis System

The Market Planner is a desktop market analysis system designed exclusively for the health-care industry that includes modeling, analysis, mapping, and graphing features. The current version of The Market Planner runs on the DOS operating system. The system includes information on demographics, health-care utilization, and competing institutions, as well as a cartographic package. The Market Planner can interface internal data (e.g., patient records or physician roster) with external market data.

The Sachs Group has also developed an OS/2 version of The Market Planner. Hospitals that can most benefit from this enhanced version are those with large competitor databases, extremely large medical staffs, many subsidiaries or hospitals, data stored on mainframes or local area networks, or the need to perform complex detailed geographic and market analyses.

The Physician Practice Planner

The Physician Practice Planner is an extension of The Market Planner that focuses on the development of physician/patient activity. By linking demographic information to health-related data, it allows analysts to forecast office visits by market segment and physician specialty, identify over- and under-served areas by comparing physician supply with demand, and estimate follow-up care related to physician visit volumes.

SachsGroups Market Segmentation System

SachsGroups is a household segmentation system designed exclusively for the health-care industry. Individuals receive care, but health-care decisions are made at the household level as families make decisions about physicians, health insurance, and hospitals. The 29 SachsGroups market segments categorize households by their propensity to use health-care services based on the factors that relate most to health care: head-of-household age, household composition, income, and household location (urban, suburban, or rural). SachsGroups can be used in conjunction with MP Target and or The Customer Management System.

OTHER RESOURCES AND DATABASES

The Contract Planner is a PC-based software system used in conjunction with The Market Planner to reduce risk and improve returns on managed-care contracts. It contains population profile templates, product-line profiles, encounter rate models, resource models, and cost models.

SPECTRA MARKETING, INC.

333 West Wacker, Suite 650
Chicago, IL 60606
(312)263-0606

Spectra Marketing provides consumer packaged goods companies with proprietary information services and facilitating the targeting of high opportunity consumer households. Through a joint venture with Market Facts, Spectra is able to provides its clients with sophisticated attitudinal segmentation capabilities. Its Advantage desktop system allows a customized, "cookie cutter" approach, made possible by new, accurate scanning technology. The focus of Spectra on the "end user" is considered a factor differenting Spectra from its cimpoetitors. The company maintains a client service team dedicated to providing sloutions to challenges faced by its consumer packaged goods clients.

PRODUCTS

Spectra Advantage

Spectra Advantage is a proprietary micro-marketing information product developed specifically for the consumer packaged goods industry. The Advantage platform represents "incremental" technology developed for the unique needs of this industry. Its developers consider it a complete "consumer intelligence system" that allows users to link the strategic who/what/where with their tactical marketing and sales execution programs. It has been used to analyze 40 product categories and hundreds of different brands.

Spectra users can directly link consumer attitudes and marketing strategies down to the household and store level. Advantage does this by utilizing a 54-cell lifestyle/lifestage consumer segmentation matrix. This consumer targeting strategy allows users to profile consumption of products in terms of penetration, buying rate, loyalty and volume consumption. Advantage offers an integrated solution that still allows for customization for the needs of the individual user.

INDEX